INDIA'S
WORLD

INDIA'S WORLD

HOW PRIME MINISTERS SHAPED FOREIGN POLICY

RAJIV DOGRA

RUPA

Published by
Rupa Publications India Pvt. Ltd 2020
7/16, Ansari Road, Daryaganj
New Delhi 110002

Sales centres:
Allahabad Bengaluru Chennai
Hyderabad Jaipur Kathmandu
Kolkata Mumbai

ISBN: 978-93-89967−40-1

First impression 2020

10 9 8 7 6 5 4 3 2 1

The moral right of the author has been asserted.

For
B K & Toshi Goswami

CONTENTS

PROLOGUE
An Independent Path in the World

Addressing the Indian Parliament on 22 March 2000, the US President Bill Clinton said, 'Time and again in my time as President, America has found that it is the weakness of great nations, not their strength, that threatens their vision for tomorrow. So we want India to be strong, to be secure, to be united, to be a force for a safe, more prosperous, more democratic world. Whatever we ask of you, we ask in that spirit alone.'[1]

They were fine words, delivered by the high priest of the world's oldest democracy in the temple of its largest. They were crafted for a country that has existed mystically before time, where emotions often trump cold calculation. Both the eloquent speaker and his enraptured audience were conscious that democracy, like happiness, is one of those elusive things whose promise is almost as important as its performance.

Clinton's words were meant sincerely, if one goes by the material available about his preparation for the visit. He wanted India to be strong, secure and united so it could be a force for a safe, more prosperous, more democratic world. What Clinton was suggesting amounted to a triple-double; if India was strong, secure and united, the second triple would follow naturally. Instead of being a mere participant in the world, he was urging it to be one of its determinants. Instead of just watching the world go by, Clinton was suggesting that India should help choose the direction it should take. Can there be any quarrel with that? More importantly, did the Indian leadership of the time share this vision, or did it have its own variation of it, with an inherent continuity? Or to put the same question differently, did the Indian leadership over the years have a shared vision about India's place in the world? And if its leadership did share that vision wholly or partly, has India made progress on the triple-double that Clinton had wished for India? Perhaps not.

There has been some movement in the last two decades towards carving a global role, but it has not been significant enough. As Karl Marx said, 'Men make their own history, but they do not make it as they please; they do not make it under self-selected circumstances, but under circumstances existing already, given and transmitted from the past...' It is these circumstances from the past that have circumscribed the Indian leaders' freedom of action. They could not wish away the fact, and the burden, of foreign rule. That past is still raw in India.

Another deep resource from its past is India's consistent faith in remaining content within its land boundaries, tolerance of the other and secularism in faith and belief. These ideas have for long been sustained and sponsored by a large Hindu-majority state brimming with ethnic, religious and linguistic diversity. This was both a source of pride and justification for the rightful Indian claim to exceptionalism. But howsoever praiseworthy these ideals are for a society, they are also singled out as reasons for India's passivity. The lack of aggression and the reluctance to covet what is others' has been blamed for the blows it has received over the centuries. Along the way, India lay defeated and wounded.

The invasions and the prolonged stay of foreign forces were certainly not blessings. During those trying centuries, India's contact with the world was through the prism and the needs of its rulers. If they went to war, their enemy was India's too, and its people the readily available cannon fodder. If the ruler needed to create a buffer stock of food for his troops engaged in war, the Indian population had to make the necessary sacrifice, even if it meant facing food shortages and a drought that killed a million people. For long, therefore, India was condemned to deal with the world second-hand.

Naturally, then, even in the early twentieth century, India had not figured in the rising America's calculations as a geographical reality to be taken note of. If at all it interested an American, it was because of the rapture that India provided to a Mark Twain for being so exotically different. Mahatma Gandhi, with his non-violent protests, was the other reason for curious interest in India. The American leadership, however, had little time for a region that was devoid of strategic value and no longer quite the jewel it once had been in the British crown.

The partition changed this. Its violence was a deep wound on the global conscience. For India, this new awakening into independent statehood should have been a long-sought joy. To an extent it was, but it was not quite a transformative event in that respect. A new beginning that kills a million plus and displaces over fifteen million cannot prod people to happiness. Still, the national attention did not take long to shift from the pain of loss to focus on putting lives together. This haemorrhaging India had come into being soon after Europe had stopped mourning its dead from the Second World War. While the financially generous Marshall Plan by the US was available to rejuvenate Europe; India and Indians were left to fend for themselves. India made a virtue of its misery by terming it self-reliance.

This smart turn of phrase was no palliative. Despite being one the oldest civilizations, with an established tradition of governance, India emerged reborn as a young, traumatized state wounded by its partition. There were also the issues of its size and heterogeneity. It has the world's second-largest population, in a landmass the size of Western Europe. This population, of every religion known to man, is divided into hundreds of ethnic groups speaking over a thousand languages, including 20 major ones. Some of the world's poorest people and some of its richest live here, uncomfortably together.

Therefore, the Indian past and present, like that of many other countries, are strongly influenced by its history, tradition and geography. So too are its contradictions. The type of neighbourhood that a country is in and the quality of its leadership should be added to this list. In today's times, the state of the world and the vastly enhanced global interaction can critically influence national destinies, as was the case during the Kargil war or even in the post-Pulwama phase. To put it differently, powers big and small can upset the established order of a country and devastate its people, as was the case with Afghanistan, Iraq and Syria. Add to all this the role of social media, and the complex picture is complete. When a first-time visitor expresses exasperation at India's complexity, his or hers is not a cry in the wilderness. Even its leaders find that India is not easy to govern.

Perhaps the fault lies in the vastness of India's population; its diversity, its poverty and its argumentative nature. Perhaps our collective memory is stained by a thousand years of bending low, by a history of accommodation, even subservience. That long dark period, and the occasional episodes of conspiring with the foreigner, may have left a psychological scar on the otherwise argumentative Indian, stunting his free flow, turning him hesitant.

THE MIDDLE PATH

These historical narratives do not merely reflect and describe realities; they can also help shape them. Let's wind the clock back for a bit and turn to the world as India might have found it on 15 August 1947. The picture it saw then could not have been pleasing or wholesome. The world war had crippled large sections of it. Most major European cities had suffered extensive bomb damage, almost all economies were gasping for breath, people were battle tired, and their expectations of a better future were low. Yet the West was readying for another battle; this time, one of ideologies—between the East, dominated by the Soviet Union, and the West, led by the US.

India was wooed by both, with offers of the benefits that come from association with the global strongman and allurements like a seat at the global high table of the United Nations Security Council (UNSC). This was tempting. India could have tied itself to the apron strings of one or the other power and simply sailed along under its steam.

What if, at that dawn in 1947, we had opted to align with the US? We wouldn't have invited the wrath of Gods, nor necessarily been thrown down from the high moral ground that we were aiming to occupy in foreign policy. On the contrary, it might have resulted in multiple benefits; perhaps a mini Marshall Plan, a permanent settlement of the Kashmir issue in line with the instrument of accession signed by the Maharaja, and the US may never have forced us to sign the iniquitous Indus Waters Treaty. Wary of the US, China may not have launched the punitive war in 1962. Nudged by the West, we may even have accepted the offer of the UNSC seat. This leap into the big league would surely have transformed India's relationship with the world. But that was not to be. India chose self-respect, and wisely so, because aligning would have meant accepting a subservient status, something close to the humiliation it had suffered for centuries.

India followed the middle path, keeping company with some of the other newly independent nations of the world. It was a difficult choice, but as is often rightly said, foreign policy is never easy. Gains are incremental and reverses common. In the Indian context, this is complicated further because domestic politics intrude sometimes to render foreign policy less than 'rational'. Sadly, it is not easy for a country to carve its own independent path in the world. This becomes even more difficult in a world divided into two bitterly opposed camps, as the world was then. Despite claims to the contrary, evidence suggests that very few leaders have the capacity or the opportunity to alter the basic direction of their nation's foreign policies. Geography, historical precedent and bureaucratic inertia prevent leaders from significantly reorienting foreign policy. This is the conventional wisdom—and for the large part, this has been the case. But sometimes exceptional circumstances require breaking free from the mould.

India was at one such crossroads in the early 1950s. Fuelled partly by the idealism of the freedom movement, and to some extent by the fear of bondage to one or the other of the two superpowers, it sought a third way. Since India did not have the economic or military heft of its own, it found non-alignment as its low-cost influence enhancer across Asia and Africa.

The West viewed these independent forays with suspicion and India's role as the leader of the developing world with some concern. The feeling that these efforts were somehow connected with and inspired by the Eastern Bloc continued to nag the Western strategic mind. This wariness began when Bandung hosted a conference in April 1955 for leaders from India and other Asian and African states. The immediate Western reaction to it was scornful. The American writer and activist Richard Wright, who attended the event, described it as the assembly of 'the despised, the insulted, the hurt and the dispossessed'[2]—in which they condemned the Cold War and railed against the West. This remark by Wright, its cynicism and suspicion, largely defined the way in which the two blocs, especially the West, were to view the subsequent assemblies of the developing world.

The Bandung conference inspired the launch of the non-aligned movement, and India, led by Prime Minister Jawaharlal Nehru, was a founding member. The world thereby also found itself divided, definitionally, into three entities; the First World, composed largely of the US and its allies in the West, a Second World, consisting of the Soviet Union and its satellites in the East, and now this latest vast mass of the decolonized and other developing countries, together labelled the Third World.

This compartmentalization lasted for nearly half a century, till the splintering of the Soviet Union into 15 states. With that, the Cold War was over and soon the world became dominated by a single super power. In this unipolar world, the question that the non-aligned countries began to ask was this: Equidistance from what and who?

All this while, non-alignment as a brand had punched far above its weight, whereas the reality was that, shorn of the moralistic hyperbole, it lacked solid foundation on which it could flaunt its muscle. Still, it had some episodic relevance during the Cold War. Once that phase was over, the brand of non-alignment had gone past its use-by date, and the policy that was the insurance of the meek of the world against domination by one bloc or the other lost its raison d'être. The Cold War, too, lasted as long as the socialist bloc stood its ground. Once the East caved in, the limits imposed by two blocs lifted. In India, the Nehruvian premises began to give way to a slightly more open view of the West.

AN EMERGING WORLDVIEW

India has long since moved away from non-alignment. But it has not yet decided what should take its place. The contours of a new worldview are emerging slowly, but remnants of the old one linger. This uncertainty about India's proper role abroad is also tied to the country's complicated situation at home. There is consequently a feeling that India may be prematurely seeking a major role in the new world.

In recent years, India has tried to convince itself that it seeks strategic autonomy. But strategic autonomy is not without constraints. How can India have meaningful autonomy without an indigenous defence industry? As long as it relies on foreign powers to equip its military, it will remain strategically dependent. Moreover, does it have the economic heft to support its strategic ambition?

Alas, these are not the only chains around India's legs. It finds itself hobbled continually by the machinations of Pakistan and the grand strategy of China. The Pakistani mischief started with the invasion by its forces in Kashmir in 1947–8. Ever since, the Pakistani trespasses have taken multiple forms, but the objective remains the same: To somehow keep chipping away at India's integrity. This continues to be a millstone around the Indian neck; an irritant that refuses to go away. The Chinese invasion of 1962 was a different matter altogether. It represented the loss of innocence for a new nation, leaving India and its citizens shell-shocked for long thereafter.

The other two links that have figured prominently in India's worldview are the US and the Soviet Union. At first, the US and India, as the two largest democracies of the world, viewed each other warily, overwhelmed by the enormity of minor quibbles. The complaints did not fade away, but gradually practical wisdom took over, guiding them to a firmer, less quarrelsome relationship. A major factor in this was the periodic disappointments of America with Pakistan and China.

Future historians might debate about the precise moment when the 'decision' was made by India to deepen her engagement with the US. They might broadly agree that it happened as the twentieth century was folding into the twenty-first. Indian techies were then making waves in the Silicon Valley, giving rise to this apocryphal anecdote. When a visiting Indian leader asked the US President, 'How's the Silicon Valley doing now?' the President quipped, 'Why are you asking me? Ask your techies. They own half the Silicon Valley.'

Nevertheless, a future historian might conclude that the decision to fast track relations with the US was not a unanimous one by the establishment in New Delhi. In fact, even when it seemed poised for a major leap, it did not enjoy consensus even within the Congress party. It was orchestrated by a small set of politicians led by Dr Manmohan Singh and aided by some diplomats.

In the beginning, the growing warmth in the Indo-US ties did not affect India's relations with Russia. On the contrary, there were solid grounds for them to be strengthened further, and for the first few years of this millennium, this is what happened, with cooperation bubbling along healthily in space technology, nuclear cooperation and the military sphere. However, over time, as the relations with the US gathered strategic strength, there were signs that the defence industry's ardour, which had once given substance to Indo-Soviet relations, was fading. The freeze set in slowly in the second decade of this millennium, and the indifference began to show most visibly in the disinterest towards the annual summit meetings. Russia, on its part, insisted that its interest had not lessened, but its amour propre had been hurt by the signals it was receiving that Indian attention was becoming US-fixated.

There were good reasons for the Russian complaint. India's US policy has settled, over the years, into a mode of steadily deepening cooperation. There are occasional irritants, but nothing of a truly strategic nature. Going by the current form, there seems reasonable assurance that nothing that Washington does will be aimed to fray India's stability, its territorial integrity, or its economic and military strength. Still, the Indo-US relationship has still to pass the test of trying times. Rather, there were stages, as in 1971, when the US worked actively against India. Insofar as the Indo-Russian relations are concerned, it is a truth acknowledged even by the severest observer that until recently, the two had stood by each other in difficult times. It will, therefore, be worthwhile remembering Kissinger's remark that 'history is to nations what character is to people.'[3]

MANDARINS OF FOREIGN POLICY

Moving on, it is useful to establish who and what influenced decision-making in India. On the subject of history it is necessary also to recall that on most major issues that affected the nation critically, the decisions were invariably taken arbitrarily by a small group of people.

This trend started with the decision to partition India and carried on to matters like referring the Kashmir issue to the UN, bartering away the bulk of the waters of the Indus river system, the Simla agreement and much more. And it still carries on; for instance, the policy regarding China and the information about its intrusions or territorial encroachments is kept mostly a closely guarded secret limited to a few, in an age where public satellites regularly beam the slightest movement forward by the Chinese troops.

Alas, it is not realized that this small, select group of policymakers making critical choices for a billion-plus people at any particular moment is not going to last forever. That one day a new crop of decision-makers will take their place. Then they, the media and strategic analysts will give their verdict on the wisdom, or otherwise, of the decisions taken by their predecessors. Such criticism is already happening with regards to referring the Kashmir issue to the UN during Nehru's time, and the alacrity with which India agreed to the Chinese demand on Tibet. Alas, the die having been cast long ago, this critical look back and the consequent lament cannot undo the damage.

But the discovery, post-event, that a flawed decision was taken, hurts people. As a case in point, the Chinese claim over Tibet is not cast in stone as the Indian people were once made to believe:

> Both Chinese and Tibetan historiography note the ad hoc nature of the influence each has had on the other through millennia... After the earliest British trade inquiries to Tibet commissioned by Warren Hastings in 1774 came to naught, the British signed a treaty with the Chinese Manchu Emperor at Chefoo in 1885-86, securing rights to travel to Tibet by way of China. That this did not yield the Tibetan government's cooperation and Tibet remained closed to foreigners for the next three decades, was further proof of the absence of Chinese writ over Tibet. This was echoed by Lord Curzon while commissioning the Young husband expedition that reached Lhasa through a long and violent incursion in 1904. He held that... China's sovereignty over Tibet is a constitutional fiction, a political affectation maintained because of its convenience to both parties.[4]

The question that should therefore be asked is: Why is it that we are generous with others to the extent of sacrificing our interests? Is it because by nature and tradition we hesitate to displease a visiting guest; that he must not leave resentfully or with an empty plate? The Indian scriptures are full of stories giving precisely this message. Or is it because we are diffident, and hesitate to say no? Or are we, by nature, generous to a fault, even with a vengeful enemy as in Simla in 1972? Or is it that, despite knowing of the policy misadventures of predecessors, every new Indian leader feels that he or she can write a new chapter on a clean slate?

Unfortunately, none of the instances noted above have been of benefit to us. In contrast, history is witness to the fact that Pakistan has been dogged in its pursuit; it has used the same old tricks and almost similar arguments to finesse every new Indian leader. It has been relentless in pursuing its agenda, regardless of whether a civilian or a military dictatorship is in charge if its affairs.

By the beginning of the 1990s, India was in a battered shape economically; a basket case, as it was referred to contemptuously by the pundits in the West. This was compounded by political uncertainty as it kept drifting from one leader to another. At that stage, all cards seemed to be stacked in Pakistan's favour. It had acquired nuclear weapons by the late 1980s, and with this, its army seemed to have neutralized India's conventional military superiority over Pakistan. Moreover, having just humbled the Soviet Union in Afghanistan through its proxies, Pakistan was on an artificial high. Its Prime Minister Nawaz Sharif proudly referred to himself as Fateh-e-Kabul (the conqueror of Kabul).

In India too, Pakistan's terror proxies were causing mayhem at will. It was under such circumstances that Prime Minister I.K. Gujral decided in 1997 to go in for composite dialogue. But Pakistan did not change its ways, and disappointment set in steadily. After repeated Pakistani betrayals over the years, the Modi government seems to have lost its enthusiasm for giving Pakistan yet another chance. Whether this is a temporary punctuation in the policy followed over the last seven decades remains to be seen.

HAS INDIA RISEN TO POWER?

The larger question, the one that is often asked in public and private debates is this—has India done well for itself?

For much of this millennium, India had been performing admirably on the economic front; however, in the recent past it has faltered. India needs 10-12 million new jobs a year, but the combined effect of demonetization and GST has been perilous. The number of unemployed is increasing by a few million every year, and so is inequality in society.

In this background, can it be asserted that India has risen to power? If for argument's sake we accept that it has, is it then a regional power on its way to becoming a global power? Or is it already a mini global power?

There is still some hesitation about where exactly it belongs, because of the ambiguity surrounding India's ambitions for itself and its global role. Meanwhile, whatever be its status, one fact has remained constant. India counts in world affairs, unlike a Brazil, a South Africa or a Pakistan. This has been the case since Nehru guided the country to the moral leadership of the developing world by championing its causes. It is in this background that India's present quest has led to speculation about its role in the emerging global order. There is expectation that India's would once again be the voice that counts. But one of the world's oldest civilizations and its largest democracy hesitates now to promote values that once gave it a special talisman abroad.

There are some sobering statistics too; in 2017 India's GDP per capita was $1,940, compared to $59,531 for USA, $4,065 for Sri Lanka and $3,110 for Bhutan. Over the years, India has performed better than Pakistan on most economic and social indicators, yet it lags far behind Brazil, China, Malaysia and South Korea on essentials like life expectancy, infant mortality and literacy. And it has miles to go before it can claim to equal China in its pool of human skills; which is so essential for a nation's rise.

But India has certainly made progress across several indicators: its vast land no longer lingers in darkness as electric supply has reached most villages, there is visible improvement in people's living standards, life expectancy shows a rising trend and there are toilets in schools and village homes. Yet job creation is a major issue and there is worry about rising religious polarization and its impact on India's management of its diversity. To add to this glum news, the World Happiness report for 2019, which evaluated 156 countries on a scale of global happiness, ranked India at the 140th position on the list—very close to the bottom, where Haiti, Botswana and Syria sit.

Still, there is reason for hope. A great asset for India, depending on how it is moulded, is its relatively young age profile. Ten years hence, in 2030, it will still be a nation with a median age of 31 years, compared to 42 in China. But having a young population can be both an advantage and a disadvantage. Put to constructive ways, they can transform India and make it truly a great power. However, this vast number of wasting youth can be easy feed for disruptive revolution. Already the signs are ominous, as the young, irritable Indian is testing our institutions and the political class. In this new age of resentment, the old idioms of patience and inaction may not remain valid.

At this critical stage—and sadly for India—its education system has delivered only selectively. The IITs, IIMs and some medical colleges have undoubtedly produced world-class graduates. But a vast majority of its educational institutions have failed expectations. It is the youth coming out of this latter system that could be a cause for concern.

Moreover, 80 per cent of the jobs are in the informal sector rather than in the formal economy. The informal sector by its very nature cannot guarantee security or permanence to its employees. Then there are state-level and regional disparities within India in terms of employment opportunities.

To complete this short list, at about 25 per cent, India has one of the lowest participation rates of working-age women in its workforce. If the goal is to increase the numbers in the formal economy, then massive investment is needed in that sector. For that to happen, India would require large-scale funds, skilled entrepreneurs and a considerable lead time. The issue then is, does India have the necessary financial cushion and luxury of time available to it, and does its youth have the patience for the long wait?

STATECRAFT VS. STAGECRAFT

Our relations with the outside world will be the other test before we can claim to be on solid ground. This essentially means dealing with other countries, especially our neighbours and the big powers, in a manner that ensures peace and security.

According to the theories that currently carry conviction, there are three basic ways of achieving this result—coercion, payment or attraction. This mix is regarded as the mantra of a good national strategy. But to be historically correct, it must be pointed out that this mantra is neither new nor a Western discovery. As a matter of fact, the basic premise of it has been around for centuries. As far back as the fourth century BC, Kautilya had propounded the concept of *saam* (advice or cajole), *daam* (pay or bribe), *dand* (punish), and *bhed* (exploit secrets) as the policies to be followed, as per need, by a ruler. Ever since, these four forms have been in use as matters of practical statecraft. Since the concept has now been given a Western touch, it has acquired the polish of a new philosophy. Soft power, smart power, hard power and the latest, sharp power, as the Western debate describes them, are in fact all derivatives of Kautilya's *saam, daam, dand* and *bhed*!

Have we in India fully and fruitfully followed this ancient wisdom? Before we come to that, let us try and understand what the modern version of it entails.

Soft power is the ability of a country to persuade others to do what it wants without force or coercion. To put the same thing differently in the manner made famous by Daniele Vare, 'Diplomacy is the art of letting someone else have your way.' But soft power alone cannot produce effective foreign policy. With the exception of Mahatma Gandhi and Nelson Mandela, it is hard to think of anybody who has been able to lead using soft power alone.

Hard power swings to the other extreme; it is the use of coercion and payment. Five hundred years ago, Niccolò Machiavelli recognized the shortcomings of both options. He wrote that 'a prince should make himself feared in such a way that if he does not gain love, he at any rate avoids hatred.'

In a way, Machiavelli was anticipating Joseph Nye and his use of the term 'smart power,' which he first introduced in 1990 in his book, *Bound to Lead*. It is just that Nye put a name to it—otherwise Teddy Roosevelt, too, had famously meant more or less the same thing when he said that 'we must speak softly and carry a big stick'. We could go back further in time on this, because for one reason or the other, 'smart power' has been in use for a long time now. There have been various interpretations of what smart power should be, but its most public articulation was given by Hillary Clinton during her Senate confirmation hearing on 13 January 2009 for the position of Secretary of State:

> We must use what has been called smart power—the full range of tools at our disposal—diplomatic, economic, military, political, legal, and cultural—picking the right tool, or combination of tools, for

each situation. With smart power, diplomacy will be the vanguard of foreign policy.[5]

A recent addition to this lexicon of power is 'sharp power'. Simply put, it is the use of manipulative diplomatic policies by one country to influence and undermine the political system of a target country. Or, as Nye had put it, sharp power is the deceptive use of information for hostile purposes. Russia and China are currently considered the ablest users of sharp power as a force that 'pierces, penetrates, or perforates the political and information environments in targeted countries.'[6]

These various types of power need not be applied exclusively or one by one. It is possible to mix and match them as per need. For instance, as a rising power, China employs 'soft power' to achieve its objectives as also the 'sharp power' of disruption and censorship. But these two goals are hard to combine, and sometimes they can boomerang. In Australia, for example, the Chinese use of deceptive sharp power has undercut its soft power. The public approval of China was growing until the revelation of its use of sharp power tools to meddle in Australian politics.

MOSAICS THAT DEFINED INDIA'S SOFT PATTERN

Where does India fit in this scheme? Is there a tag that could uniformly be applied to India over the last seven decades? Given the tragic circumstance of its independence, its fragile beginnings, the shape of the world then and the changes since, it is difficult for a standard formula to hold good. Accordingly, the Indian position has adjusted.

Nehru did well to recognize India's weak internal basics and the dominance of the two great powers. Many of his policy decisions have to be viewed in that light, and because of those compulsions. Whether each one of these was consciously thought through as an exercise in soft power is debatable. But taken together, they do present a picture that does not say otherwise. Non-alignment, anti-colonialism, anti-racism and the promotion of Indian culture were mosaics that formed India's soft pattern.

It was in 1971 that Indira Gandhi introduced a mixture of smart and sharp power. Getting the world's opinion on her side through extensive meetings with leaders and using the media and mega stars like Bob Dylan and the Beatles to spread the message of atrocities by the Pakistani army in East Pakistan were as much parts of her exercise of smart power as was her success in outwitting the Nixon and Kissinger combine.

Since then India has been alternating between being a soft power and a smart power state. Kargil, and to some extent, Balakot are cited as examples of a smart power that was quick to respond militarily to defend itself. There were other instances where critics accused India of being a 'confused' power, for instance during the Kandahar hijacking, Operation Parakram and after 26/11.

While a certain amount of flexibility is inherent in any policy, the lack of a well-drafted, long-term approach can have its pitfalls. What, for instance, is the signal sent if, despite the passage of a resolution in 1994 by the Indian parliament asserting that the entire area of J&K, including that under present occupation by Pakistan, is ours, India commits itself to a composite dialogue with Pakistan on J&K? This was agreed to by Gujral in 1997, and the dialogue itself started in 1998, to questions from analysts. Since Pakistan claims ownership of the entire territory of J&K, it makes no bones about the fact that it approaches these talks to get the rest of the state. The message that we, thereby, conveyed to Pakistan in 1997-8, and to the outside world, is that we are willing to talk about our part of Kashmir. A smart power would not have allowed itself to be snared into such a situation. Nor would a smart power have gotten trapped into signing a treaty like the one regarding the Indus Waters, by which we gave away to Pakistan 80 per cent of the waters of the six Indus system rivers. These missteps can be avoided if the state has a long-term strategic view and the policy it then sets is followed through. It may not work all the time and in every situation, but at least it serves as a guide to avoid diplomatic traps set up by the other side.

The larger question that we started with was whether in this present age of instant communication—where a president tunes in to CNN to learn about the nuclear tests in Pokhran, where leaders follow TV debates to help formulate their views, where social media influences policy issues—should decision-making remain the arbitrary preserve of a few in India?

Alas, this practice is unlikely to change. The few will continue to be the sole arbiters of policy.

Still, there is merit in considering change. It should be possible for leaders, for their own good, to follow the practice adopted by victorious Roman generals. An enduring image from the victorious Roman armies is the figure of the slave who was supposed to ride behind the triumphant general. He holds a laurel crown some inches above the general's head and whispers in his ear, 'Memento homo (Remember, you are only a man).'[7] This message is meant to keep the general's feet planted firmly on the ground.

Measured on this scale, have the Indian leaders kept their feet planted on the ground? It is difficult to judge because there is no one standing behind them to whisper in the ear, 'Memento homo.' In power, they appear larger than life, and their actions beyond reproach. But out of power and in a humbler position, the same leader might repeat what Shakespeare wrote in *Richard II*, 'For you have but mistook me all this while: I live with bread like you, feel want, taste grief, need friends: subjected thus, how can you say to me, I am a king?'

Alas, such an admission happens when the leader is one among us—when the aphrodisiac of power no longer keeps him perched above everyone else. At those rarefied heights, the modern day leaders of men do not feel the need to employ someone to whisper into their ears, 'Memento homo'. But the coming times portend change. A thousand voices on social media will constantly be sitting in judgment over their actions. There, the reminder of mortality will distinguish leaders of character from those of whimsy.

THE FATE OF A NATION

This leads naturally to the other thought that people have had throughout recorded history: What if they had a different leader? Would the fate of their nation have been different? Or was it in the course ordained by nature that they had to have a particular type of leader at a given moment in their national destiny?

This debate will go on inconclusively for many more years. However, it can be said with a fair degree of authority that only an Alexander, a Napoleon or a Hitler can mould national destiny decisively, to their will. Others—the time-serving leaders—would have been just as effective or ineffective if they were to rule in another period or at another place.

Our task is to analyse and record as fairly as possible the imprint these leaders have left behind. Have their efforts ennobled the 'idea of India'? Or have they left this 'idea' grander in promise than in fulfillment? India, in its post-colonial independence, is a young country, and it is too early to make a truly objective assessment of this idea. Still, some conclusions can be drawn fairly reasonably.

One of the more fundamental issues is that of identity. It is sometimes mistakenly said that India and Pakistan were born of the same womb. The fact is, we were not. India was born many millennia ago, at the dawn of civilization. Pakistan was cruelly carved out of a bleeding India. This amputation was illegal and ill-conceived.

As if that trauma was not enough, there was a vast difference in the priorities of the two leaderships. With the passage of time, and in the casualness of retrospective debate, it is sometimes forgotten that leadership can make or mar a new nation's foundation. Despite the pain of partition, Indian leaders like Gandhi, Nehru, Patel and many others advocated honesty of purpose, right action and hard work as the secular mantras for people. It was this that built the moral fibre of free India's first generation; from Bollywood films to the neighbourhood elders, the message was the same—there is no substitute to right thought and right action.

The Pakistani leadership was different; it was so self-seeking in the race to the top that a dying Jinnah was left to ponder on a Karachi road where he had gone wrong. The rickety van sent to fetch him from the airport broke down midway, with a very ill Jinnah inside. Ever since, this pattern of conspiracy against the leader has continued there; intrigue and impatience have become that nation's signature tune.

When people shifted from what had become Pakistan to the divided part of India, they had to start life afresh, slogging their way up through hard work. On the other hand, the western part of pre-partition Punjab was its industrial base; it was also the agricultural heartland, where a major share of the business and landholdings was controlled by the Hindus and Sikhs. After the partition, people of Pakistan received a bonanza of vacant homes and active businesses abandoned by fleeing Hindus and Sikhs. Those who had the muscle or influence became busy vying with each other to grab these readily available trophies. The lust for taking property by any means became a national characteristic, with the army as an eager participant.

Yet another test is the contrast of the Indian experience with that of the other newly independent countries. Many of them quickly fell into the hands of dictators. Instead of the British or the French colonial bosses, native leaders took over. The rest of the population remained more or less in the same trap of bondage that they had recently been freed from—only the masters had changed. India was a rare exception to this rule; it was fortunate that democracy grew deep roots in it.

This does not mean that democracy has had a smooth ride in India all the way through; there have been aberrations like the Emergency. Nor does it mean that India has been fortunate in consistently having leaders of exceptional ability. On the contrary, there were some of patchy quality; lucky individuals who were pushed to the top by the force of circumstance. However, the intention here is not to point accusing fingers at them, but to draw attention to the mark that some others have left on the Indian brow.

Since India's Independence in 1947, it has had 14 prime ministers heading a parliamentary form of government.[8] As a result, the same person can serve as prime minister for multiple terms. Some have served several terms; however, their longevity is no measure of their success or otherwise. Of these 14, my focus is on eight. These eight are also people of flesh and blood, they also made mistakes, but overall, they have made significant contributions to the country. In one case—that of Narendra Modi—it is a continuing chapter, so the reading and assessment of his policies cannot be considered complete. Still, since he has already left a mark in his own special way on the international platform, an attempt has been made to assess the impact of his style and of his stay at the top.

It should also be pointed out that historically, Indians have tended to forgive and forget where others in a similar position would have gone in for the jugular. From Prithviraj Chauhan with Mohammad Ghori in the battlefield to Indira Gandhi with Bhutto at the negotiating table in Simla, the Indian leadership has invariably succumbed to appeals for generosity and large-heartedness. It is a shade of this vain faith, that generosity might change the errant behaviour of Pakistan, which affected some major decisions taken by Pandit Nehru. Years later, Vajpayee fell more or less into a similar trap. The appeals for generosity were certainly a factor, as he kept trying repeatedly, like a later day Robert the Bruce, to make peace with Pakistan.

By holding a mirror to the past, and to the effect that the decisions taken then continue to have on India, the hope here is that we would be forewarned, because history, especially in our subcontinent, is prone to repeating itself. It is essential here to add a qualification—this book is about the prime ministers, but their decisions can be, and often are, influenced by the advice they get from their aides.

INDISPENSABLE MEN

Let's dwell a bit on the role that an advisor plays in the success or failure of a leader. Leading can be gratifying, but it is also lonely. There is the constant fear of failure. That's why a good advisor is indispensable. History is replete with examples of leaders whose success became synonymous with the quality of their advisors. Chandragupta Maurya's glory is attributed as much to his ability as to the wisdom of his advisor Kautilya. Otto von Bismarck was another such, who created Germany. The Prussian King Wilhelm needed him for the task; but theirs was not an easy relationship. Wilhelm used to complain that it was hard to be King under Bismarck, but he was equally firm in acknowledging the quality of advice he received from the latter.

Closer home, Indira Gandhi had a dream team of exceptionally able people before and during the Bangladesh war. To mention just a few—Jagjivan Ram was heading the Defence Ministry and Swaran Singh the External Affairs Ministry. At the bureaucratic level, P.N. Haksar was her principal secretary, R.N. Kao the chief of RAW and General Sam Manekshaw the army chief. But the same high standards were not maintained in some other periods.

Conversely, there is also the view that a leader suffers if he does not pay heed to good advice. For instance, 44-year-old John F. Kennedy was meeting Nikita Khrushchev in Vienna for their first and only summit barely weeks after the 1961 Bay of Pigs disaster. At that time, he had been the president for less than five months. Still, he ignored warnings from his advisors not to debate communist ideology with the 61-year-old Soviet. This got him stuck in time-wasting discussions about Marxism, where he was totally out of his league. At the summit, Khrushchev told his interpreter, 'This man is very inexperienced, even immature…' JFK admitted the scale of his disastrous performance to a *New York Times* reporter: 'Worst thing in my life. He savaged me.'[9] But JFK was a quick learner; he rarely faltered thereafter.

However, all advice need not be good. And advisors can be an evil influence too. In the front ranks of any such list would be Rasputin, the advisor to Nicholas II, last Czar of Russia.

Therefore, technically speaking, the blame for misjudgements as also for the credit for the right calls must be equally apportioned between the prime minister and his/her advisors. Yet, since the buck stops with the boss, the prime minister remains our reference point.

The last word in this regard must refer to a remarkable chapter of history, immortalized by Shakespeare. The reference is to the funeral of Julius Caesar, who had been betrayed by his own and killed cruelly. Defending him and his good deeds, Marc Antony said,

'The evil that men do lives after them;
The good is oft interred with their bones.'

Marc Antony's words from those distant times hold good even now—perhaps to an even greater degree. Today, social media and the fake news industry manufacture stories that are often far removed from reality. So, evil, or the allegations of such, has a considerable chance of living on long after a politician has met his maker. But the good that he does often gets clouded by the fog of criticism.

Yet, on calm reflection, we in India can say without exaggeration that by and large, we have been fortunate with the leaders who became India's prime ministers. It is true that they were people of varying abilities; some may even have taken questionable decisions. But a majority of them acted in the country's best interests. It is also true that some of their decisions were in bad judgement, but even gods err sometimes.

Finally, a word about the inspiration for this book. What should be a writer's guide when he sets his pen to paper? From ancient times this has been a dilemma, as also a catalyst, for some of the finest works of history. Tacitus is widely regarded as the greatest historian of ancient Rome. Explaining his approach to writing the history of those times, he says in his book *The Annals & The Histories*, 'The histories of Tiberius, Caius, Claudius and Nero, while they were in power, were falsified through terror, and after their death were written under the irritation of a recent hatred.' As against these two extremes, he says of his way of writing history, '…my purpose is to relate a few facts about Augustus…without either bitterness or partiality…'

The history that he wrote brought alive, cinematically and colourfully, the times and deeds of the emperors. As the French dramatist Racine remarked, 'Tacitus was the greatest painter of antiquity.' Thomas Macaulay was more practical in saying, 'Tacitus is unrivalled among historians… All the persons…in his works have an individuality of character… We know them as if we had lived with them.'

Going by the comments above, a good account of history must bring passion yet aloofness to it. Importantly, there should be objectivity towards, and absence of rancour against, the figure one is writing about. Moreover, the basic quest in writing about the past should be a combination of 'what set it off' and a desire that 'the actions of people do not fade with time.'

It is, therefore, good to follow the great, and their time-tested formula for putting pen to paper. But sometimes, it is best to leave it all to your instincts to do a job well and as honestly as possible. Homer left it to his Muse when he began *The Odyssey* with these lines, 'Sing in me, Muse, and through me tell the story of that man skilled in all ways of contending…'

The invocation to the Muse worked well and *The Odyssey* continues to fascinate, thousands of years after it was first told. Perhaps because the characters it spoke about were believable. It is not the intention of this book to airbrush the warts of the eight leaders, or to exaggerate their abilities. It is to present the leaders as they were, and to reflect on their policies as they affected the country.

1

JAWAHARLAL NEHRU: GANDHI'S CHOICE

I am the beginning and the middle and the end of all that is.
Of all knowledge I am the knowledge of the Soul.
Of the many paths of reason I am the one that leads to Truth.

—BHAGAVAD GITA

W as Jawaharlal Nehru the first accidental Prime Minister of India? Or was he the first imposed Prime Minister of India? Perhaps he was a bit of both. In the elections held in April 1946 to choose its new president, the Congress party had voted in favour of Sardar Patel. Had Patel stood his ground and asked that the democratic mandate be respected, Mahatma Gandhi may have yielded. But Patel himself withdrew in favour of Nehru, giving rise to the argument that the history of India may have taken a different turn under the former.

The political happenings of April 1946 were dramatic and came at a time when the Congress party was facing a stiff challenge from the Muslim League, which had made no secret of their wish to have a separate homeland for Muslims. Internally, too, there were differences among the leaders of the Congress. During his lifetime, Subhash Chandra Bose had not been on the same page as Nehru on many issues. Some of the other tall leaders of the party had also differed sharply with Nehru. By and large, these differences had been kept in check by the force of the Mahatma's personality. But this latest development during the elections was different, coming as it did on the eve of anticipated independence and at a time when the Congress party needed to show a united front not just to the British, but more importantly to the Muslim League.

The intrigues and whispers that accompany such an event must have kept the Congress leadership on edge. Moreover, it must have come as a blow to Nehru that he did not command the support within the party that he thought was his for the asking. As per the party's constitution at the time, only the Pradesh Congress Committees (PCCs) could nominate and elect the Congress president.

This time, however, it was not going to be just another annual ritual of electing a new president and passing on the party's baton to him. This time, the president-elect would automatically become the party's nominee for the first Prime Minister of India. It was going to be a historic election for the person elected, for the party and for the new nation.

The party had kept 29 April 1946 as the last date for filing the nominations for the post of the Congress president. It was hoped that unlike on some previous occasions when he had been partial to Nehru, this time Gandhi would let free choice prevail. But this was not to be, and as in the past, this time too he let it be known that Nehru, not his fellow Gujarati (Patel), was his choice for the post.

Normally that should have been enough to get Nehru elected, because, till then, Gandhi's word was law. But the party cadre held Patel in high esteem as a strong leader who could deliver at this critical time for the party and for the new country. Therefore, despite Gandhi's appeal in favour of Nehru, 12 out of 15 PCCs nominated Patel. The remaining three abstained from the nomination process. Nehru's name was proposed by a few working committee members who had no authority to do so.

When the results were announced, the party's message was clear and unambiguous. It wanted Patel to be the first Prime Minister of India. But soon after the results were declared, efforts began to persuade Patel to withdraw in favour of Nehru. To resolve the issue, Gandhiji said to Nehru, 'No PCC has put forward your name…only [a few members of] the working committee has.'[1]

Nehru did not respond. Instead there was petulant silence on his part and a vacant look into distant space. After some time, he left the room, but his disappointment continued to linger, troubling the Mahatma. When

Gandhi was given the final word that Nehru would not take second place, he asked Patel to withdraw.

Rajendra Prasad, who was later to become the first President of India, remarked that Gandhi 'had once again sacrificed his trusted lieutenant for the sake of the "glamorous Nehru"' and feared that 'Nehru would follow the British ways'.

Patel could not say no to the Mahatma. He agreed to step back and take the second position in the first government of independent India. He had reasoned that whereas office was likely to moderate Nehru, rejection would drive him into opposition; an outcome that would bitterly divide India.

Many years later, Maulana Azad wrote in his autobiography, '...the election of Sardar Patel would not be desirable in the existing circumstances... it seemed to me that Jawaharlal should be the new President... I acted according to my best judgment but the way things have shaped since then have made me realise that this was perhaps the greatest blunder of my political life... [It was a great mistake that] I did not support Sardar Patel...'[2]

Maulana's regret was in retrospect. Much before that, on 15 August 1947, Nehru had fulfilled his life's ambition. As he took the oath of high office, Nehru the thinker must have also reflected on the ruinous state of the nation that he was going to lead.

WRITING ON A CLEAN SLATE

Nehru had become the leader of a nation that was suffering from economic shortages, the weak integration of its regions, the after-effects of religious conflict and tensions with the new neighbour. He was the leader of a large nation, but without an inherited pattern of how to act in the world. What Nehru inherited was Britain's foreign policy, which was driven by its imperialistic ambitions and the adrenalin high of the 'great game'. But this was hardly a suitable model for a new nation, pacifist by nature and weak in every respect. It could hardly have an imperialistic agenda if it was struggling to establish its identity. All he had as a guide were a jumble of Indian ideas and legends about civilizational solidarity. He had to forge an international identity and the ways of practical action for India more or less from scratch.

Therefore, for all practical purposes, Nehru was writing on a clean slate; he could have moulded a new nation of four hundred million people in any shape and form he wanted. There were also dangers aplenty, because the country was poor and the task enormous. But Nehru had some unique gifts: the intellectual capacity to motivate people with the idealism of a new beginning, the ability to fire their imagination with passionate rhetoric and the vision to aim high. All this wasn't merely the wishlist of a desperate man whistling in the dark. The nobility of Nehru's words provided a newly born India with a lodestone that was ambitious and humane.

Nehru's vision of India was of a modern, secular state that would be inclusive and liberal. Once, when advised to outlaw communal parties as they flouted the spirit of the Constitution, he declared that communalism had to be defeated politically, not by the use of legal instruments. When asked why he was so strident in attacking Hindu communalism while he soft-pedalled on Muslim communalism, he replied that it was because majority communalism was far more dangerous, since it could easily be passed off as Indian nationalism. He had warned about hyper-nationalism in 1947: 'Nationalism…has a tendency to limit one, give one thoughts of one's country as something different from the rest of the world. The result is that the same nationalism which is the symbol of growth for a people becomes a symbol of the cessation of that growth in the mind…'[3]

It wasn't just nationalism that bothered him at that stage. Nehru was also concerned that the pluralistic India should not continue to be buffeted by the ill winds that began to flow with the partition. The essence of what Nehru gifted to his people then has been distilled in these words by a wise Pakistani scientist: '…in Pakistan we never…believed Nehru when he declared India's intent to become a pluralistic, liberal, syncretic state whose strength would lie in diversity. For us, all these were just fine words justifying Hindu majoritarianism under the cloak of democracy. Only now…have some Pakistanis realized what loss of secularism—even imperfect secularism—actually means.'[4]

In the beginning, the outside world, especially the United Kingdom (UK) and the United States (US), was not impressed by the abstemious and moralistic ways of the Indian leadership. After a visit to India and Pakistan, US Secretary of State John Foster Dulles briefed the

National Security Council (NSC) in June 1953. At that meeting he expressed high regard for the martial and religious qualities of Pakistan and contrasted this with his view of Jawaharlal Nehru as an utterly impractical statesman. Nehru may have anticipated such criticism, because in *The Discovery of India*, which he wrote in 1946, he mentions, 'The practical statesman took precedence over the uncompromising prophet.' But Dulles had come to hasty judgment. Had he asked, his fellow countryman Norman Cousins would have told him, 'Nehru was not one man, but a procession of men.'

Nehru was a statesman and a gifted writer; his sentences were finely crafted and memorable. His *Discovery of India* read just as well then as it does now. He spoke in the language that came naturally to him—English acquired through Harrow and Cambridge. When he rose to speak at the midnight hour, the sleeping world listened and remembered the fluently chiselled words. It wasn't just the 'tryst with destiny' that echoed long after Nehru had spoken but also his veiled reference to the partition when he said, freedom will be redeemed 'not wholly or in full measure'. And he had in mind the communal slaughter when he added, 'pains that continue even now.'

This multiplicity, sometimes mutually contradictory, is the closest we can come to a true description of the man. Nehru was no saint, nor was he an unblemished icon of Gandhi's stature. In fact, in the iconography of Indian independence, Gandhi was the saint and Nehru the prince. He was an aristocrat who belonged to the masses, a dictatorial taskmaster who was a great democrat. He was not comfortable with the negative-sounding term 'non-alignment', yet became its high priest.

He was a visionary who sometimes saw things wrong. When French journalist Jacques Marcuse interviewed Nehru in 1946, the latter had made three assertions: 'One, India would never be a Dominion. Two, there will never be a Pakistan. Three, when the British go, there will be no more communal trouble in India.'

Marcuse came back to Delhi soon after the Partition to interview Nehru again. He hesitated to bring up the issue of Nehru's three predictions. But Nehru himself brought up the subject and said, 'You remember, Marcuse, what I told you, "No Dominion, No Pakistan, No..."' After a pause he added, 'Wasn't I wrong?'[5]

Nehru was also a great diplomat who made major mistakes. Had he not appointed Mountbatten as independent India's first Governor General, he may not have taken decisions concerning Kashmir that have, for long, haunted India and its policymakers. On his own, and despite his idealistic streak, he may not have referred the issue to the United Nations (UN).

Conceptually, he gave moorings to India's foreign policy at a time when one part of the world was recovering from war and another was emerging from the dark spaces of colonialism. His advice to countries, including India, was to interpret their national interests in a way that did not conflict with overall international cooperation.

After Gandhi's assassination, Nehru became the most visible embodiment of India's struggle for its place in the world. It helped that Nehru's stature was so great as an incorruptible leader, a visionary and a politician above politics. Since then India has moved on, but Nehru remains a compelling figure, irresistible to historians, biographers and politicians.

THE ESSENCE OF HIS IMPRINT

Almost half a century after his death, the question is often asked whether India has moved radically away from much of Nehru's beliefs. Or is it still clad in the essentials of Nehruvianism?

Dispassionately viewed, a good deal of Nehru's legacy appears intact. It may be hotly contested, and admonishing fingers are often raised at his mistakes, but the canvas that he created for India remains largely intact. If a count were to be made of his legacies, the most lasting in impact and the most cherished should include democracy, pluralistic society, modern and liberal vision, free media and the soft power of India's people.

When Cousins asked him what might be his legacy to India, Nehru replied, 'Four hundred million people capable of governing themselves.'[6] If nearly a billion people have celebrated democracy in the latest Indian elections, it must in part be regarded as a tribute to Nehru and his scrupulous regard for the form and the substance of democracy.

Whether he accepted the partition of India or tried to prevent it is a subject of inconclusive debate. It is certain however that he never accepted the logic or the need of division. He remained convinced that multiple religions should not only coexist, but thrive in India. This gave the country its special quality as an 'ancient palimpsest' on which successive generations had inscribed their visions without erasing the past.

Undoubtedly, Nehru was a man of paradoxes; a moody, idealist intellectual who felt an almost mystical empathy for the peasant masses; an aristocrat, accustomed to privilege, who had passionate socialist convictions. Yet, he had concerns and apprehensions that anyone would have before an important appointment. For instance, here is Nehru worrying in a letter to Vijay Lakshmi Pandit about his first visit to the US: 'Which facet of myself should I put before the American public—the Indian or the European?... I am inclined to think that the best preparation for America is not to prepare and to trust to my native wit and mood of the moment... I go there to learn more than to teach.'

If he was tentative there, he was certain about where he wanted to take India. Nehru's vision for the newly independent India was sweeping in its range. It brought in the IIMs, IITs, medical colleges, agricultural universities, specialized laboratories, steel plants and hydro schemes besides the two modern cities of Chandigarh and Bhubaneswar. Pakistani commentator Pervez Hoodbhoy captures the essence of Nehru's imprint in these words, 'Nehru's stamp upon Indian science can be seen across the length and breadth of India in the form of dozens of scientific institutes and universities that owe to him. India is probably the world's only country whose constitution explicitly declares commitment to the "scientific temper"—a quintessential Nehruvian notion.'[7]

As early as the 1940s, he was preparing himself for a new India. He was seeking ideas from scientists to match an Asia that was rapidly becoming a continent of new states, where notions of self-esteem and historical injury allied with the new instrumentalities of state power. In 1946, Nehru articulated the need for India to pursue atomic energy research, 'I have no doubt India will develop her scientific researches and I hope Indian scientists will use the atomic force for constructive purposes.' Then, anticipating the 'No First Use' concept, he went on to add, 'But if India is threatened, she will inevitably try to defend herself by all means at her disposal.'

It is also worth recording that Pandit Nehru had been thinking about the military uses of nuclear energy ever since 1945. Finally, in a report of 3 February 1947 on 'Defence Policy and National Development',

Nehru articulated the role that nuclear energy should play in the Indian defence strategy, 'The probable use of atomic energy in warfare is likely to revolutionise all our concepts of war and defence…it makes it absolutely necessary for us to develop the methods of using atomic energy for both civil and military purposes.'[8]

Both the civil and military uses of atomic energy came about in course of time, but it is worth remembering that the initial push in that direction was given by Nehru. India's first nuclear reactor, CIRUS, was built with Canadian technical assistance. Just after CIRUS came online in 1960, Nehru told the National Development Council in 1961, 'We are approaching a stage when it is possible for us…to make atomic weapons.' Just about a dozen years later, the 40-megawatt CIRUS provided the plutonium for India's first nuclear test in 1974.

As with the setting up of the steel plants, advanced learning institutes and the areas of frontier technology like atomic power, Nehru was ploughing virgin soil in the field of national policy. And for all practical purposes, his was a lonely furrow.

DIFFERENT PULLS; MANY CONSIDERATIONS

Overall, there was a gap between what Nehru had set his sights on and what could be achieved. Nehru has been criticized for confusing the country's strategic interests with his personal idealism. His handling of the Kashmir issue and his China policy are often cited as cases in point. He did ensure that India should express its views on many international issues, but could not defend its interests.

Long after Nehru's death, his ideas live on; though the debate is vigorous about their effect on national destiny. Among the largely undisputed achievements Nehru is credited with is the practice of non-alignment. But the jury is out on whether it was anything more than a mantra: Did it actually protect the non-aligned from being subsumed by the powerful? Or was the truth far more modest—that the big powers were simply not interested in getting messed up with the affairs of so many of the non-aligned?

On the negative side of the ledger, the list is rather long. His handling of the Kashmir issue and its reference to the UN is the most vexing. His

China policy is almost unanimously attacked whenever and wherever it is discussed. And he is faulted invariably for missing the chance of getting a seat in the UNSC. There are many more issues that could be listed on both sides of the ledger, but even this short list should be enough for an assessment of the man and of the issues that linger long after him.

However, it is unfortunate that critics should see his actions in terms of the end product. Rarely is the attempt made to view his decisions in the frame of the larger picture obtaining then. India had barely put salve on the wounds of partition when it was attacked by Pakistan in Kashmir. Even as the government was engaged in that operation, it had to work overtime to calm the communal nerves. There was also the gigantic task of resettling the refugees from Pakistan and encouraging them to start life all over again.

Overall, India was then scraping the very bottom of the global poor countries list; it was food deficient and short of foreign exchange. There were undoubtedly some able officials to assist him—the civil servants who came to be known as the steel frame of India. But the fact is that they were trained to be maintainers of law and order for the colonial masters, not innovative pushers of development projects. Nor were there diplomats who had the experience of negotiating their way through the minefield that statecraft often can be. Nehru, himself without training or expertise in these various fields, had to learn quickly on the job to become a mentor to others and to guide the national destiny. Under the circumstances, and with such a diverse and fraught plate, it is unfair to judge the man only by his mistakes.

Conventional wisdom has it that Nehru was the prima donna of non-alignment, and that his commitment to the cause was absolute. It is the second part of that assumption that is in dispute. The fact is that he had tried to scuttle the first Summit of the Non-Aligned Countries. There were reasons for his reluctance, which he shared with the then US Ambassador to India, John K. Galbraith:

> …he was wary of his peers among the non-aligned countries; Josip Broz Tito of Yugoslavia and Gamal Abdel Nasser of Egypt. And he found the leaders of the newly independent states too radical and unpredictable for his taste. For another, Nehru was all too aware of

India's dependence on American and western aid and had no desire to see a contretemps such as the one over the Bandung Conference. Tito and Nasser, however, forced his hand by publicly announcing a conference in Belgrade in September 1961. Nehru told Galbraith that he would attend but without much enthusiasm...[9]

This is representative of the different pulls and the many considerations that acted to shape Nehru's policy. It was a tough tightrope walk for a new nation, especially when other leaders in many of the emerging countries were succumbing to the temptations of quick fixes. India was fortunate that it was safely led to the tranquil waters of democracy. But Nehru's record in foreign affairs has also been the subject of conflicting interpretations.

Sympathetic voices have defended him for piloting India with prudence through an uncertain period. They have praised him for opting in favour of a world of diversity at a time when it was divided rigidly between two blocs. That choice, plus his championing the struggle against colonialism and racism, raised India's standing in the developing world. Those who talk now of 'Look East' and 'Act East' should also remember that it was Nehru who hosted the Asian Relations Conference in Delhi as far back as 1947.

India had also suffered grave humiliations during his time. It lost the Northern Areas and a part of Jammu and Kashmir (J&K) to Pakistan in 1947–8. Later, in 1962, it lost Aksai Chin to China. In fact, Nehru has the unfortunate distinction of being the only prime minister in whose tenure India lost large portions of its territory in battle. (The loss of territory in the Rann of Kutch in 1966 was due to an arbitration award.)

MISADVENTURES IN KASHMIR

There is one issue, however, that continues to baffle people. Pakistani tribals, supported in large numbers by its army, had invaded J&K in October 1947. In the battles that followed, the Indian army repulsed the attack, forcing the invaders to vacate some of the area they had occupied. Yet, a large portion of J&K continued to be under their occupation. The US and the Soviet Union were sympathetic to the

Indian view that Pakistan was the aggressor. But UK, the erstwhile colonial power, chose to side with Pakistan. Ironically, it was under the British pressure, articulated by the Governor General Mountbatten, that Nehru decided to take the matter to the UN in the belief that this newly created world body would weigh in on India's side and ensure that Pakistan vacated its aggression.

Ever since, the debate has continued over the wisdom of this move. Why, critics ask, should Nehru have approached the UN when the Indian army was winning the battles? Had it been given free hand, they suggest, the army would have pushed the Pakistani invaders out of the entire territory of J&K. There is a counterview, however, that suggests that the two battling armies had reached a stalemate on ground, and that reference to the world body was the prudent option.

But critics remain sceptical, and the argument persists; why did Nehru take the Kashmir issue to the UNSC? Some Nehru apologists have tried to explain it away by suggesting that had India not made the move, Pakistan would have taken the issue to the UN. Nothing could be more far-fetched than this. There was no way Pakistan could have done this; after all, Pakistan was the aggressor in Kashmir. And the entire point in this reference to the UN was that the aggression should be vacated.

It was not the apprehension that Pakistan may pre-empt India and approach the UN that forced Nehru's hand. Instead, British machinations in favour of Pakistan did the trick. In pursuance of that plan, Mountbatten convinced Nehru that it was morally the right course to make the reference to the world body. It was Nehru's fault that he succumbed.

Having made the reference, he was quick to realize his mistake. Nehru was also conscious of the anger of the Indian people that this reference was made unnecessarily. In a statement he made at a press conference in New Delhi, he explained the parameters within which India had approached the UNSC:

> On 30 December 1947, a formal reference was made to the Security Council through the Representative of Government of India with the United Nations... The Government of India requested the Security Council, therefore, to ask the Government of Pakistan;

1. to prevent Pakistan Government personnel, military and civil, participating in or assisting the invasion of J&K State;
2. to call upon other Pakistan nationals to desist from taking any part in the fighting in the J&K State;
3. to deny to the invaders: (a) access to and use of its territory for operations against Kashmir; (b) military and other supplies; (c) all other kinds of aid that might tend to prolong the present struggle.

Nehru then explained that the reference to UNSC was limited to the issues he had mentioned and that there was urgency to the matter: '...the first step that must be taken is to put a stop to the fighting and this can only be done if the invaders withdraw.'

Sadly, the passage of history has obscured this important fact. Pakistan has taken full advantage of this amnesia to claim that the very fact that Nehru had made a reference to the UN indicates that Kashmir is a disputed territory. It was in consciousness of this that Nehru then went on to stress at that press conference, 'It must be remembered that all the fighting has taken place on Indian Union territory and it is the inherent right of the Government of India to drive back any invaders on its territory. Till the Kashmir State is free of invaders, no other matter can be considered.'[10] But critics are not convinced by this explanation. They argue, and largely correctly, that Nehru fell for British scheming in favour of Pakistan, and Mountbatten's persuasion.

Having made the reference, Nehru was soon showing signs of disillusionment with the UN and the trust he had reposed in it. In a statement in the Constituent Assembly on 5 March 1948 his cri de coeur came through clearly:

> Our making a reference on this issue to the UN Security Council was an act of faith, because we believe in the progressive realization of a world order and a world government. In spite of many shocks, we have adhered to the ideals represented by the UN and its charter. But those very ideals teach us also certain duties and responsibilities to our own people and to those who put their trust in us. To betray these people would be to betray the basic ideals for which the UN stands or should stand.[11]

Unfortunately for him and for the succeeding generations of Indians, both his idealism and the trust he placed in that world body were betrayed. Can the inference be made from Nehru's statement that he had misjudged the world body? Or worse still, was it an error of judgment on his part to have rushed to the UN? These questions have been asked, but more in remorse or anger. Sometimes, the blame is shifted conveniently to Mountbatten. It is true that he was the evil spirit goading Nehru to make the reference to the UN, but Nehru was not a novice. He had spent a lifetime dealing with the British and observing their devious ways. Surely, as a statesman, he should have known that the world body could be a snake pit and that once you have placed yourself at its mercy, there would be diverse pulls and pressures. Yet, he experimented and called it idealism.

In a speech in the Parliament on 28 March 1951, Nehru reverted to the theme that had been troubling him and the entire nation:

> The accession of Kashmir to India is entirely in conformity with the Indian Independence Act...it is also fully in accord with all that has happened in the case of other princely States which acceded to India...We did not ask the UN to adjudge the validity of Kashmir's accession or to determine where the sovereignty lay. We did not seek arbitration but we went to them to complain about aggression by Pakistan which we thought might jeopardize world peace. The UN took advantage of our initiative in our referring the matter to them and thus enlarged the scope of their enquiry...Until now neither the UN Commission nor the Security Council has suggested that the accession was open to question.[12]

There can be no contest with the explanatory first part of Nehru's statement, but even this did not clarify why he chose to approach the world body.

Nehru said, 'We went to them to complain about aggression by Pakistan which we thought might jeopardize world peace.' But he forgot to elaborate on how a localized aggression, in what was then a remote part of the world, could jeopardize world peace. Besides, if world peace was indeed at risk, the UN itself could have taken the initiative to prevent such a major war.

It is a cardinal principle of diplomacy that once you bring your dispute out in the open, the busybodies of the world will take over. Anyone and everyone feels free to interject. It happened in this case too. The US, at first because of nagging by the UK and later due to the military pacts it had signed with Pakistan, began to take increasing interest in the Indo-Pak affairs. It irritated Nehru so much that he had to bluntly tell the US ambassador that he was 'tired of receiving moral advice from the United States.' Nehru went on to warn that he would not back down, 'even if Kashmir, India, and the whole world went to pieces.'

Nehru had visited the US in 1949 to be welcomed warmly by its people and somewhat correctly by the establishment. Nehru found the Americans rather materialistic and the Truman administration bristled at Nehru's suggestion that the West recognize Communist China and deal more amicably with the Soviets. On its part, Washington betrayed even greater insensitivity by inviting Pakistan's Prime Minister Liaquat Ali Khan shortly after Nehru's visit. This riled Nehru sufficiently to make him write to his sister Mrs Pandit, 'The Americans are either very naïve or singularly lacking in intelligence. They go through the same routine whether it is Nehru…or Liaquat Ali… It does appear that there is a concerted attempt to build up Pakistan and build down, if I may say, India.'[13]

Nehru went a second time to the US in 1956. This time, Dwight Eisenhower went out of his way to make the visit special. As Bruce Riedel notes, 'Eisenhower was…fascinated by Nehru, whom he regarded…as "a somewhat inexplicable and occasionally exasperating personality" because he often seemed to condemn American and British actions more vigorously than he condemned Soviet behavior.'[14]

Eisenhower took Nehru to his farmhouse in Gettysburg, where they spent 14 hours talking of the world and its state. Eisenhower recorded this conversation in fourteen pages of notes. Some of the more pleasing parts of their conversation, first at the White House and then in Gettysburg, must have included this:

> In private, he found Nehru much more critical of Soviet behavior in Hungary than he had been in public. Nehru was 'horrified' at the Soviet invasion and predicted that it 'spelled the eventual death knell of international communism', because 'nationalism is stronger than communism'.[15]

Yet this did not stop Eisenhower from proposing American mediation in the Kashmir issue, nor did it prevent Nehru from rebuffing the offer.

But Pakistan was not deterred. It kept persisting with the new US President, Kennedy, that he should do something to help Pakistan, and this time the Pakistani appeal was more blunt than usual:

Ayub Khan says, I've been betrayed. The president has promised me, first at Mount Vernon and then when his wife came, that I was the favorite of the Americans. After all, I've always signed treaties. I have all these CIA operations going on. I should be his best friend. Why is he coming to the defense of India?' Then Khan begins writing letters to the president and saying publicly, 'If you're going to help India, I should get something in return.'

And...what does Pakistan want? It wants the rest of Kashmir... It was Pakistan's raison d'être, and particularly Ayub Khan's, as a military dictator, raison d'être to recover control of Kashmir. Galbraith and Kennedy saw this as extremely dangerous. Not only would they potentially have a war with China, they could have a two-front war.

So Kennedy writes to Ayub Khan, '...our treaty obligations are with you in the event of war with communism. Not war with India... if you invade India at this moment, we will see that as a hostile act.'[16]

If Ayub had been blunt in pursuing his agenda, Kennedy was equally blunt in setting the record straight when he said that America's treaty obligations related to war with communism, not war with India. Still Ayub Khan's efforts paid off handsomely in another matter: he did not get the rest of Kashmir that he was pleading for, but he got the most generous Indus Waters Treaty as a result of the American pressure on India. But before we come to that, let us resume the thread on Kashmir from where we had left off.

The issue has preoccupied the Indian Parliament often. In a Lok Sabha session on 6 December 1978, Dr Karan Singh, son of the former ruler of J&K, clarified, 'Our ancestors had established this State nearly 120 years ago. It has been a unique State from the plains of Jammu to the hills of Gilgit and Chitral and from Poonch to Ladakh...what steps are you taking to recapture 84,000 sq miles of land in Kashmir which is under foreign occupation?'

In the same debate, Atal Bihari Vajpayee, who was the External Affairs minister then, asserted, '... It [J&K] is not merely a piece of land for us, it is a symbol of certain ideals. J&K became a part of India under the same procedure under which the other princely States had joined India...'[17]

As then, there is unanimity in the country and across the political class that the entire territory of J&K is an integral part of India even now. But as we will soon note, that intent has remained just that. Therefore if Nehru made a mistake, the subsequent leadership has not found it possible to correct it; at least not so far.

Interestingly, the two stalwarts of Indian politics, Nehru and Vajpayee, shared almost a similar view of Pakistan. Nehru had not yet been broken by the Chinese invasion, and Vajpayee was a rising star on the Indian political firmament. There was a clear difference in age, experience and viewpoints on many issues; one was a prime minister constrained by the responsibilities of office, the other an opposition leader gifted with a silver tongue. The older man was a national icon and international statesman. He saw in the young opponent a potential prime minister. They crossed verbal swords in parliament, yet on Pakistan their views were remarkably similar.

On 16 August 1961, in a debate in Lok Sabha about the international situation, Nehru said, '...the foundation of Pakistan was based on opposition to India... Hatred towards India is the genesis of the birth of Pakistan...if the problem of Kashmir is resolved the rulers of Pakistan will raise some other bogey to continue tensions between the two countries.'[18]

Agreeing with the prime minister, Vajpayee went on to say:

... An [Indus] agreement was reached about canal waters with the hope that it would create goodwill between the two countries. Berubari was given to Pakistan in the hope that it would improve relations between us. But what was the result of all this? Pakistan always raises new obstacles...should we not review our policy towards Pakistan? The day Pakistan will end its enmity towards India, Pakistan's existence would come to an end. The very foundation of Pakistan is hatred of India.[19]

370: A WASTEFUL MILLSTONE?

Barely had India recovered from Pakistani aggression in Kashmir, when it created yet another complication for itself. This, despite the warning by Babasaheb Ambedkar and the reluctance of Sardar Patel to be associated with what came to be known as Article 370 of the Indian constitution on 17 October 1949.

We tend to forget some important markers from our past; otherwise we should have set in stone these words spoken wisely by B.R. Ambedkar when he refused to draft Article 370. He told Sheikh Abdullah in 1948:

> You wish India should protect your borders, she should build roads in your area, she should supply you food grains, and Kashmir should get equal status as India. But the Government of India should have only limited powers and Indian people should have no rights in Kashmir. To give consent to this proposal would be a treacherous thing against the interests of India, and I, as the law minister of India, will never do it.[20]

Ambedkar was prophetically correct in saying that this proposal would be treacherous. Yet, Nehru had insisted that Article 370 be adopted by the parliament. Besides the gap this created between Kashmir and the rest of the country, it also retarded the development of the region because of the restrictions it put on settlement and the practical difficulties in setting up industries there. Ever since, it has proved to be a wasteful millstone for the country and ruinous for the state itself.

According to the statements in the parliament, and by common consensus, it was meant to be a temporary provision. But Article 370 lingered on out of fear of the reaction from the Valley's politicians should it be repealed. Added to this was the worry about Pakistan's mischief. However, the background to its introduction was once again the idealism of Nehru and his strong belief that temporary aberrations like Article 370 would be taken in the spirit that they were first introduced in. As Faizan Mustafa explains,

> It (Article 370) is the first article of Part XXI of the Constitution. The heading of this part is 'Temporary, Transitional and Special Provisions'... Article 3 of the J&K Constitution declares J&K to

be an integral part of India... Moreover people of state are referred as 'permanent residents' not 'citizens'.[21]

In fact, the preamble to that constitution, adopted by J&K in 1956, states categorically,

> We, the people of the state of J&K, having solemnly resolved, in pursuance of the accession of this State to India which took place on the twenty sixth day of October, 1947, to further define the existing relationship of the State with the Union of India as an integral part thereof...

Once you are an integral part of something, and acknowledge yourself to be so, there can be no room for ifs and buts. It was the hesitations pointed out above that stayed the subsequent governments' hand, and in the process, this indecision helped the Pakistani propaganda. It cited this as yet another case in its point that the Indian state itself is not sure about J&K's exact relationship with it.

Twice (on 22 November 1968 and 19 November 1971) Vajpayee had moved a resolution in the Lok Sabha seeking the abrogation of Article 370 of the Constitution. Introducing the resolution in 1968, Vajpayee had mentioned that 'a psychological barrier stands between J&K and the rest of the country...this barrier strengthens the anti-India elements.' He then described the situation in J&K as 'explosive, where pro-Pakistan elements were inciting people and army jawans were being stoned.'[22]

The exclusionary damage done by Article 370 was bad enough, but the Nehru government compounded the mistake by bringing in Article 35-A in 1954. It gave the J&K government the right to decide who qualifies as a 'permanent resident'. In practice, this provision had shut out the possibility of settlement in J&K for anyone from outside the state. Only the permanent residents of J&K could acquire land, settle, and get government jobs, etc. in the state. To make it virtually impossible for others to settle in J&K, the article also provided that none of the above laws could be held as void on the ground that it takes away the rights conferred on other citizens of the country.

This Constitutional Order was given sanctity by President Rajendra Prasad in 1954 upon the advice of the Nehru government. Since then, this presidential order has led to debate and considerable controversy. It is often pointed out by critics that the process prescribed by the constitution is to introduce the bill in the Parliament. That course must be followed to make any changes to the constitution or add a new law. But those arguing in favour insist that under Article 370(1)(d), the President is allowed to make exceptions and modifications with the concurrence of the government of the state for the benefit of the subjects of the state of J&K.

However, the fact is that both Article 370 and 35A were anomalies. There is hardly any other example in the world where a country wilfully, and for so long, continues to discriminate against its own citizens. Most other countries in a similar situation would have swung to the other extreme and forcibly changed the demographic profile of that part of the country to ensure that people living there did not have the numbers and the scope for mischief against the State. Italy did so successfully in South Tyrol, Pakistan settled large numbers from Punjab in POK and China introduced Han in substantial numbers in both Tibet and Xinjiang.

On the rare occasion when a country has introduced a special measure to give protection to a part, such provisions are, by their very nature, temporary, to ward off a particular difficulty at a certain point of time. That was Nehru's intention too when he introduced these two articles. But somewhere along the way, he forgot the fundamental point on which his intention was based.

If he had caved to pressure from Mountbatten in agreeing to make a reference to the UN on Kashmir issue, it is also alleged that Sheikh Abdullah was instrumental in persuading him to introduce Articles 370 and 35A. He had taken the plea that it was necessary as a temporary measure to protect the economic interests of the residents of J&K, who would otherwise be overwhelmed by refugees coming in from Pakistan. They, the Sheikh argued successfully, would buy out the properties of Kashmiris. Over a period of time, this original argument got replaced by the emotive twist given conveniently by Kashmiri politicians, which somehow correlated accession with Article 370.

MISSED OPPORTUNITIES TO SHAPE OUR DESTINY

It wasn't just on issues relating to Pakistan and Kashmir that Nehru went against the advice given to him by the senior Indian leaders of the time. He had misjudged China as well. Ever since the 1950s, curious scholars have asked: Was the offer of a UNSC seat made to India? The more inquisitive follow it up with the query: Was the offer genuine? The hint of an answer, if at all there was one, remained ambiguous. All this, while the possibility remained suspended hopefully in the air that one day some secret vault might open to reveal what was, or wasn't, the truth.

The reason for this frustrating wait was the archaic system that treats the smallest scrap of confidential information as a State secret. But with the passage of time, and a more relaxed bureaucratic regime in many parts of the world, the long-buried archives are opening up. It is now possible to draw a reasonably accurate picture of what may have actually transpired.

There is now both circumstantial and archival evidence that the UNSC seat was indeed offered to India by the US in 1950 and by the USSR in 1955. Anton Harder, a scholar who has studied the subject, claims that the US offer should 'be regarded as quite sincere'.[23]

This offer came at a time when Washington was looking to shape the UN's decision-making in its favour. The Soviet Union had walked out of the UN in January 1950 in protest against the US (and others) blocking the People's Republic of China (PRC) from taking up Nationalist China's seat in the UNSC. The US used the Soviet Union's absence to push resolutions against North Korea's aggression in the Korean War, which began in 1950.

At this and other such moves by the US, the USSR realized that it had miscalculated the harm to its interests that its absence from the UN could cause. Reversing its earlier decision, the Soviet Union returned to its seat in August 1950.

The offer of the Security Council seat to India was made shortly thereafter. India had voted with the US on two of the three resolutions passed on the Korean War during the Soviet Union's absence from the UN. This, the US regarded as a positive sign that India could be wooed to its camp if it was incentivized with offers like the seat at the global high table.

The curious also ask if, besides this, there was some other context to the US offer. It is difficult to say so categorically, but the very fact of getting one of the leading lights of the developing world on its side may have been one motivation. Nehru's public statements do not make us any wiser on the issue. However, his correspondence with Vijaya Lakshmi Pandit, holder of various major diplomatic positions in the late 1940s and early 1950s, is more enlightening. In late August 1950, Pandit wrote to her brother from Washington, DC, where she was then posted as India's Ambassador to the US:

> One matter that is being cooked up in the State Department should be known to you. This is the unseating of China as a Permanent Member in the Security Council and of India being put in her place. I have just seen Reuter's report of your answer to the same question. Last week, I had interviews with [John Foster] Dulles and [Philip] Jessup,[24] reports of which I have sent to Bajpai.[25] Both brought up this question and Dulles seemed particularly anxious that a move in this direction should be started. Last night I heard from Marquis Childs, an influential columnist of Washington, that Dulles has asked him on behalf of the State Department to build up public opinion along these lines. I told him our attitude and advised him to go slow in the matter as it would not be received with any warmth in India.[26]

There is a Hindi phrase that aptly describes this situation—'*Muddai Sust, Gawah Chust* (the complainant is lazy, but the witness is agile).' Still, in retrospect, it is hard to believe that Mrs Pandit actually advised Childs to 'Go Slow' on the American offer of a Security Council seat to India!

Regarded now, at our distance today, this advice seems bizarre. Which other country would have forgone an offer like that? Alas, Nehru's response within the week did not carry any hopeful sign either,

> In your letter you mention that the State Department is trying to unseat China as a Permanent Member of the Security Council and to put India in her place. So far as we are concerned, we are not going to countenance it. That would be bad from every point of view. It would be a clear affront to China and it would mean some kind of a break between us and China. I suppose the state department would not like that, but we have no intention of following that course.[27]

The widely admired statesman had erred. Why did he discard the first and the most important principle of diplomacy, that your national interests are supreme? How did he presume that if India were to take the Security Council seat, it 'would mean some kind of a break between us and China'? Did China worry about the possible 'break with India' when it was advancing into Tibet? Or when it was occupying Aksai Chin? Or when it gladly gobbled up the Shaksgam valley of Pakistan Occupied Kashmir (PoK), which was illegally gifted to it by Pakistan?

But Nehru did not stop there. Instead of agreeing with the US that India deserved a seat in the Security Council, Nehru went on to assert that India would adopt a proactive role on China's behalf:

> We shall go on pressing for China's admission in the UN and the Security Council. I suppose that a crisis will come during the next session of the General Assembly of the UN on this issue. The people's government of China is sending a full delegation there. If they fail to get in, there will be trouble which might even result in the USSR and some other countries finally quitting the UN. That may please the State Department, but it would mean the end of the UN as we have known it. That would also mean a further drift towards war.[28]

Reading it now, with the benefit of hindsight, it seems surreal that he should have painted such an alarmist picture. How could a man acknowledged widely as a statesman, so readily jump to conclusions like 'the end of the UN' and 'drift towards war'? At our distance, as we consider Nehru's decision and the logic of it, this seems rather extreme. In fact, it could be argued that nothing of the sort may have happened in case India had decided to take the place that was on offer to it. Rather, we missed a great opportunity to shape our destiny in league with the high rollers of the world.

As for the American motivation in offering the Security Council seat to India, the context for this move by the US needs to be put in perspective. As Anton Harder writes:

> The tensions of the Cold War were spreading to East Asia, while Europe appeared to be in deadlock. Specifically, the emergence of an apparently communist government in control of China had created a new fault-line. The other mega-state of Asia, democratic India, was burnishing its independence from the democratic camp by refusing

to acknowledge this fault-line and had gone as far as transferring its diplomatic recognition of China from the defeated nationalists in Taiwan to the unknown revolutionary guerrillas in Beijing.[29]

It wasn't just the American observers who were bewildered by Nehru's fascination for the 'revolutionary guerrillas' of Beijing. Patel was also deeply sceptical of the Indian policy of giving one-sided favours to China. He warned Nehru in a letter in 1950:

> During the last several months, outside the Russian camp, we have practically been alone in championing the cause of Chinese entry into UN and in securing from the Americans assurances on the question of Formosa. We have done everything we could to assuage Chinese feelings, to allay its apprehensions and to defend its legitimate claims in our discussions and correspondence with America and Britain and in the UN. Inspite of this, China is not convinced about our disinterestedness; it continues to regard us with suspicion and the whole psychology is one, at least outwardly, of scepticism perhaps mixed with a little hostility. I doubt if we can go any further than we have done already to convince China of our good intentions, friendliness and goodwill...[30]

While Patel's letter was in the context of China's admission into the UN in place of Formosa (Taiwan), the logic of it was to apply equally when India began championing for China the Security Council seat that was being offered to it. It is to the credit of Patel that unlike the trend in recent times, he chose not to whisper a word about this to a helpful journalist.

Still, India got a second chance within five years.

This time, the offer was made by the Soviet Union during a visit to India in 1955 by Nikita Khrushchev, the first secretary of the Communist Party of the Soviet Union, and Nikolai Bulganin, the prime minister of the Soviet Union. The record of the conversation between Bulganin and Nehru in 1955 speaks for itself,

> [Nikolai] Bulganin: Regarding your suggestion about the four power conference we would take appropriate action. While we are discussing the general international situation and reducing tension, we propose

suggesting at a later stage India's inclusion as the sixth member of the Security Council.

JN [Jawaharlal Nehru]: Perhaps you know that some people in USA have suggested that India should replace China in the Security Council. This is to create trouble between us and China. We are, of course, wholly opposed to it. Further, we are opposed to pushing ourselves forward to occupy certain positions because that may itself create difficulties and India might itself become a subject to controversy. If India is to be admitted to the Security Council, it raises the question of the revision of the Charter of the UN. We feel that this should not be done till the question of China's admission and possibly of others is first solved. I feel that we should first concentrate on getting China admitted. What is your opinion about the revision of the Charter? In our opinion, this does not seem to be an appropriate time for it.

Bulganin: We proposed the question of India's membership of the Security Council to get your views, but agree that this is not the time for it and it will have to wait for the right moment later on. We also agree that things should be taken one by one.[31]

This conversation makes painful reading. If it was an international post that was being offered to him personally, that would have been Nehru's business. He could have accepted or rejected it as he pleased. But should he not have consulted his cabinet before rejecting the offer that was being made to India? Moreover, the intermixing of China's Security Council seat and the revision of the UN Charter with regard to India's membership of the Security Council could only indicate to Bulganin Nehru's disinterest, bordering on disdain.

Normally, when such an unexpected bonanza comes a country's way and the leader is not sure whether he should accept it, he seeks time. He is likely to respond gracefully and tell the other leader that he would revert soon after internal consultations, or something of that nature. In this case, there was no risk of upsetting China as before, because what was being offered was a sixth seat in the Security Council. Bulganin must have thought the entire matter through before suggesting India's inclusion.

Yet Nehru dismissed the offer. By declining it in the manner that he did, he was also putting the future generations at a disadvantage, because such offers don't come easily and often. Today, India is struggling with half-a-dozen other countries to get a foot in to the Security Council, and that too as a half member at best.

There was an interesting sidelight to Bulganin's visit. Nehru was unhappy by the negative coverage in the British press about the visit and he complained about it in a letter to Edwina Mountbatten, 'The visit of Bulganin and Khrushchev has evidently raised the temperature of some of the British newspapers... Some have...worked themselves up into frenzy... I associated some restraint and some balance of mind with them but evidently this is lacking now. I am distressed...'[32]

INDIA'S TRYST WITH PERFIDY

Nehru may have had his reasons for keeping China's friendship and its interests in view while interacting with the leaders from the US and the Soviet Union. But his colleagues were not equally sanguine about China's intentions. For instance, Patel had expressed his doubts as early as 1950 in a letter to Nehru:

> I have carefully gone through the correspondence between the External Affairs Ministry and our Ambassador in Peking [K.M. Panikkar] and through him the Chinese Government. I have tried to peruse this correspondence as favourably to our Ambassador and the Chinese Government as possible, but I regret to say that neither of them comes out well as a result of this study. The Chinese Government has tried to delude us by professions of peaceful intention. My own feeling is that at a crucial period they managed to instill into our Ambassador a false sense of confidence in their so-called desire to settle the Tibetan problem by peaceful means. There can be no doubt that during the period covered by this correspondence, the Chinese must have been concentrating for an onslaught on Tibet. The final action of the Chinese, in my judgement, is little short of perfidy. The tragedy of it is that the Tibetans put faith in us; they chose to be guided by us; and

we have been unable to get them out of the meshes of Chinese diplomacy or Chinese malevolence...[33]

So while India was busy espousing the Chinese case, China was advancing into Tibet. It wasn't just a case, however, of misreading Chinese intentions in Tibet. Nehru had enormous faith in China's good behaviour even on matters of bilateral concern. The enormity of his trust in China was obvious in this conversation with President Eisenhower in 1956:

> Nehru pressed Eisenhower to support giving Communist China the seat in the United Nations Security Council...The prime minister dismissed any possibility that China would attack India, given the 'fortunate location of the Himalayan mountain chain' on their 1,800 miles of common border. India could not afford the cost of building a defence along this long border: Taking part in an arms race would jeopardize its hopes of development. Better, Nehru concluded, that India stay neutral in the cold war and seek to build friendly ties with China. Eisenhower, with China's role in the Korean War still fresh in his memory, refused to budge on China and the UN seat...[34]

On the few occasions when the border issue was raised within India, Nehru smothered it with a dismissive hand. Prior to the signing of the Panchsheel Treaty in 1954,[35] Nehru wrote a note to the Ministry of External Affairs (MEA) rejecting a proposal to strengthen the border by providing military training to border inhabitants in large numbers: 'The defence of our border depends far more on [road] communications than on men. It would be [a] waste of men to place them in remote places on the border where they cannot be easily reached. Therefore, the plan of making roads should be pushed ahead... I think this is important. Without such roads, no proper defence can be organized.'

Complex issues don't fade away. Instead, they keep cropping up till one side decides to settle them finally or offers a solution that satisfies the other party. But this was a bizarre situation, where China was not required to make any effort to meet India's concerns even halfway. Instead of safeguarding its own interests, India was making all effort to promote China's interests, both globally with the major powers and in Tibet.

Sadly, this contagion had spread down the line. During Nehru's China visit in October 1954, the Indian ambassador, N. Raghavan, hosted a dinner. In the Chinese transcript of the discussion at the banquet, Mao Zedong, chairman of the PRC, told Nehru soothingly that there were only 10,000 troops in Tibet and another 10,000 in Chengdu, which were there just for road construction, after which they would leave. Nehru did not respond. But Raghavan interceded to say, 'What China does in Tibet is China's own business. India trusts China.'

It wasn't just the Chinese intentions in Tibet that we had read wrong. The Indian establishment's assessment of the Chinese plans vis-à-vis India, too, was way off the mark. In June 1962, a few months before the Chinese attacked India, the chief of army staff, General Pran Nath Thapar, wrote to the defence ministry, 'I am convinced that the Chinese will not attack any of our positions even if they [Indian posts] are relatively weaker than theirs.'[36]

Three months later, in mid-September 1962, when the moves to evict China from the Nam Ka Chu area were being debated, the foreign secretary M.J. Desai insisted: '"The Chinese would not escalate the fighting"…The foreign secretary's confidence stemmed from yet another source. The MEA's China division and the director of military operations at army headquarters had concluded that the (Chinese) infrastructure was incapable of supporting a full-scale invasion deep into Indian territory.'[37]

The officially appointed Brooks-Bhagat committee, which went into the reasons for India's debacle in 1962, was scathing in its conclusion. It damned the government squarely on almost all counts: 'Against all evidence of increasing military disadvantage, and all the warnings that the Chinese gave us by actions like those at Galwan and Dhola, the government had convinced itself that when forced to choose between going to war against India and withdrawing, the Chinese would withdraw.'[38]

It's a pity that the entire system had misread China and its intentions. There could have been two reasons for it: a genuine slip on their part or a desire not to go against the political current because Prime Minister Nehru kept vouching for China's good behaviour, and the Soviet support for India that he thought would restrain China.[39]

The Chinese attack started before the first morning light on 20 October 1962. When the fog lifted across the Himalayas at 5 a.m., the

Chinese were there. To give just one example of how ferocious the attack was—at one point across the Thagla Ridge, 150 artillery guns and mortars boomed together to begin an intense bombardment. China attacked India over multiple points across the border, leading to a month-long war between about 15,000 Indian soldiers and 80,000 Chinese troops.

The fighting was spread across the western sector in Aksai Chin, over almost 600 kms. Most of the attacks by the People's Liberation Army (PLA) were aimed at dislodging Indian troops from the outposts that had been established as a result of Nehru's Forward Policy, rather than capturing territory. A thousand kilometres away, in the eastern sector in North East Frontier Agency (NEFA) and Assam, the Chinese forces advanced equally easily.

The Chinese knew exactly where the Indians were, how many there were at each position, and what kind of weaponry they had. As was the case in NEFA in the east, pre-war intelligence gathering had been carried out in the Aksai Chin area by small teams of surveyors who could move freely and, presumably, undetected on the barren plateau. Since the Chinese were already in occupation of most of the Aksai Chin plateau, further occupation of territory in this sector was not their objective.

By 18 November, the Chinese had penetrated close to the outskirts of Tezpur in Assam. Having achieved all their objectives, they declared a unilateral ceasefire on 21 November. Later, the Chinese forces withdrew 20 km behind the McMahon Line, which China called 'the 1959 line of actual control' in the Eastern Sector, and 20 km behind the line of its latest position in Ladakh.

After the war, the Chinese President Liu Shaoqi told the Sri Lankan leader Felix Bandaranaike that the conflict was 'to demolish India's arrogance and illusions of grandeur'.

President Liu was not wide of the mark. The scars of that demolition still linger in the national psyche. India's military defeat in 1962 was a dividing line between the post-Independence Nehruvian idealism and a man betrayed by realpolitik. Nehru was never the same man again; from a conjurer of lofty words, he was busy counting the national losses of territory, international prestige and domestic morale. He was a broken man. There is no doubt that he had become weak physically and of will as well.

An observant Lee Kuan Yew recalls:

> I visited Nehru again in 1964 when I stopped in Delhi on my way
> back from a tour of Africa. He was a shadow of his former self; weary,
> weak in voice and posture, slumped on a sofa. His concentration
> was poor. The Chinese attack across the Himalayas had been a blow
> to his hopes of Afro-Asian solidarity. I left the meeting filled with
> sadness. He died a few months later in May.[40]

But Nehru's disillusionment was not merely on account of the Chinese
perfidy or the weakness of the people he had trusted the country's defences
with. It was compounded by the blow that India stood virtually alone
in the world; his championing of the Third World, the non-alignment
that he had nurtured as its high priest, amounted to nothing when India
needed the Third World to stand by it.

The non-aligned countries remained largely non-involved. Of them,
just six—Egypt, Burma, Cambodia, Sri Lanka, Ghana and Indonesia—met
in Colombo on 10 December 1962. Their proposals stipulated a Chinese
withdrawal of 20 km from the customary lines without any reciprocal
withdrawal on India's behalf. But the failure of these six nations to
unequivocally condemn China deeply disappointed India.

Kennedy was sympathetic to Nehru's desperate letters beseeching
American military aid. What Nehru sought would have amounted to
the setting up of a large American air force in India with dozens of
squadrons of military aircraft and about 10,000 personnel. But the war
was over before the Americans could get it all together. To be fair to the
US, it must also be recalled that this was the time when America was
confronting the Soviet Union in the Cuban missile crisis.

Nehru, however, had learnt a bitter lesson from this war. Writing to
Vijaya Lakshmi, Nehru reflected,

> A country today is completely helpless if it has not got proper
> defence forces as well as the machinery to produce the necessary
> equipment. I am anxious to avoid any dependence on the USA.
> I do not like the way they are going and they have a method of
> trying to get their pound's flesh...[41]

Though late in the day for such a realization, Nehru was presciently correct regarding the defence preparedness of countries. Sadly, six decades later, the Indian defence industry is still not able to produce the necessary equipment.

The second part of his statement regarding USA and its Shylockian manner, however, needs to be considered in tandem with other observations. His wariness of America was not absolute. Moreover, marinated in the bitter experience of 1962, he found himself drawn in to the protective and somewhat eager arms of USA to the extent that seasoned observers began to wonder if India was truly non-aligned any longer.

Another major change was with regard to equipping the defence forces. Post-Independence, Nehru had been a reluctant spender of money on defence purchases, preferring instead to use it for developmental purposes. But after 1962 and a hard look at the security policy, India decided to increase its defence spending. This led to the creation of a million-strong army with ten new mountain divisions equipped and trained for high-altitude warfare, a 45-squadron air force with supersonic aircraft and a modest increase in naval strength. Incidentally, that is more or less the size of India's defence establishment today, with the rider that the strength of its air force is now far short of the 45 squadrons.

HOLDING FIRM AGAINST WESTERN PRESSURE

America did eventually come forward to help with material but it also wanted its pound of flesh. It was encouraged in this demand by the British. Kennedy and the British Prime Minister Harold Macmillan put it bluntly: they were ready to help militarily provided India made up with Pakistan on Kashmir![42] Nehru and the Indian establishment refused to bend, and in the end, Kennedy grudgingly acknowledged that 'Kashmir was perhaps more complicated than Americans realized'.

This odious behaviour of pressurizing India when it was down was to be expected from Britain. But Kennedy was held in high esteem in India, and the US was, by and large, viewed favourably by its masses. The hurt of the US squeezing India at a time of vulnerability lasted long. It is true that Nehru took some wrong turns as prime minister, including initially on the Kashmir issue. But his steadfastness in this instance has not been sufficiently acknowledged. Under similar circumstances, another leader may have wilted.

However, it is worth recounting briefly what the UK–US combination had planned. Had they succeeded, it would have resulted in loss of territory for India at the very least. It was in pursuance of their pressure that India agreed to hold a series of talks with Pakistan on the Kashmir issue in 1962.

The first round of Indo-Pak talks got off to a negative start in December that year. On the evening of their arrival in Pakistan, the Indian delegation got an unpleasant surprise when, by chance, they heard on the Karachi Radio the announcement that Pakistan and China have reached an agreement whereby the former would gift a part of POK to the latter. In that background, the talks themselves did not produce any forward movement. Despite this unpleasant surprise, the US-UK pressure in favour of talks continued, and a month later in January 1963, Zulfikar Ali Bhutto led a Pakistani delegation for a second round of talks in Delhi.

It was here, during this second round, that the 'soft borders' approach was first broached. The idea was floated in a document prepared by Roger Hilsman, a foreign policy adviser in the Kennedy administration, and it involved an undivided J&K jointly administered by India and Pakistan. However, the plan could not get any traction in this round because of the political pressure against it in Delhi.

Prior to the third round in Karachi in February 1963, Americans had been pressing behind the scenes for an even bolder proposal involving joint administration and the ceding of territory west of the valley and of Jammu by India. Once again, the Indian delegation stood firm.

In all, six rounds of talks were held in quick succession between the two delegations, the last being in Delhi in May 1963. Britain and the US were blatant in their partiality towards Pakistan and in their efforts to push through an agreement that would involve concessions by India. Fortunately for India, its delegation stonewalled all these efforts.

OF SOPHISTRY AND PARADOX

How should Nehru be remembered? Will it be fair to say that he was a majestic man prone to committing Himalayan blunders? Or should it simply be said that he was a great man who made some mistakes in the service of his country?

There is no doubt that Nehru was a great statesman and a profound thinker. But his contradictions, and later in life his moody silences, baffled his interlocutors. For example, Eisenhower had liked Nehru but was puzzled by his views: 'Pandit Jawaharlal Nehru was not easy to understand: few people are, but his was a personality of unusual contradictions.'[43]

Even Pakistanis, our mirror image in more ways than one, could not quite fathom the man. Many blame him for the partition, citing his ambition to become the first Prime Minister of India as a catalyst for division. Yet there are others in Pakistan who hold quite the opposite view: 'Pandit Jawaharlal Nehru would never have won a popularity contest in Pakistan quite simply because he did his best to oppose our country's creation.'[44]

To further this argument about his contradictions, take for instance these two phases of Nehru during two separate visits to the US. Speaking to the US Congress on 13 October 1949 he said inspiringly, 'I have come here, therefore, on a voyage of discovery of the mind and heart of America and to place before you our own mind and heart.'[45]

Yet the same man was lost in his thoughts when he visited the US again in 1961. Kennedy was an admirer of Nehru till then. He tried to get Nehru's opinion on the Vietnam issue. But Nehru chose to remain silent throughout. However, later he told his foreign secretary M.J. Desai, 'Tell them, tell them not to go into Vietnam. They will be bogged down and they will never be able to get out.'[46] Had he mentioned this to Kennedy himself, things may have turned out differently for the US in Vietnam.

During their meeting, Nehru's moody silence irritated Kennedy. Arthur M. Schlesinger Jr. writes in his book *A Thousand Days*, 'Reminiscing about the meeting, Kennedy described it to me as "a disaster—the worst head-of-state visit I have had".'

Still, it will be simplistic to assess Nehru by his moods or his contradictions; he himself would have admitted to these failings. Instead, he should rightly be assessed by the very lofty perch he gave to his ideas. An example of this paradox was the reverence that the deeply conservative and religious masses of rural India gave to an avowed agnostic determined to break through ancient obstructions to modernization. In the drive to modernize, as in other ways, Nehru's India gave a lead to the other newly independent countries. India's starring role in the new 'Third World' was frequently resented; but India's influence, in countless forms, made its mark almost everywhere in that world.

The international credibility of India's position of 'positive neutrality' was established by the stand it took in Korea. Guided by the principle of impartiality, India's stance was, at first, resisted by China, US and the Soviet Union. This was a unique distinction because at first sight, it seemed that Nehru had succeeded in getting all sides to the dispute to gang up against India. Gradually, however, they were almost all equally convinced that India's view had merit.

Undoubtedly, the Western ears were often irritated by the sound of his pronouncements on the virtues of coexistence and non-alignment. It was equally logical that Nehru should have been the spokesman of the third world on global platforms. He developed a role for India based largely on its civilizational history and moral standing, making India the voice of the oppressed and the marginalized against the world's big powers. This gave it enormous prestige across the world for some years, but the humiliation of the 1962 war with China demonstrated its limitations.

In the decades after Nehru's death, much of the structure that he had assembled so painstakingly began to crumble. One by one, the new nations whose independence Nehru had championed sank into deep crisis. Dictatorships replaced faltering democracies in most countries, corruption became the norm in public life and military dictators took over the governance. Every such fall was a painful reminder that Nehru's dreams of a new world order had a short shelf life.

It was once said that India did not have a foreign policy, Nehru did: so completely was India's place in the world identified with him. This reluctance to delegate and his reliance on confidants like Krishna Menon contributed to his failure.

Yet there was a lot that he achieved and was credited for. Much before the term 'soft power' came into use in the West, Nehru saw in its practice enormous potential to unite the developing world. To him, India had an extraordinary ability to inspire through ideas that were persuasive and attractive. The fact that it succeeded was remarkable at a time when the West had a near total monopoly over the global media.

In discussions regarding Nehru, it is sometimes said dismissively that he was an idealist, meaning thereby that his ideals were not suited for a practical world. However, this is an unfair judgment. It disregards the fact that he wrote in his book, *Discovery of India*, 'But the ideal is terribly difficult to grasp or to hold.' It is true that some of his efforts did not endure. Yet, his oft-criticized idealism may hold out a message for today's Asia, which is at once vigorous in growth and riven by tensions.

In his personal life, Nehru was not irreligious, but he was against religious rituals. Even Gandhi's use of religious symbols exasperated him. 'The spectacle of what is called religion…in India and elsewhere has filled me with horror,' Nehru wrote, 'and I have frequently condemned it and wished to make a clean sweep of it.'[47]

Among Nehru's many achievements, some stand out. He reaffirmed India's faith in secularism despite the partition. And he ensured the firm establishment of democracy in India. In contrast to his contemporaries like Sukarno who ended up as dictators-for-life, Nehru put in place the tradition of civilian supremacy over military. This prevented India from becoming another newly independent country-turned-military dictatorship.

But his sanctimonious attitude towards the actions of the great powers, which he viewed through his idealistic prism, irritated those in the West. It prompted the poet Ogden Nash to write,

Just how shall we define a Pandit?
It's not a Panda, nor a bandit.
But rather a Pandora's box.
Of sophistry and paradox.[48]

Upon his death *The Guardian* wrote despondently:

He led his people out of bondage, but like Moses he did not himself live to enter the Promised Land, and the grumblings in the wilderness grew louder. He inspired the great series of five-year plans, but although they have created much additional wealth, they have still not brought about that 'take-off' into self-sustained growth… And poverty aggravates all the other dangers that Mr Nehru devoted his life to fighting: the divisiveness of India, its regionalism, its conflicts of religion…corruption, and the abuses of power.[49]

The Guardian's assessment is unduly harsh on Nehru and his country. It does not take into account the fact that India was born miserably poor in 1947. It was a brutalized, bleeding land with negligible industry and inadequate agriculture. So the task of nation-building that Nehru faced was enormous, with hardly any expert support.

Moreover, no leader, not even one as tall as Nehru, is perfect. As Lee Kuan Yew records, '... Nehru was a man of ideas; concepts he had polished and repolished: secularism, multiculturalism, rapid industrialisation of the state by heavy industries, in the fashion of the Soviet Union. Right or wrong, he was a thinker.'[50] What distinguished Nehru from other leaders were his absolute personal honesty and a lofty vision for India.

Finally, we must rely on an adoring daughter to sum up her father best. In a tribute to him in the *Selected Works of Jawaharlal Nehru*, Indira Gandhi describes the great man with this sentence, '...the story of Jawaharlal is that of a man who evolved, who grew in storm and stress till he became the representative figure of much that was noble in his time...'

2

LAL BAHADUR SHASTRI: NO SMALL MAN

In liberty from the bonds of attachment, do thou therefore the work to be done: for the man whose work is pure attains indeed the Supreme.

—BHAGAVAD GITA

Worrying over the fate of India after Nehru's death, *The New York Times* wrote in an editorial:

> Starting with independence in 1947, India was so heavily dependent on Jawaharlal Nehru that there is no way of predicting what will now happen... The burning question is: How much was India's devotion to democracy, to communal harmony and to nonalignment due solely to Jawaharlal Nehru? Not only the internal peace of India, but the peace of Asia and perhaps of the world hangs on the answer.[1]

It wasn't just the outside world that was watching anxiously. India itself held its breath apprehensively. A principal reason for this uncertainty was the oft-quoted criticism of Nehru that like the massive Barghad tree, he did not let a second line of leadership grow under him. So instead of an orderly transition of power, what followed immediately after Nehru's death was an acrimonious struggle for it.

Fortunately, it was short-lived and the issue was settled quickly. But the scars of an intense political struggle leave their mark. The new leader remains on guard, constantly looking over his shoulder. As Michael

Brecher notes in his book, *Succession in India: A Study in Decision-Making*, 'In the six days following Nehru's demise, many hats were thrown into the ring.'[2]

The jockeying for the top job and the negotiations for it had already started while Nehru's corpse lay in state. As an immediate arrangement, Gulzarilal Nanda was sworn in as caretaker prime minister, to the annoyance of V.K. Krishna Menon, who called it unconstitutional. When Nanda sat in what was Nehru's seat in Parliament, there were gasps.

The crusty, puritanical, but quietly ambitious Morarji Desai considered himself a suitable successor to Nehru. He arrived at the prime ministerial residence of Nehru and tried to direct the funeral proceedings, provoking an angry remark from the health minister Sushila Nayar: 'Who are you to give orders?'[3]

As if in response, a day after Nehru's death, Morarji declared that he was a candidate for the prime ministerial position. It was a typically tactless move on Morarji's part, which allowed his rivals to castigate him for this blatant lust for power. It also gave the Maharashtrian lobby in the Congress the opportunity to make it clear that they would not support him. Finally, it was K. Kamaraj who took a straw poll with the parliamentarians of the Congress party. His gentle prodding in favour of Lal Bahadur Shastri worked, and Shastri, rather than Morarji emerged as a non-controversial, consensus candidate. Shastri became the second Prime Minister of India on 9 June 1964.

Alas, he was not in good health. He had been in office only for 17 days when he was ordered to bed. The official handout said he was suffering from 'physical and nervous exhaustion and strain.' But it was widely believed that this was a heart attack, the first in a series of bad news about his health.

He should have taken some rest to recover fully, or at least lessened somewhat the pace of his work. But the worries of office were relentless, and they tested Shastri's steel from the very beginning. When the Chinese nuclear test came on 16 October 1964, Shastri's initial reaction was to reiterate his opposition to India following the nuclear path. But this was soon to change. On 24 October, the then Chairman of the Atomic Energy Commission of India, Dr Homi Bhabha, speaking on All India Radio (AIR), argued famously that 'atomic weapons give a State possessing them in adequate numbers a deterrent power against attack from a much stronger State.'[4]

The logic of Bhabha's argument appealed to Shastri and on 27 November, in reply to a debate on the nuclear issue in Lok Sabha, Shastri said that he had just come from a meeting with Bhabha in which the latter had suggested that India pursue the development of peaceful nuclear devices for future engineering use. Then he indicated that he and Bhabha were now in full agreement that work should be conducted on such devices.

Bhabha knew (and in fact had said so publicly in the past) that nuclear explosives for peaceful and weapon use were essentially the same. The major issue from his point of view was getting Shastri's nod for the development of the nuclear programme, and he succeeded in resolving it. After all, there is a saying in the nuclear non-proliferation community, 'The difference between a peaceful nuclear explosive and a bomb are the tail fins.'

TESTING TIMES

Shastri had barely settled into his office when he ran into uncharted waters on the external front. The mild-mannered prime minister got off to an unhappy start with the US for no fault of his own. In January 1965, soon after his election victory, US President Lyndon Johnson invited Pakistan President Ayub Khan to Washington. The background to this was the growing testiness in their bilateral relations, made worse still by the increasing warmth in Pakistan's relations with China. Therefore, to send a message to Pakistan that the US had other options in the subcontinent and to balance this gesture towards it, an invitation was also extended to Prime Minister Shastri.

Though Pakistan had given the US the use of its airbases and helped it undertake anti-China operations in Tibet, there were areas of discord too. Pakistan had not responded positively to the US expectation that as a member of the Southeast Asia Treaty Organization (SEATO) and Central Treaty Organization (CENTO), it would send troops to Vietnam to fight by America's side. What irritated Washington even more was the fact that before his planned trip to the US, Ayub went to Beijing and Moscow on official visits. Johnson was already upset by the active opposition of Moscow and Beijing to America's war in Vietnam. Ayub's trip to these two countries riled Johnson sufficiently to cancel his visit. To balance that snub to Pakistan, the invitation to Shastri was also withdrawn. Shastri regarded it as a personal embarrassment at a time when India was trying to take as helpful a stance as possible towards America and its global concerns.

Explaining this cancellation to the domestic constituency was a task in itself. It was made more difficult by his rivals in the party, who were busy finding fault with his policies. At first, his critics suggested that Shastri was a small man for a big job, and that he would soon be subsumed by the enormity of challenges facing the country. There were indeed dire warnings of drought and food shortages, made worse still by a red-taped decision-making system. But in the short time available to him, he did a remarkable job of tackling the fundamentals. As P.N. Dhar writes in his book *Indira Gandhi, the 'Emergency', and Indian Democracy*:

> Lal Bahadur Shastri...seemed an unlikely person to face up to the (economic) situation. But in his own quiet way he did initiate a series of steps which would have not only brought the economy out of the existing crisis but possibly put it on a high-growth path in the long run. He wore no ideological blinkers; he saw facts as they were in all their starkness. Chronic food shortages made him shift investment from basic industries to agriculture. Roaring black markets persuaded him to make a relative shift from controls to incentives, and the glaring inefficiency of the public sector made him accept a larger role for the private sector and foreign investment. He also took measures to shift the locus of economic decision-making from the Planning Commission to the ministries and from the Centre to the states. These measures reduced the influence of the Planning Commission—which had developed a rigid, almost doctrinaire outlook on economic policies—and at the same time decentralized decision-making.[5]

These course corrections and shifts in policies were enormous in themselves. It may have taken a lesser man many more years of pondering to introduce them, if at all. Still, there was no shortage of other trials for Shastri during his short tenure.

The first major external challenge was given by Pakistan from an unexpected direction—in the Great Rann of Kutch. At about 7,505.22 sq kms in size, it is a seasonal salt marsh and one of the largest salt deserts in the world, located in the Thar Desert in the Kutch district of Gujarat in India and the Sindh Province of Pakistan. The northern boundary of the Greater Rann of Kutch forms the international border between India and Pakistan. In January 1965, Pakistan established a security post in the Kanjarkot area belonging to India. India objected to this intrusion, but Ayub dismissed it by saying that Pakistan had long been occupying the area. In response, India moved heavy forces in March-April and established forward military posts. By the second week of April 1965, the skirmishes between the two armies had turned into small-scale battles. Pakistan held the advantage because of its superior strategic position in the Bets,[6] and India lost some territory as a result. But international pressure forced the two sides to agree to a ceasefire.

In June 1965, at the urging of the British Prime Minister Harold Wilson, the two sides agreed to the setting up of an arbitration tribunal. Its award, announced in February 1966, resulted in India ceding 910 sq kms of its territory to Pakistan. Besides gaining territory, the relative military success of Pakistan in these skirmishes confirmed for Ayub his boast that one Pakistani soldier was equal to ten Indian soldiers.

NOW OR NEVER

For Pakistan, the Rann of Kutch intrusion was a test probe for something bigger, somewhere else. That bigger objective became clear a few months later in September when the 1965 Indo-Pak war started.

At first, groups of infiltrators led by Pakistani army regulars were pushed into Kashmir in August 1965. This operation, code-named Operation Gibraltar, was the brainchild of Pakistan's foreign minister, Zulfiqar Ali Bhutto. Pakistan chose this name to draw a parallel to the Muslim invasion of Spain that was launched from the Port of Gibraltar in AD 711.

On his own, Ayub was a cautious man; he was most reluctant to risk a war with India. But Bhutto talked him into it. If Pakistan wanted to wrest

Kashmir by armed force, he argued, 1965 was the 'last chance'. The time was most opportune, Bhutto added, because India was badly shaken by its 'humiliating' defeat in the 1962 war with China. Moreover, after Nehru's death, his successor Shastri was ineffectual; there was acute food shortage and a virulent anti-Hindi agitation in the South. This opportunity, Bhutto added, would vanish once the expansion and reorganization of the Indian Army was complete in a few years' time. 'It is now or never,' Bhutto insisted.

After Bhutto succeeded in convincing him, Ayub suddenly put his finger on Akhnoor in the sand model used during the briefing and said, 'Why don't you go for the jugular and cut Kashmir off from India?' He also declared, 'Hindu morale would not stand more than a couple of hard blows at the right time and place.'[7] The irony, as his information secretary and biographer Altaf Gauhar was to reveal later, is that while Ayub was making this assertion, he 'did not know that the Operation Gibraltar had failed'.[8]

Ayub also gave the go-ahead to 'Operation Grand Slam', which was launched on 1 September 1965. Pakistan's principal military thrust during this operation was to seize the vital Akhnoor Bridge in J&K to cut off the road between India and Srinagar, and it almost succeeded in doing so. Militarily, India was vulnerable in the sector. Its soldiers were demoralized by the Pakistani advance, so much so that the Pakistani media mocked the retreat of the Indian forces in some sectors by descriptions of their desperation. From London, *The Sunday Times* reported, 'Indian troops had departed so hastily that they left behind all sorts of daily use things, like pyjamas and boots and half-eaten chapatis.'[9]

Diversion was the only way to stop the Pakistani advance, and Lieutenant General Harbaksh Singh, the general officer commanding-in-chief (GOC-in-C), Western Command, wanted to open a second front to achieve this. But his predicament was that the fight, so far, had been limited to the disputed ceasefire line. There had been no exchange of fire along the international border, because India has traditionally restrained itself from doing so to maintain the myth that all is still well between the two brothers.

When he met Shastri, General Harbaksh explained to him how the second front was essential to lessen the pressure from Pakistani forces.

Shastri asked him what hindered him from opening it. He said he would have to cross the international border. 'Cross it,' said Shastri.

What is not generally known, however, is the fact that this bold decision was facilitated by two unrelated factors. First, a Pakistani unit had, in a burst of enthusiasm, crossed the international border, giving India the excuse to retaliate. Second, the Indian public was greatly agitated by the news filtering in from the front of its losses. It was this anguish that led nearly a hundred thousand people to march to the Indian Parliament, urging Shastri to take bold action against Pakistan. What was also in the minds of Indians at that time was the humiliation that had only recently been inflicted by China. The Pakistani army's advance now threatened to multiply that humiliation. It was this combination that steeled Shastri's resolve.

The war lasted 23 days, from 1–23 September 1965. India won 1,920 sq km of territory; Pakistan won 540 sq km. 2,862 Indian soldiers were killed; Pakistan lost 5,800 soldiers. India lost 97 tanks; 450 Pakistani tanks were destroyed or captured.

Among the more celebrated and hard-fought battles was the one for Haji Pir. The 8,652 feet-high Haji Pir Pass is a dominating feature located on the western fringe of the Pir Panjal range. Apart from significantly reducing the road distance between Poonch and Uri to just 56 km, compared to the then 282 km, the Haji Pir Bulge provides a direct ingress to both the Jammu region and the Kashmir Valley. It is through this that Islamabad has been infiltrating terrorists into J&K for the last three decades and more.

Ever since, both sides have claimed victory in the 1965 war; it is recalled as the 'finest hour' in Pakistan, and for India it symbolized the redemption of the honour it had lost in 1962 to the Chinese.

But honour of a different nature had also to be retrieved, this time on the media front. The Western media, particularly from London, had not been kind to India, and one particularly galling BBC report claimed, 'Since India's Prime Minister Lal Bahadur Shastri is a Hindu, he is ready for war with Pakistan.'

Shastri waited for the war to end. Then he gave his response to BBC's unfair remark. Addressing a public meeting at Delhi's Ram Lila ground on 26 September, he said,

Mir Mushtaq who is presiding over this meeting is a Muslim. Mr Frank Anthony who has addressed you is a Christian. There are also Sikhs and Parsis here. The unique thing about our country is that we have Hindus, Muslims, Christians, Sikhs, Parsis and people of all other religions. We have temples and mosques, gurdwaras and churches. But we do not bring this all into politics... This is the difference between India and Pakistan. Whereas Pakistan proclaims herself to be an Islamic State and uses religion as a political factor, we Indians have the freedom to follow whatever religion we may choose [and] worship in any way we please. So far as politics is concerned, each of us is as much an Indian as the other.[10]

SETBACK AT TASHKENT

When guns are silenced by governments, their hope is that they do not fire again, because war is deadly business. If the two combatants cannot or will not come to the negotiating table on their own, others step in. The Soviet Union saw in the war an opportunity to establish its credentials as a superpower with influence in the region. Accordingly, it succeeded in persuading Ayub and Shastri to come to Tashkent, where its role was going to be that of an honest broker.

The meeting was held in Tashkent from 4–10 January 1966. The Soviet Premier Alexei Kosygin moderated the discussions between the two leaders. On arriving in Tashkent on 3 January, Ayub infuriated Kosygin, because 'when the India-Pakistan conference opened the next morning, he would not shake hands with the Indian Prime Minister. He did not want Pakistanis back home to see images of their brave Muslim leader shaking hands with a Hindu. He backed down in the face of Kosygin's fury.'[11]

The negotiations that followed between the two sides were contentious, largely because of the bellicose role played by the Pakistani foreign minister, Zulfikar Ali Bhutto. At one stage, a frustrated Shastri conveyed to Kosygin that he would be unable to sign the declaration. It was largely due to Kosygin's persuasive role that a diplomatic disaster was averted.

Almost all through, there was intense pressure on Shastri from the Ayub-Bhutto combine, and Kosygin as well, to restore the status quo along the ceasefire line. The Soviets, in particular, were keen that the Tashkent talks should not fail, for the sake of the USSR's own image as a global leader who could successfully mediate and resolve issues. Another factor that weighed on Shastri's mind was the capture of parts of Chhamb territory by Pakistan. This would have posed a constant strategic threat to India.

The eventual declaration was not a game-changer. It did not cause Delhi and Islamabad to move towards changing the basic mistrust in their relationship. What it did do,[12] however, was compel India and Pakistan to accept status quo ante, return the captured territories and revert to the 1949 ceasefire line in Kashmir.

The big setback at Tashkent was the death of Shastri on the night he signed the agreement. Many conspiracy theories have been spun about the cause of his death, but the fact is that he died of a heart attack.

That night Bhutto was awakened from sleep by his foreign secretary Aziz Ahmed with these words, 'Sir, the bastard is dead.'

Bhutto responded, 'Which one?'[13]

Shastri's death toned down the criticism that was brewing in the country over the declaration, particularly over the commitment that India would return strategically important features like Haji Pir. This was a prominent Indian gain in this see-saw battle, which witnessed India and Pakistan alternately making gains.

Still, there continued to be important voices in India against the decision to return the Haji Pir pass to Pakistan. On 21 February 1966, the issue was debated in Rajya Sabha, where an anguished Vajpayee echoed the lament of many in India, 'Three hours after signing the Tashkent Declaration the Foreign Secretary of Pakistan said in Tashkent that the Declaration did not apply to Pakistani infiltrators...' Moving then to the issue about the territories won by the Indian army, Vajpayee said, 'Haji Pir, Kargil and Tithwal are part of India legally and constitutionally. Why should we vacate it?'[14]

If there was heartburn in India at losing on the diplomatic front the gains made in battle, and if Tashkent had taken the life of its prime minister, the signs for Pakistan were far more ominous. Bhutto saw a political opportunity in bad-mouthing the Tashkent agreement. He began to sulk about the agreement from the moment it was signed, leading to his dismissal from the cabinet and eventually to the downfall of Ayub himself.

More importantly, it marked an important dividing line in Pakistan's destiny. From then on, a relatively stable, liberal and prosperous Pakistan began its slide towards a politically divided, economically declining and rigidly Islamic Pakistan. The division of Pakistan and the creation of Bangladesh in 1971 can in significant ways be traced back to Bhutto's sulk that began in Tashkent, and the political intrigues that were set in motion by him thereafter.

Had Shastri not died at the age of 61 in Tashkent, the history of India may also have taken a different turn. Indira Gandhi may not have become the prime minister, nor would her son have followed her into the job. And both may have lived to ripe old ages. But fate had willed otherwise.

Even in the short span of just about a year and a half, Shastri was constantly on trial. There were challenges from within the country and outside. To counter droughts and the consequent food shortages that were occurring on a regular basis, he laid the foundation of the Green Revolution. He shifted C. Subramaniam from the steel ministry to the agriculture ministry, setting in motion policy measures that truly led to the greening of the country. After some reluctance initially, he gave the enthusiastic go-ahead to India's nuclear programme. And on the military front, the task of reorganizing and equipping the army well was put into fast gear.

As for the 1965 war, the opinion is divided as to who, if anyone, won it. But what is sometimes not taken into account is the fact that post the 1962 war with China, the Indian army was still in recovery mode. Moreover, the initial Pakistani thrust had almost succeeded in cutting off the road linking the rest of India to Kashmir. It was Shastri's bold go-ahead to the army to cross the international border that retrieved the situation. The leader whom Ayub had contemptuously referred to as a 'small man' had proved to be more than his match in war.

Shastri must have been conscious of what Ayub had said, and what his critics in the party were saying. Perhaps that's why he kept these lines of Guru Nanak on his desk: 'O Nanak! Be tiny like the grass, for other plants will wither away, but grass will remain ever green.'

3

INDIRA GANDHI:
A GODDESS EMERGES

Prepare for war with peace in thy soul.

—BHAGAVAD GITA

On 11 January 1966, within hours of the death of Lal Bahadur Shastri, the Central Intelligence Agency (CIA) had prepared its assessment of the scenario after him. Speculating on his possible successors it said, 'Kamaraj probably has the broadest support within the [Congress] party...' The CIA paper went on to assert that the 'former Finance Minister Morarji Desai, Defence Minister Y.B. Chavan and party chief, Kamaraj were the front-runners for the top job.'[1] Indira Gandhi was considered the least likely in the CIA's list of dark horses to become prime minister.

Just days after the CIA had made this assessment, she was elected the leader of the Congress legislature party, defeating Morarji by 355 votes to 169. On 24 January 1966, Indira Priyadarshini Gandhi became the third Prime Minister of India.

The party stalwarts known as the 'Syndicate'[2] had picked her as someone who enjoyed national recognition but could be counted upon to take instructions from the party. They saw her as a 'goongi gudiya', a 'dumb doll' who could be manipulated according to their wishes while in power. She must have anticipated these conspiracies, because as early as 1 May 1958, she wrote a letter to her father reminding him of his frustrations with the party intrigues and his desire to resign. She wrote there, 'Let them try to manage by themselves, otherwise they will drag you down with their own rottenness...'[3]

The wish to get away from it all must have persisted with her, as just before Nehru died, she wrote to her friend Dorothy Norman, a New York-based writer and editor, 'The desire to be out of India and the malice, jealousies and envy, with which one is surrounded, is now overwhelming.'[4]

Interestingly, within two months of taking office, she visited the US, making it her first overseas trip. According to a presidential aide, Robert Komer, she 'vamped' Lyndon Johnson, who was moved to declare that he wanted to make sure 'no harm comes to this girl.' He promised $9 million in aid to India; she in turn offered India's understanding of the American position in the latter's war in Vietnam.

A condition of the US, in lieu of aid, had been the devaluation of the Indian currency. But her announcement of a huge 60 per cent devaluation of the rupee provoked fierce criticism at home and the fear that India was vulnerable again to foreign pressure. These reactions were formative for her as a leader. The twin, and in some ways conjoined, experience of the Syndicate's continuing intrigues against her and the disappointment with the American pressure regarding devaluation convinced her to stick with protectionist measures, adopt populist policies, and mistrust dependence on foreign hand. Singed particularly by her confrontation with the Syndicate, Indira began to surround herself with loyalists rather than equals. Along with this slow but steady transformation in her style of governance, she was responsible for a more fundamental shift in Indian politics. This heir of the nationalist founding father was now on her way to becoming an autocrat who would accept no opposition in her determination to provide firm governance. After the break with the Syndicate in 1969, her hold over the party became absolute. As she remarked to a journalist, 'Where is the party? I am the party.'[5]

Before that assertive avatar, she fumbled in the initial months as the prime minister. Her job was made tougher still by political rivals who kept sniping constantly at her. Ram Manohar Lohia, a socialist leader, for personal and political reasons, had taken it upon himself to trip her with toxic remarks in parliament and acidic speeches outside it. The coinage 'goongi gudiya' was his gift to the lexicon of Indian political barbs, and this comment by him during a speech was representative of the venom that Indira had to endure during those early years. Lohia said, 'Indira should be defeated in the election so that "this pretty woman does not have to suffer pain and trouble beyond her endurance..."'[6]

Indira's transformation from a 'goongi gudiya' to a confident, assertive and decisive prime minister did not take long. Along the way, she took care to discard almost all who had mistakenly considered her a 'dumb doll'. When her marginalized opponents said, '*Indira hatao* (Remove Indira)', she countered them with the slogan, '*Garibi hatao* (Remove poverty)'. In fact, some of India's greatest achievements came about when she was the prime minister. To name just one, the Green Revolution, encouraged by Shastri in his short tenure, saw its full flowering during her rule. With food security for the first time, India no longer had to beseech others for grain, bowl in hand.

But the period that she was the prime minister was tumultuous; she won great victories and suffered some spectacular losses. In one such phase in 1978, Indira was on a comeback trail politically, involving endless campaign travels across the country. One late evening after addressing a gathering, all the while holding a torch that could focus its light on her face in the gathering dark, she turned to the journalist Bruce Chatwin who was accompanying her and remarked, 'You have no idea how tiring it is to be a goddess.'[7]

Indira is the only goddess that the Indian political constellation has had so far. She may have been flawed, but she loved India and gave it its proudest possible moment. In that period, the US tried to obstruct her with all its might, including by sending a mighty flotilla, the Seventh Fleet, to cow her down. She, in turn, more than matched the Nixon-Kissinger duo trick for trick, frustrating them at every turn. This was no mean feat considering the fact that these two were considered wizards of statecraft.

One of her many diplomatic masterstrokes was the signing, in August 1971, of the Treaty of Peace, Friendship and Cooperation between the USSR and India. It sent out a strong signal to Washington and Beijing that India was no longer alone in the struggle for Bangladesh that it was soon to engage in. Article IX of the treaty said it all:

Each High Contracting Party undertakes to abstain from providing any assistance to any third country that engages in armed conflict with the other Party. In the event of either being subjected to an attack or a threat thereof, the High Contracting Parties shall immediately enter into mutual consultations in order to remove such threat and to take appropriate effective measures to ensure peace and the security of their countries.[8]

It wasn't the fear of Pakistani might that made India opt for the bear hug, but the possibility that the US and China might directly or indirectly come to Pakistan's aid. Whatever shine India may have put thereafter on describing the treaty with the Soviet Union as one to promote peace, the world was far from convinced that it was still truly non-aligned. But that labelling, or lack of it, was not a major cause of concern for India, nor was it the first time that such criticism was being made. After all, India had faced a similar verdict when Pandit Nehru wrote to Kennedy in 1962 seeking military help. The principal difference this time was the message that the Indo-Soviet treaty sent out. It spoke clearly of the measures that could be taken in case one of the treaty partners came under attack. This was a significant morale booster for India, at a time when China's stand remained unclear and the US was doing all it could to trip India.

One example of that attitude was President Nixon's remark shortly after meeting Mrs Gandhi at the White House in 1971, 'We really slobbered over the old witch.' Echoing his boss, Kissinger said, 'The Indians are bastards anyway.' Much later in 2005, in a half-hearted attempt at repentance, Kissinger told an interviewer, '[The foul language has] to be seen in the context of a cold war atmosphere 35 years ago, when I had paid a secret visit to China when President Nixon had not yet been there and India had made a kind of an alliance with the Soviet Union.'[9] Kissinger was not being entirely truthful, because that interview was tailored to the interviewer's taste. His more candid assessment of Mrs Gandhi was in his memoirs: 'My own views of Mrs Gandhi were similar to Nixon's, the chief difference being that I did not take her condescension personally.'[10]

Looking back from this distance in time, it was clearly an issue of the egos of two American leaders bent on making their mark in history through an opening to China, which they thought would transform the world and checkmate the Soviet Union. In the American perception,

India's actions were souring that passage. In contrast, the Indian view was coloured by the immediate problem on hand. For India and Indira, the issue was one of morality in international affairs and respect for the human rights of millions of Bengalis who were being targeted by the Pakistani army's guns, as a result of which ten million East Bengali Hindus and Muslims had fled their land to seek refuge in India while another million plus had been killed by the Pakistani army by that time.

Still, Nixon and Kissinger were fixated on the mythical benefits of their trip to China. Since then, the US has had reason to look back with mixed feelings at that journey and its uncertain results. In contrast, history records the liberation of Bangladesh as Indira's greatest achievement. But this episode also reflects the sharp differences that two of the world's largest democracies can be prone to.

It wasn't just Nixon who had underestimated Indira—so had the Pakistani President General Yahya Khan. He never thought 'that woman', as he contemptuously called Indira Gandhi,[11] would risk a military response. Much to his surprise, within a few hours of the Pakistani air strikes on Indian airbases on 3 December 1971, the Indian Army had moved into the then East Pakistan.

The Indian victory over the Pakistani army in East Pakistan was swift and complete. Because it was so overwhelming, the world pondered anxiously if that rout would be extended to the western side of Pakistan, because the Indian army had already advanced significantly in that part as well. But as in her previous moves, this time too, Indira surprised the world by ordering her army to cease fire all along the western front as of 8 p.m. on 17 December 1971.

Kissinger was delighted on hearing this decision. He telephoned Nixon to report the ceasefire in the west, 'Congratulations, Mr. President. You saved W[est] Pakistan.'

Nixon brooded over it, not wanting Indira Gandhi to gloat in victory. 'She shouldn't get credit for starting the fire and then calling in the fire department,' he said. As noted by Gary J. Bass, 'Kissinger...spent the rest of the day calling reporters to claim credit... About the Indians, he told the British ambassador, "I don't know how you tolerated them for those years."'[12]

A SUAVE STRATEGIST

It wasn't the US that saved West Pakistan. No effort by Nixon could have stopped Indira from pushing further into West Pakistan, if she had so decided. The Pakistani army was a bruised, defeated and leaderless force at that time and there were voices within India urging Indira to let the army complete the job once and for all. But she had reasons to stay her hand. Her principal aide, P.N. Haksar, recorded these in a note to the prime minister on 1 April 1972:

- The continuation of conflict would not have produced a decisive military victory and,
- Even in the event of a victory it was quite unthinkable for us to enter Pakistan as occupying power. Informed circles in India were conscious of the risks involved in pushing any further. A hostile population in major cities would have acted like a vast guerrilla force, stalling and sabotaging the Indian army. The victorious army of East Pakistan would have found itself struggling in an urban quagmire.

As Haksar explained in his note:

> If we had allowed ourselves to be carried away by our emotions and carried out the war, we would have been in complete mess with our garrisons in Lahore, Rawalpindi, Islamabad, Peshawar, Karachi, Hyderabad etc. Even to think of it is nightmarish because we have no political base specially in Punjab on which to restructure west Pakistan. In Bangladesh, we had political allies. In west Pakistan, we had none except marginally speaking people in Baluchistan and Frontier province.[13]

Haksar's note from 1 April was post-event; quite a while after the war had ended. He could therefore, view the issue relatively dispassionately and then record the reasons for not carrying on deep into West Pakistan. Besides, it was prudent to record them as pointers for future leaders to ponder over. However, even as the war was going on, Indira had factored in the imponderables of extending the war in this manner. She also took care that both the superpowers were kept informed and assured that India's military intentions did not include aggression into West Pakistan, except to the extent that it was necessary to deter the Pakistani army.

On 11 December 1971, when the war was in full swing, Haksar sent a telegram marked 'personal' to India's ambassador to the US, L.K. Jha. It read:

> We have no claims against the territory of West Pakistan. However, this does not mean that Pakistanis can continue to savagely attack our forces and occupy our territory and that we should in advance, declare to them that they can do all this and we shall sit with our hands tied and surrender meekly to their attacks.[14]

Three days later, on 14 December, he sent a cable to D.P. Dhar, who was then the Indian ambassador in Moscow, saying, 'Please reassure Chairman Kosygin that we have no repeat no territorial ambitions anywhere in east Pakistan or in west Pakistan.'[15]

Of the two telegrams above, the one to Moscow had the salutary effect of keeping in confidence a state that had proved to be of great help. The mere fact that the Soviet Union was standing by India's side was a psychological plus for India. It was also needed to counter the US and China against carrying on with ill-advised moves like that of dispatching the Seventh Fleet to the Indian Ocean.

But insofar as the telegram to Washington is concerned, even this move on India's part left Nixon and Kissinger seething. They did not trust Indira and they were hardly in the mood to tamp down their prejudice. It is unfortunate when leaders turn their personal likes and dislikes into national policy, as these two had done during the Bangladesh crisis. It is doubly unfortunate when that policy is forged into conviction through low-level intelligence of the kind that Nixon was receiving from his CIA unit at the American embassy in New Delhi.

It was about this that Jha wrote to Haksar on 17 February 1972. Jha's letter mentions that according to his information, Nixon and Kissinger had based their conclusions on a CIA report, saying that once Bangladesh had been liberated, the Indian forces would turn their full attention to West Pakistan.[16] When Indira was informed of this by Haksar, she told him to convey categorically to the Americans through Jha that no such discussion had taken place in the cabinet, nor had she made any statement to that effect.[17]

This is not all. Indira's decision not to foray deep into West Pakistan was based on a solid assessment of the risks involved in undertaking a venture that would stretch the Indian army's resources to the limit and lose India the moral support it was receiving then from the rest of the world despite America's exhortations otherwise.

Yet the issue of Indian intentions continued to preoccupy the world. When Haksar went to Iran in January 1973 and met the Shah of Iran on 24 January, the Shah asked him anxiously whether India was interested in breaking up Pakistan. This was an unusually blunt question to ask, and Haksar responded on a philosophical plane arguing that Iranians and Indians belong to civilizations, cultures and languages with long histories. These give their people mooring and a certain stability. But these basics, Haksar asserted, were lacking in the case of Pakistan, and '…[i]t is merely a label attached to those portions of India carved out on the sole criterion that the majority of inhabitants in these areas were allegedly united not by allegiance to a common culture, a common language, a tradition, a civilization but to a religion…'[18]

Despite all this, the question still continues to persist among people as to why a strong leader like Indira did not finish the job by dividing West Pakistan as well. The cogent answer to that is available in the notes and arguments recorded above. At first reading, it might appear that what Haksar advised Indira to do and what he told the Shah of Iran were two different things; to her he reasoned that the break-up of Pakistan was not feasible, but to the Shah he seemed to be saying that it was an inevitable eventuality, because Pakistan was 'merely a label'.

But a closer second reading would reveal that he was essentially conveying the same message to both: that Pakistan was an unviable project. But to Indira he attached the rider that the ingredients for a revolution in West Pakistan were not ready as they had been in East Pakistan, where almost the entire population had stood up in revolt against the Pakistani army and where the Mukti Bahini had become a reasonably well-organized guerilla force.[19]

FALTERING AT SIMLA

The complete victory in 1971 was, without doubt, the finest diplomatic and military success that any Indian prime minister has achieved so far. But questions continue to persist as to why she gave in at Simla, losing in negotiation all that her soldiers had won in battle? What was the point of releasing 93,000 Pakistani Prisoners of War (PoWs) merely on the basis of an assurance of good behaviour on Kashmir given by Bhutto?

A hint of this intent was given by Mrs Gandhi in her statement in Parliament on 17 December 1971, when she made the announcement of the Indian army's victory and the decision to declare a ceasefire: 'It is natural that the people of India should be elated. We can also understand the great rejoicing of the people of Bangladesh. I share the elation and the joy. But as the Gita says, neither joy nor sorrow should tilt the balance of our equanimity or blur our vision of the future.'[20]

It was in this spirit of magnanimity that she went on to add a message for the people of Pakistan, '...we have no enmity towards them. There are more things in common than those [that] divide us. We should like to fashion our relations with the people of Pakistan on the basis of friendship and understanding. Let them live as masters in their house...'

There was grace in speaking these words at a moment of overwhelming victory, and a clear hint that unlike how other leaders might have acted in a similar situation, she was not going to set arrogant conditions.

According to a former official, Sashanka S. Banerjee, one important reason why Indira did so was her concern that no harm should come to Mujibur Rahman, who was then in Pakistani custody. A deal of sorts was arranged at the London airport when Bhutto was on his way back from the US to take up his position as the head of a new Pakistani government. According to Banerjee, Laila, a former close friend of Bhutto, met him at the airport and passed on the message about the safe release of Mujibur. Banerjee described the result of that meeting thus to Delhi. According to his report, Bhutto told Laila:

Laila, I know what you want. I can imagine you are [carrying a request] from Mrs. Indira Gandhi. Do please pass a message to her, that after I take charge of office back home, I will shortly thereafter release Mujibur Rahman, allowing him to return home. What I want in return, I will let Mrs. Indira Gandhi know through another channel. You may now go.[21]

There is no reason to disbelieve Banerjee's account. But whether this was the only reason that compelled Indira to release 93,000 PoWs remains unvalidated. If she had recorded her views somewhere, they remain under wraps so far. But the officials accompanying her to Simla had, in their accounts, maintained that the decision to return the captured territories and the PoWs was sprung as a last-minute surprise on them. This may have been so at the mid-level officialdom that was accompanying Mrs Gandhi to Simla. But those at the helm were clear that a punitive agreement was neither enforceable nor desirable. There was also a mistaken belief that events in Pakistan had taken a democratic turn for the better and that this trend needed to be encouraged by conciliatory gestures in Simla. Thus, in one assessment before the Simla talks, P.N. Haksar suggested, 'The military-bureaucratic and feudal social order had crumbled… Pakistan of Yahya Khan had suffered political and military defeat. It is a nation in ferment seeking new identity for itself.'[22]

As later events have shown, the otherwise astute Haksar had misread the internal dynamics of Pakistan. The establishment had suffered a temporary reverse, but it bounced back quickly and once again the army and the feudal lords were the arbiters of Pakistan's destiny. Add to this the fact that the shrewd Minister of State for Foreign Affairs, Aziz Ahmed, had skilfully manipulated the negotiations to Pakistan's advantage. As he remarked once, 'despite holding "all the bargaining chips", India's excessive anxiety to avoid the failure of the talks at any cost became its major handicap.'[23]

Besides all this, there was considerable international pressure too, particularly from Moscow, that India should come to an amicable settlement on all issues, including Kashmir.

As it turned out, it was the issue of Kashmir and Pakistan's reluctance to turn the ceasefire line into a border that became the stumbling block. By the evening of 2 July 1972, the talks in Simla between the Indian delegation led by P.N. Haksar and the Pakistani delegation led by Aziz Ahmed had broken down, and the two delegations were resigned to leaving the next morning without an agreement. Suddenly, out of the blue, Bhutto suggested that he and Indira go out for a walk in the garden of the guest house. When they returned, they called Haksar and Rafi Raza, who was special assistant to Prime Minister Bhutto, to the room where they were carrying on their discussions. A little later, Haksar stepped out of the room. When the prime minister's social secretary, Usha Bhagat, asked him, '*Haksar Sahib, ladka hua ya ladki* (Is it a boy or a girl)?' Haksar beamed broadly to say, '*Ladka hua, woh bhi MA pass* (It's a boy, and that too, MA passed).'[24] In today's times, the query might sound offensive, but in those tense moments, it was phrased by Mrs Bhagat spontaneously in a fashion that was in traditional usage in the subcontinent, and so was Haksar's ebullient response.

Haksar may have been pleased with the result, but Bhutto had reason to beam far more broadly. He had got his 93,000 men as well as the territory captured by India. In return, he had given nothing much away, except soothing words said charmingly: '*Aap mujh par bharosa keejiye* (Please trust me).' Insofar as Kashmir was concerned, Bhutto had solemnly assured her that 'he would "gradually" make the LoC the permanent border, but he just could not put it in writing.'[25] All this, as well as the solemn words of bilateralism exchanged in the formal document, turned out to be just thin air. Bhutto had no intention of taking his promise seriously. As he told a close political confidant on his return to Pakistan, 'I have made a fool of that woman.'[26]

In effect, that's what it was. Having got back his PoWs, Bhutto did not release any of the Indian PoWs, who kept languishing in Pakistani prisons till their deaths. And soon after his return to Pakistan, he put into fast gear the effort to make the nuclear bomb. He had the chance of reciprocating Indira's magnanimity by moulding his country's opinion towards a stable relationship with India. Instead, and characteristically, he chose the path of acrimony and bitterness.

Ever since, the debate and anxiety regarding the state of the relationship between India and Pakistan has carried on. There is a difference, though, in the type of enquiries that foreign observers have begun to make in the last three decades. The questions are now directed more towards Pakistan's intentions and the objective behind its support for terrorism in and against India. What is the ultimate aim of Pakistan? Is it just to keep bleeding India by a thousand cuts, or to divide India?

Enquiries like this may be driven by curiosity or by the professional motivation of a foreign interlocutor, but these set the Indian mind thinking. What if Bangladesh had not happened and Pakistan had not splintered? The immediate and reflexive response to that is likely to be a shudder. It is tough enough handling Pakistan in the shape it is now. It would have been perilous if a hostile Pakistan was squeezing India with terror from its eastern part as well.

Therefore, if an assessment were to be made today, then it could be said that Indira was flawless as a strategist up to the Bangladesh war. But she erred at Simla. She could have given the concession she wanted, but only in phases; one concession to be followed by the other based on proof of good behaviour from Pakistan. For instance, India could have held on to the territory captured in West Pakistan. Moreover, India need not have released all Pakistani PoWs in one go. The war criminals among the PoWs could have been put on trial in Bangladesh or even in India. There was also the option of holding back the officers among the PoWs. However, India opted to sign a blank cheque.

Still, a final word must be said about Indira Gandhi as to what motivated her to put her signature on an agreement that suited Bhutto. On the day following the agreement, she told her top aides that, 'while she did not trust Bhutto, she wanted to make a gesture to the people of Pakistan with whom we have ultimately to settle this question.'[27] Alas, this formidable strategist, whom Atal Bihari Vajpayee had called 'Durga' and the Western media 'The Empress of India', had failed to realize that when it comes to dealing with India, the people of Pakistan stand as one with their army and their political leaders.

ON THE WORLD STAGE

However, given the odds that she was working under, it will be fair to characterize Indira's foreign policy as bold in conception and execution. If the test of a great leader is the ability and the will to take quick and transformative decisions, then too she qualifies eminently for the honour. That's why the political icons of that time, ranging from Fidel Castro of Cuba to Yasser Arafat of Palestine, held her high in their esteem. Singapore's first prime minister, Lee Kuan Yew, may have been echoing that high regard when he described Indira in this manner:

Indira Gandhi was the toughest woman prime minister I have met. She was feminine but there was nothing soft about her. She was more determined and ruthless a political leader than Margaret Thatcher, Mrs Bandaranaike or Benazir Bhutto. She had a handsome face with an aquiline nose and a smart hairstyle with a broad streak of white against a jet black mass of hair combed back from her forehead. And she was always dressed elegantly in a sari. She affected some feminine ways, smiling coquettishly at men during social conversation, but once into the flow of an argument there was the steel in her that could match any Kremlin leader.[28]

It wasn't just Pakistan that occupied her strategic calculus. The fact is that the 1962 humiliation of her father by China continued to rankle her. She was also acutely conscious of the fact that China was a nuclear power, recognized as such by the world, while India was not. As early as 1968—much before the 1971 war was in anyone's thoughts—she had already started worrying about the long-term disadvantage for India due to this disparity. Haksar reflected this concern when he recorded a note in 1968 titled 'Need for India in a Changing World to Reassess Her National Interest and Foreign Policy.'[29] In essence it advocated that India's strategic calculus had to look beyond Pakistan to other potential threats; the principal of which could be China:

> ...the making of nuclear arms in the shape of medium range missiles (2,000-3,000 miles) capable, from sites within India's frontiers, of striking with success not only a few chosen targets in Tibet but of ranging as far afield as the industrial heart of China in Manchuria and in the great river valleys south of it which include some of her principal industries and urban centres of population.[30]

In that same year, the world had been divided into the nuclear haves and have-nots after the international community concluded the Nuclear non-Proliferation Treaty (NPT). But Indira waited for another six years before reacting on the ground to this nuclear apartheid. On 18 May 1974, Raja Ramanna, the director of Bhabha Atomic Research Centre (BARC), placed a call to PM Indira Gandhi to say, 'The Buddha has smiled.'[31] India's first nuclear test had been conducted in Pokhran on

Buddha Purnima (Buddha's birthday). It was the first confirmed nuclear test by a nation that was not a permanent member of the UNSC.

As expected, the Western world imposed sanctions on India. But the nuclear test had successfully breached the artificial ceiling that the five nuclear haves had built—that only they could be trusted to act responsibly with the 'bomb'. The unstated axiom to that assertion was that the others, the have-nots, could not be trusted to act responsibly and hence must be dissuaded from following the nuclear path. The threat of sanctions was the deterrent that the group of five had employed with great effect so far. When India broke free of these chains and conducted the nuclear test, it did so in full consciousness of the fact that it would have to contend with the odium of the nuclear five— and more so because the test was conducted within three years of the Bangladesh war. But the Indian riposte to the barbs, somewhat amusing in retrospect, had irrefutable logic to it. The test, it was said, tongue firmly in cheek, was for 'peaceful purposes' because India needed to use the atomic power to blast out irrigation canals![32] An important factor that somewhat softened the Western reaction against India was the American preoccupation—and frustration—with the way the war was going in Vietnam. Moreover, the memory of their inability to stare down Indira during the Bangladesh war was still fresh for the Nixon-Kissinger duo.

If she was firm on these major concerns for India, there was flexibility and grace in Indira's dealings with the smaller neighbours. With Nepal, for instance, she took the soft approach generally and dealt with the King courteously but with firmness when needed. There was also the recognition that India's strategic resources, limited as they were, could not be stretched far beyond its borders. This was reflected in the response to a probing enquiry by Lee Kuan Yew:

> When I visited India in 1970, I asked her [Indira Gandhi] whether India intended to extend its naval interests into southeast Asia? Their foreign minister Swaran Singh who was present intervened to say, India was interested in increasing economic ties but its greater interest was in keeping its western sea lanes open. I sensed that India's primary defence concern was Pakistan, fearing a US-China-Pakistan line up.[33]

Swaran Singh had astutely described the limits of India's strategic reach, which, by and large, should continue to remain valid even now: That India's greater interest was in keeping the western lanes open. Sensitive to the possibility that China, Pakistan and the US could become a potent grouping, Indira began to soften her approach towards the US. At first, though, the period after 1971 was marked by uncertainty in Indo-US relations; the Indian triumph in the Bangladesh war was viewed as a humiliation of sorts by the Nixon-Kissinger combine. The American misery was further compounded when it had to withdraw in defeat from Vietnam in the mid-1970s. Indira exploited the anti-American mood domestically by playing up, during elections, the fear of American interference.

But by the end of 1970s, she was ready for a course correction. She did not want India to be solely dependent on the Soviet Union. On its part, the US under Ronald Reagan was keen that a new opening be made towards India, to prise it away from too tight a Soviet hug. One sign of the thaw and the gradual warming of relations was the US agreement to provide dual-use technology to India.

GRANDEUR EVEN IN FAILURE

If there was success on the external front, her record domestically was mixed. She made the steel frame of the Indian bureaucracy bend to her will. She increased socialist economic controls and nationalized the large privately held banks, opening the doors to the widespread corruption that leading politicians now routinely practice. Instinctively and by inheritance, she was drawn, at least in her first term, to socialism. This was embraced by a deeply impoverished electorate, but over time, the narrative alone ceased to be adequate. Poverty continued to be rampant and economic crises kept piling up. Labour unrest, railway strikes and student agitations seemed to spread like a virus across the country. Oil prices multiplied and drought conditions were bringing misery to many parts of the country by the mid-seventies.

The last straw for her was the verdict delivered by Allahabad High Court on 12 June 1975, declaring her election victory invalid on account of malpractice. Indira responded to all this by imposing Emergency on 26 June 1975, which lasted till 21 March 1977. It is often referred to as the darkest period in the history of independent India because of the brutalities that followed against her political opponents. A few days after the Emergency was imposed, the Bombay edition of *The Times of India* carried an obituary claiming that 'Democracy, beloved husband of Truth, loving father of Liberty, brother of Faith, Hope and Justice, expired on June 26.' This echoed the popular sentiment, and it was only natural that she lost in the elections of 1977. Wisened by this experience, she quietly discarded socialism when she returned to power in 1980 and began to reinvent herself, favouring new solutions to old problems.

She also made some political compromises of doubtful validity. In the late 1970s her party had supported the Sikh extremist Jarnail Singh Bhindranwale in a bid to split the Sikh votes and weaken the Akali Dal, the chief political rival of Congress in Punjab. Her momentarily convenient indulgence of Sikh extremists for political gains led to her death, and her encouragement of the Tamil rebels in the neighbouring Sri Lanka was eventually the cause of her son Rajiv Gandhi's death. These were aberrations that proved costly for the country, but have they significantly tarnished her legacy as a great leader? One view has it that she could have left a deeper mark. 'If Nehru was greater than his deeds, as many people say, Indira was not as great as she should have been, and her deeds were more damaging than she probably intended...'[34]

Perhaps it was so. Had she not made an entire nation cower during the period of Emergency imposed by her, her legacy may have been less flawed. But as another commentator observed:

Indira Gandhi had a personality replete with contradictions. Greatness and pettiness went hand in hand. Richness of heritage and opportunity were not fully translated into positive action despite numerous opportunities that came her way. Good intentions were often sabotaged by the exigencies of politics. Yet there is grandeur even in failure.[35]

But what about Indira—what was her opinion of herself? Once, a visiting journalist asked her to describe 'Indira Gandhi, the woman'. She replied that 'in spite of always living in the public glare, she has remained a very private person. Her life has been hard. This has made her self-reliant but has not hardened her.'[36]

Perhaps more in jest, she confided to one of her close friends a few days before her death, 'I was so sure I had nothing in me to be admired.'[37] For once, she was wide of the mark, because she was admired like a goddess after the Bangladesh war. Nothing that she did thereafter, not even the cruellest of her mistakes, could wipe out that single image that the Indian people had enshrined of her. It is true that she was feared by people during the Emergency and resented by politicians spurned by her. To the latter she seemed to personify a ruthless instinct for political survival. During her lifetime, she was also accused by her opponents of being the greatest threat to democracy in India. Soon after she imposed Emergency, over 50,000 were put in prison. This was just one of the many extremes that the people suffered then. Addressing the country on 15 August 1975, she tried to explain them away by saying, 'Sometimes bitter medicine has to be administered to a patient only to cure him.'[38] That was her view, but among the critics there is a unanimous view that she weakened the constitutional regularities.

Paradoxically though, she also made democracy more participative. In a series of radical moves intended to resonate with people, banks were nationalized, the princely families were divested of the privileges they had been constitutionally promised, and an electoral slogan at once superbly simple and blissfully hazy was coined: '*Garibi hatao*'. Some of these were contested achievements, but it is worth repeating that the Bangladesh war and the nuclear test stand out as testimonies to the boldness of her vision and the clinical efficiency in its implementation. She did falter in Simla, but then there was no one to whisper caution in her ears, as was done in case of victorious Roman Generals: '*Memento mori* (You are only mortal).'

On her death, *The New York Times* described her as 'Strong-willed, autocratic and determined to govern an almost ungovernable nation that seemed always in strife, Indira Gandhi was Prime Minister four times and the dominant figure in India for almost two decades.'[39] The report went on to add, 'She was physically frail. She had suffered from tuberculosis, low blood pressure, kidney problems and muscle spasms in the neck and had ignored doctors' orders not to have children. She worked 14 hours a day and seemed lonely and isolated.'

As if in answer to those curious about why she was a self-willed recluse, she once said, 'I think the only reason I'm able to survive this with equanimity is that I'm just myself, regardless of the situation in the country.'[40]

Did she have the premonition that the end was near? It would seem so, going by the speech she delivered on 30 October 1984 in Bhubaneswar, just a day before her assassination:

> I am here today; I may not be here tomorrow. But the responsibility to look after national interest is on the shoulder of every citizen of India...Nobody knows how many attempts have been made to shoot me, lathis have been used to beat me. In Bhubaneswar itself, a brickbat hit me. They have attacked me in every possible manner. I do not care whether I live or die. I have lived a long life and I am proud that I spent the whole of my life in the service of my country...and when I die, I can say that every drop of my blood will invigorate India and strengthen it.[41]

The following morning, on 31 October 1984, a little after 9 a.m., she walked briskly down the winding path from her home to her office in the bungalow next door at 1 Akbar Road. There, Peter Ustinov was waiting with his TV crew to interview her. As she approached the wicket gate connecting the two houses, her bodyguard, Sub-inspector Beant Singh, loomed into view. She greeted him as she always did, with a namaste. Beant Singh raised his revolver in response.

'What are you doing?' she asked.

Singh fired five shots at point-blank range. Across the lawn, another Sikh guard, Satwant Singh, appeared to fire 25 bullets from his sten gun.

The frail goddess fell and her blood began to seep into the ground below her, just as she had said the previous day at Bhubaneswar: '...when I die...every drop of my blood will invigorate India and strengthen it.'

4

RAJIV GANDHI:
INDIA'S RELUCTANT PRINCE

At the end of the night of time all things return to my nature;
and when the new day of time begins I bring them again to light.

—BHAGAVAD GITA

31 October 1984 dawned as a mild autumn day in Kanthi in West Bengal. That morning, Rajiv Gandhi happened to be in this wayside town on an initiation tour in politics with Congress heavyweights like Pranab Mukherjee and Ghani Khan Choudhury. Suddenly, the police wireless crackled to convey the news that Indira Gandhi had been assassinated. Pranab Mukherjee describes the events that followed: '… Rajiv went into the cockpit. After some time, he came back and announced, "She is dead." There was absolute silence. Tears started rolling down my face… Rajiv was exceptionally calm and displayed total control and fortitude, possibly a trait he had inherited from his mother.'[1]

Pranab goes on to describe the consultations during the flight back to Delhi that led to Rajiv Gandhi being sworn in as the sixth Prime Minister of India:

Once we were able to regain some semblance of composure, we began discussions on what was to be done next… I cited precedents from the time when Prime Minister Nehru and, later, Shastri passed away while in office… In both instances, an interim government was formed with Gulzarilal Nanda, the senior-most minister, as the interim

Prime Minister. However, that took place when the incumbents died a natural death. This was an extraordinary situation... At the conclusion of the discussion, it was decided that we should request Rajiv Gandhi to take over as the full-fledged Prime Minister... I took Rajiv to the rear of the aircraft and requested him to take over as Prime Minister. His immediate question to me was, 'Do you think I can manage?' 'Yes,' I told him, 'we are all there to help you. You will have everyone's support...'[2]

Rajiv had been a reluctant entrant in politics. At 40, when he took over as the Prime Minister of India on 31 October 1984, he was the youngest incumbent in the post. As a relatively young leader of a country struggling with multiple problems, he was in a hurry to find a quick fix for all the complex issues, including Punjab, Assam and Sri Lanka.

This impatience with red tape and his anxiety to get things done quickly paid off in many spheres. One of his strongest desires was to transform India through a technological revolution. The country's success in information technology (IT) can largely be ascribed to that motivation. He also brought in far-reaching changes in some spheres of the polity. He had taken over against a backdrop where political defections by elected representatives, termed the 'Aaya Ram, Gaya Ram' (turncoats), were leading to abrupt changes of government. A major reason for this was the lure of money for the politicians, making them defect from the party they had been elected from. It was to bring some stability in the system that one of Rajiv's first acts as prime minister was to get the Parliament to pass the Anti-Defection Act in January 1985. Another of Rajiv's fundamental reforms traces its roots to Mahatma Gandhi's vision. Gandhi had advocated 'Panchayati Raj' as the foundation of India's political system, as a decentralized form of government in which each village would be responsible for its own affairs. Rajiv gave it practical shape by introducing the panchayat raj system. He also took early steps to puncture the licence-permit-quota raj, which had really meant licencing a black market in scarce items, which were imported through a quota system. Rajiv did open up the economy as well, but his mistrust of multinationals, still seen as symbols of Western imperialism, led him to finance this modernization through borrowing. This had unintended consequences.

By 1991, India's external debt had risen to $72 billion and the balance of payments (BoP) crisis was so acute that in June that year, India could afford only four more weeks of imports.

But Rajiv's instincts were basically sound and he wanted to speed march India into the twenty-first century. On 15 August 1985, when he unfurled the national flag for the first time from the Red Fort, he told his countrymen that a change was in the air: 'When the tricolor was unfurled here for the first time, I was only three years old. Today, two-thirds of the people of India are like me, who have not participated in the country's struggle for independence. A new generation has come to the fore.'

But the odds against this new generation were enormous. Besides the considerable problems internally, India's relations with its neighbours were tepid at best. Bangladesh was in a sulk over India's decision to build a border fence to stop the flow of illegal immigrants. For quite the opposite reason, Nepal resented the inflow of Indians into its Terai areas. Down in the south, Sri Lanka suspected that India was giving support to its Tamil rebels. Relations with China continued to be frozen and Pakistan was eying a new opportunity with the US after the Soviet intrusion, in December 1979, into Afghanistan. Taking the bait, the US responded with interest and opened, in generous proportions, its aid and arms supplies to Pakistan.

All told, it was quite a plate full of problems for Rajiv when he slid into the prime ministerial chair. Indira had inherited a far more tranquil foreign policy slate when she took over in 1966, and she had the advantage of having been groomed by her father. Rajiv Gandhi's was an unexpected entry into politics, forced by the tragedy of his mother's death. But he was a quick learner on the job.

When the US Secretary of State George P. Shultz first met Rajiv Gandhi in 1984, he commented that Rajiv had come through 'with a quiet sort of strength that I found reassuring.'[3] The impression that this was a self-assured but open-minded man lingered with his interlocutors almost throughout his tenure as PM.

There were some sceptical voices too. Lee Kuan Yew wrote about him, 'I saw him as an airline pilot with a straightforward worldview. In our discussions, he often turned to Natwar Singh. I wondered who guided him through Indian politics but was certain many would want to hold his hand and lead him their way.'

Rajiv may have given the impression of an overgrown public school boy, but he was not naive, nor a simpleton lost in the devious political woods. And Lee Kuan's view was not wholly correct. It did not take into account the complex and rather trying circumstances obtaining in and around India. Moreover, as a long-time family confidant and a minister in his cabinet, Natwar Singh was performing his expected role of easing Rajiv's transition into the subtler nuances of diplomacy.

PROVING THE CASSANDRAS WRONG

Public memory is notoriously short, otherwise people would have also remembered the extremely troubling times that the country was going through in the 1980s. The situation in Punjab was deeply worrying, with terror at its peak and terrorists receiving ample support from Pakistan. The situation in Kashmir, never quite tepid, was beginning to become volatile again. Some political experts in India had started wondering whether India would be able to sail through this turbulence with a novice at the helm.

Rajiv's own had once been scathing in their criticism. Sanjay Gandhi, his younger brother, used to take delight in telling friends accounts of Rajiv's indecisive nature. One of his favourite stories was that when at the breakfast table Rajiv would be asked whether he wanted tea or coffee, he would vacillate. Even after he had made a choice, he would change his mind many more times, stopping the waiter on his way out of the room to tell him of his revised preference between tea and coffee. Expectedly, this spiced-up account produced great mirth among Sanjay's rough clique.

Regardless of what happened at the Gandhi household's breakfast table when they were young, as a leader Rajiv was no Hamlet. Rather, he faced the problems head on. Terrorism was the biggest of the problems he had inherited. It had been gathering strength for some time. It started during 1978–9 when General Zia-ul-Haq, as the president of Pakistan, authorized the Inter-Services Intelligence (ISI) to set in motion plans to encourage separatist terrorism amongst the Sikhs in Punjab. The first step it took as part of this move was to allow a larger number of Sikhs from

India to visit the holy Sikh shrines in Pakistan. Simultaneously, Pakistan invited expatriate Sikhs living in Canada and the UK to visit these holy shrines while the pilgrim jathas from India were visiting Pakistan.

Zia gave the entire operation his personal attention. He would often receive the leaders of these Sikh pilgrim groups. ISI provided them with special care and facilities and subjected them to subtle and sustained propaganda. Once a reasonable-sized cadre of extremism-leaning Sikhs had been formed, the ISI began to finance and equip the separatist movement. This led to large-scale terrorism in Punjab and its neighbouring northern states in India in the 1980s. As an aside, and as a note of caution, it is worth comparing the tactics employed by Pakistan then, with its pretended generosity now for the Kartarpur Sahib corridor, where both Prime Minister Imran Khan and Army Chief General Qamar Bajwa have gone the extra mile to provide road connections and special facilities to the Sikh pilgrims.

But it wasn't just the issue of terror in Punjab that was preoccupying Rajiv. Pakistan had begun stoking the fire in Kashmir as well. More worryingly for India, this time the radical Islam angle was introduced in Kashmir's terror lexicon.

It was during the phase of terrorism in the 1980s that some foreign commentators began to ask whether India would be able to survive as a nation. They were of the view that the Indian experiment was at an end and would slowly give way to chaos. Despite these ominous reports, it was during Rajiv's term in office that terrorism was dealt with effectively and a political touch was added to the effort. One of the important initiatives that he took in Punjab was the Rajiv-Longowal accord that he signed with Akali Dal President Sant Harchand Singh Longowal in July 1985. Basically, the accord offered palliatives in terms of compensation, recruitment, etc. to the people of Punjab. Though well intentioned, it had very little effect on the extremists. Terrorism in Punjab continued up to the mid-nineties in one form or the other, killing people in thousands. But Rajiv had started the process of confronting the issue both by the force of the State and at a political level. As a result, the Punjab problem lost some of its sting during his lifetime. The resulting calm, though not in full measure yet, was sound enough to confirm to the world that the Cassandras were wrong: India was there to stay.

Two thousand kilometres away from Punjab, the agitation in Assam during the 1970s and 1980s over the influx of foreigners from Bangladesh was also violent. But it was taking place a long distance away from Delhi. To that extent, it did not occupy the national and international media space in the same way as the terrorism in Punjab did. But this too was bloody and deeply disturbing. It was the agreement that Rajiv signed with the All Assam Students Union (AASU) and the erstwhile All Assam Gana Sangram Parishad (AAGSP) on 15 August 1985—the Assam Accord—that brought the situation gradually back to normal.[4]

RAPPROCHEMENT ACROSS THE HIMALAYAS

If he was deft of touch in dealing with the prickly domestic issues, Rajiv was also at ease interacting with other leaders in the world. One of his first major visits was to the US in June 1985, signifying that the Indo-US differences of 1971 were a distant memory. His host, President Ronald Reagan, recalled Nehru's visit to USA in 1949 and his remark, '…though we may know the history and something of the culture of our respective countries, what is required is a true understanding and appreciation of each other.'[5] To some extent that process of mutual discovery between the US and India began then, during his grandson's visit.

Sadly though, the warmth did not last long. The relationship soon began to stagnate and then soured because of American support for Pakistan, which was backing the most radical factions of the Afghan mujahideen. Another irritant in the Indo-US relations was the former's complaint that the US was looking on indulgently while Pakistan was developing its secret nuclear programme.

Still, if the visit to the US was smooth, there were problems nearer home. Pakistan continued to be a troublesome neighbour. But more worryingly, the already fraught relationship between India and China was coming under new strains. Perhaps that's why, on the morning of 22 December 1988 in the bitterly cold Beijing, the principal leaders of India and China were awaiting their meeting a bit tentatively, with hope and anticipation. At precisely 10.30 a.m., China's 'Paramount Leader' and Chairman of China's Central Military Commission Deng Xiaoping appeared at the Great Hall of People wearing a grey Mao coat. 'I welcome you to China, my young friend,' Deng said, clutching Rajiv Gandhi's hand. 'This is your first visit to China?'

'Yes,' Rajiv replied, a half-smile betraying an initial nervousness. It must have been a coincidence but Rajiv was also wearing a dark grey suit, a bandhgala.

This was the first visit by a Prime Minister of India to China in nearly 30 years, after that of Nehru in 1954. As they stood there shaking hands for what seemed like an eternity (according to one report, for eight minutes) and smiling for the cameras, they must have thought of the armed exchanges in 1962. A brief thought must have crossed their minds about the recent past as well; Indian forces had confronted the Chinese when they had intruded at Sumdorong Chu.[6]

There was another major development regarding Arunachal Pradesh that the two leaders may have thought of as well. It must have been more than mere coincidence that a new resolve about the state was made public in the spring of 1988. Mani Shankar Aiyar describes the surprise announcement by Rajiv at Itanagar in this manner:

> I was standing at the foot of the stage when I heard to my astonishment the Prime Minister conferring full statehood on Arunachal Pradesh! When we were back in the plane, I sought him out in his cabin and asked but what was going to be the impact of this announcement on the proposed China visit. Rajiv Gandhi beamed at me and said, 'Mani, if we do not know where the borders of our country lie, how can we expect the Chinese to know?'[7]

Both India and China had been wanting for some time to normalize relations with each other, putting aside the controversial memories of the border dispute and the Sino-Indian war of 1962. At their meeting, after the initial tentativeness, their personal chemistry began to sparkle and Deng urged both sides to 'forget the unpleasant past.'

> Deng: ...in 1954, when your grandfather...visited China...I was Vice-Premier at that time. At that time, the relations between our two countries were very good.

> Rajiv: We have been through a few difficulties in between. I hope we can bring things back and get over these difficulties.

Deng: So this is our common wish. In the considerable period of time in between, there was unpleasantness at each other. Let's forget it. We should look forward.

Rajiv: There's so much work to do in both countries.[8]

Some voices from China maintain that during this visit, Rajiv lost an opportunity to settle the Indo-China border issue. Former Chinese diplomat Yang Wenchang, later president of the Chinese People's Institute of Foreign Affairs (CPIFA), in an interaction with the Indian media a few years after Rajiv's China visit recalled:

...the Chinese leader had even suggested the existing McMahon Line be renamed the China-India line... [M]ore could have been achieved during the talks between Gandhi and Deng... As a diplomat in the late 1980s, I was witness to a chance to solve the problem with Prime Minister Rajiv and Deng, who was also a strong man. Deng said, 'We do some compromise on the west wing, you do some on the east wing, then we can have a new border.' We offered but Prime Minister Gandhi didn't have a response. After that I felt very sad we lost the chance.[9]

Alas, this was not the only time we missed the opportunity to at least give the possibility of border settlement a real try. It is useful to recall here that Rajiv's grandfather, Pandit Nehru, has been variously accused of having spurned a few such offers. One account maintains that a chance came by during Zhou En Lai's visit to Delhi in April 1960. In their meeting on 26 April, Zhou set out five points as forming 'a common ground'. They were:

(i) Our boundaries are not delimited and, therefore, there is a dispute about these; (ii) however there is a line of actual control both in the eastern sector as well as the western sector and also in the middle sector; (iii) geographical features should be taken into account in settling the border. One of the principles would be watershed and there would be also other features, like valleys and mountain passes, etc. These principles should be applicable to all sectors, eastern, western and middle; (iv) each side should keep to this line and make no territorial claims. This does not discount individual adjustments along the border later; (v) national sentiments should be respected. For both countries a lot of sentiment is tied around the Himalayas and the Karakoram.[10]

Nehru's approach to this offer was radically different: 'We should take each sector of the border and convince the other side of what it believes to be right...'

On the fourth point—renunciation of territorial claims by both—Nehru had already responded to Zhou on 24 April, saying, 'Our accepting things as they are would mean that basically there is no dispute and the question ends there; that we are unable to do.'[11] After this rejection the Chinese stance on the border issue underwent subtle changes; the offer made to Rajiv during his visit being one such. Rajiv's reaction to the offer may have been coloured, unfortunately, by his grandfather's rejection three decades earlier. It is also likely that his aides reminded him that if Nehru had rejected a relatively more equitable offer back then, Rajiv would be asking for political trouble at home by impulsively agreeing on the spot to this latest Chinese proposal. Even the visit itself was a bold move on Rajiv's part, because there were critical voices in India wondering if he wasn't taking a leap into the unknown.

One main motivation for Rajiv was his conviction that this estrangement with China, despite the humiliation of 1962, had to be bridged over at some time or the other for India to sharpen its focus on development. Eventually his instinct worked; the first visit by an Indian prime minister in over three decades had achieved the purpose he had in mind. The thaw began to set in, replacing steadily the bitterness of the past. The tensions on the Line of Actual Control (LAC) reduced considerably and the prospects on the trade side started to look up.

WINS AND LOSSES DOWN SOUTH

If things were beginning to smoothen with China up in the north, there was trouble brewing down south.

The roots of the internal conflict in Sri Lanka are often traced back to its independence in 1948, when the Sinhala majority government began to pass legislation that was deemed discriminatory against the substantial

Tamil minority population. By the 1980s, it had become a full-blown civil war. Had India chosen a wait-and-watch attitude, there would have been a risk of some other power gaining a foothold in Sri Lanka. There was also the additional worry that LTTE's (Liberation Tigers of Tamil Eelam) larger agenda of Tamil Elam may have found sympathizers in India, affecting its integrity.

It was in this background that the Indo–Sri Lanka Peace Accord was signed in Colombo on 29 July 1987 between Rajiv Gandhi and Sri Lankan President J.R. Jayewardene. It was hoped that the terms of the accord would help put an end to the Sri Lankan civil war. By this agreement, Colombo agreed to a devolution of powers to the provinces; the Sri Lankan troops were to be withdrawn to their barracks in the north and the Tamil rebels were to surrender their arms. Following the peace accord, an Indian army contingent, euphemistically called the Indian Peace Keeping Force (IPKF), was sent to Sri Lanka to take control of Jaffna from the rebel LTTEs and disarm it. After three weeks of fighting, the IPKF took control of Jaffna, something that the Sri Lankan army had failed to do for several years. But in this operation alone, India lost 214 soldiers. One of the more ill-planned military moves in this enterprise was the decision to paradrop troops into the LTTE battle zone. The entire helicopter-borne force of 29 Sikh Light Infantry troops along with six para-commandos was shot down by Tamil rebels as they were being dropped into the fighting zone in Jaffna University.

In fact, the entire IPKF venture—Operation Pawan—was called out as a blunder, badly conceived and executed at the diplomatic and military level. As the losses of men and material mounted, the Indian army officers and soldiers were left wondering as to what objective they were fighting for. Within India, too, the sentiment against this foray into Sri Lanka began to build up.

In an ironic turn of events, in April 1989, the government of President Ranasinghe Premadasa ordered the Sri Lanka Army to clandestinely hand over arms consignments to the LTTE to fight the IPKF![12] All this while, the Indian casualties kept mounting. But Rajiv, under the advice of diplomats and generals, refused to withdraw the IPKF from Sri Lanka. It was only after Rajiv's defeat in the elections in December 1989 that the new prime minister, V.P. Singh, decided to do so. In this 32-month-long misadventure, India had lost nearly 1,200 soldiers. The cost of this strategic miscalculation was over ₹10.3 billion.

Commenting on this misadventure, Natwar Singh maintains that Rajiv was 'badly advised... Rajiv Gandhi sent troops to Sri Lanka without telling the Cabinet... The IPKF was not prepared for what they were undertaking in Sri Lanka. There was no coherence in India's policy. MGR [then Tamil Nadu Chief Minister M.G. Ramachandran] had his own Tamil Nadu policy; India had its own policy.'[13]

If the Sri Lankan affair was a disaster, the intervention in Maldives in November 1988 to checkmate the coup was a quick success. A group of about a hundred Sri Lankan militants from the People's Liberation Organisation of Tamil Eelam (PLOTE), backed by Maldivian businessman Abdulla Luthufi, mounted a coup in the Maldives. The militants spread out and seized key areas in the capital, Male, to overthrow the then President Abdul Gayoom. Gayoom, however, reached out to a number of nations, including India, Pakistan, US, Britain, Malaysia and Sri Lanka, for military help. Sri Lanka had commandos on standby at its Ratmalana Air Base at Colombo. The US and Britain decided they wouldn't intervene directly, but would coordinate a response with India. Rajiv saw in this a chance to demonstrate that India was the regional satrap. In less than 16 hours after President Gayoom's SOS call, Indian paratroopers were en route on an IL-76 aircraft and Operation Cactus was launched.

When they landed at the Male airport, a stroke of luck favoured them. Though the militants had seized many key points across the city, the one area they had forgotten to capture was the airport. The Indian troops landed there safely and quickly took control of the airport. They then made their way into the capital, rescued President Gayoom and drove out the militants. It was a simple operation in the end, but one that boosted Rajiv's image as a quick-on-his-feet decisive leader, who could be depended upon to ensure regional security.

Rajiv earned praise from all quarters for this quick response to an appeal by a small neighbouring democracy, just as he was praised for restoring relations with China. But sometimes he also got carried away, and in that sudden rush of adrenalin, he would overreach himself. His brand of diplomacy was aspirational and arrogant as well, depending upon who the interlocutor was going to be. He tried ambitiously, but with limited success, to bridge the differences that were growing then between the US and the Soviet Union.

On the whole, however, the first assessments of him by the foreign observers were largely in positive terms. According to a CIA document, Rajiv's visits to the then Soviet Union, the Gulf, France, and the US in May 1985 'showed he is able to move Indian foreign policy in new directions and to do so in a more pragmatic, less emotionally charged style than his predecessors.'[14]

But he failed to show sensitivity when it came to handling India's long-time ally, Nepal, or for that matter, even a country like Bangladesh, which his mother had helped bring to life.

BIG BULLY OF SOUTH ASIA

By and large, his dealings with the smaller states in the neighbourhood could be heavy-handed. For instance, the threat to build a fence along the entire border with Bangladesh, the economic strangling into submission of landlocked Nepal and the training of a Tamil guerrilla force to fuel the ethnic war in Sri Lanka were all ill-conceived and shoddily executed. In each of these, the remedy employed failed to solve the problem. Instead, they firmed up India's reputation as the 'bully-boy' of South Asia.

The Illustrated Weekly of India asked irately: 'Is Super India emerging as the Big Bully?'[15] From London, *The Economist* admonished editorially, 'India is even bigger than it looks. Its soldiers control a large part of Sri Lanka and keep order in the Maldives. It treats Bangladesh as supplicant. It leans arrogantly across Pakistan to give support to the Afghan government in Kabul, which is Pakistan's enemy. Now it is trying to turn Nepal into a vassal.'[16] Unimpressed with the suggestion that India was merely being a good neighbour, it went on to accuse Rajiv of expansionism at a time when, it said, 'the real superpowers of the world are at least trying to look less menacing...'

Besides this judgment, there was criticism from other quarters too that Rajiv's government asserted its power so often because it wanted India to be the overlord of the region. In that task, Rajiv was poorly served by some of his advisors. One such impulsive act, which seemed inspired then, but was to eventually cost Rajiv his life, was the bizarre incident of bringing the LTTE supreme leader, Velupillai Prabhakaran, to Delhi and keeping him as a virtual prisoner in Ashoka Hotel. This episode is said to have infuriated the supreme leader; some even link it to the LTTE's eventual decision to kill Rajiv.

DAWN OF A NEW ERA: ONLY A DREAM?

When an equally young and liberal Benazir Bhutto became the Prime Minister of Pakistan in December 1988, there were hopes that relations between the two countries would at last change for the better. The portents were good. Rajiv's visit to Islamabad in December 1988 was to attend the SAARC Summit, but it also marked the first time in 28 years that an Indian prime minister had set foot in Pakistan. The last such visit had been in 1960, when his grandfather came to sign the Indus Waters Treaty.

On the first day of the visit, an enthusiastic Benazir remarked, 'I hope the time would come when historians would point to your time in India and my time in Pakistan for heralding the dawn of a new era.'[17] But these post-dinner sentiments from Benazir were not carried on to the official discussions the next day. There, under the watchful eye of her ISI minders, she stuck to the standard Pakistani line of conceding nothing on the issue of Kashmir. A somewhat frustrated Rajiv concluded the discussion by calling the Kashmir issue a 'dead horse'.

Yet it was not altogether a wasted opportunity. There was clear goodwill between the two leaders and an important confidence-building measure on the nuclear field was pushed through. Both India and Pakistan had a sense of insecurity about their nuclear plants, and with this accord, both prime ministers pledged not to attack or assist foreign powers to attack either country's nuclear installations and facilities.

Not long thereafter, in July 1989, Rajiv went on a bilateral visit to Pakistan. In a clear indication of his intent to move on from the Bangladesh chapter he said, 'We do not have any intention of establishing our hegemony on Pakistan; now the time has come for the two of us to restructure our relations on correct foundations.'[18]

When they met formally, Benazir concentrated more on the Kashmir issue and wanted Rajiv to signal some shift in India's stand on it. She had her reasons for doing so, the foremost being that it would gain her brownie points with the army and the Islamic constituencies of Pakistan. Rajiv reminded her of the discussion that had led to the signing of the Simla agreement and told her that a practical and realistic approach was required rather than demands of unilateral concessions by India. Benazir had misjudged Rajiv. She had expected that since Rajiv was of a post-Partition generation, he might not be as rigid as his predecessors were on the Kashmir issue.

It wasn't just Benazir. Earlier in Zia's interactions with Rajiv as well, the Pakistani strategy was to talk him into making one-sided concessions. All the suggestions that he had made to Zia, and to some extent to Benazir, were of confidence-building and risk-reduction measures. Sadly, though, the Pakistani response was sceptical, bordering on negative.

On his part, Rajiv kept persisting, hoping that someday the Pakistani response would get better. He had tried, in lesser or greater measure, most of Chanakya's sutra of '*Saam, Daam, Dand, Bhed* (Advice, Incentive, Punishment, Secrets)' in dealing with Pakistan. Sometimes, though, the *Dand* part of it was wielded without Rajiv's knowledge. One such rather dangerously ambitious plan was set in motion in December 1986, when the army chief, General Krishnaswami Sundarji, rolled out an army exercise called 'Operation Brasstacks'. Ordinarily armies conduct these exercises as a matter of routine to keep their troops in readiness, but the scale and location of Brasstacks set it apart from the routine. At its full swing, the operation was bigger than any North Atlantic Treaty Organization (NATO) exercise till then. It was also the biggest land exercise by any army since World War II. Initially, around 600,000–800,000 troops were mobilized and stationed in Rajasthan's western border, less than 100 miles away from Pakistan. When India launched the final stage of this huge military exercise, with more than 10,000 armoured vehicles spread across its western desert, it set off alarm bells in Pakistan. The Pakistani army had reason to be concerned, because as an exercise, Brasstacks was aimed at cutting the southern Pakistani province of Sindh in two to make it easy for India to push into Pakistan's heartland of Punjab.

Some maintain that Rajiv was not informed in advance that Operation Brasstacks was being set in motion. Regardless, the sheer scale of it soon threatened to bring the two sides to actual conflict, because Pakistan was quick to mobilize troops on its side of the border. Alongside this, fears began to heighten in major global capitals that in case of hostilities breaking out, the conflict might not be confined to conventional weapons; the nuclear card could be brought into play. Following a nudge from both Washington and Moscow, the situation was brought back to near normal with some patient diplomacy. This scaling down of tensions happened after an agreement in March 1987 by the two sides to withdraw 1.5 lakh soldiers each from their respective sides of the LoC. A second agreement to thin out the military presence in the desert area followed later in March. But till then, both sides had kept their fingers crossed.

THE LAST GANDHI?

Like his grandfather and his mother, Rajiv too had his share of military engagements with neighbours; for instance, the IPKF misadventure in Sri Lanka and the successful intervention in countering the coup in Maldives, besides the near conflict with Pakistan during Operation Brasstacks and the standoff with China at Sumdorong Chu. But unlike in their case, Rajiv's was a shorter one-term stay at the top. And unlike them, he had allowed people around him to grow. Only the future will tell whether he remains the last Gandhi to occupy the prime ministerial high chair in India.

On the whole, however, Rajiv had fared reasonably well in his conduct of external relations, where he liked to be proactive as the country's chief diplomat. He felt at home meeting the likes of Margaret Thatcher, whom the family had known for a long time. He had also taken initiatives like nuclear disarmament, which caused, at least for some time, an agreeable flutter at the UN.

By the middle of his term, he had accumulated more pluses than minuses in his ledger. But all that was soon to be in vain. Even his worst critics could not have imagined the windfall that was coming their way in the shape of what became known as the Bofors scandal.

In March 1986, the Government of India had signed a $285 million contract with the Swedish company Bofors for a supply of 410 155-mm Howitzer field guns. Just a year later, on 16 April 1987, the Swedish Radio alleged that Bofors had paid kickbacks to people from a number of countries, including top Swedish and Indian politicians and key defence officials, to seal the deal.

This was just the opportunity that Rajiv's opponents were looking for. The scandal that erupted was made spicier still by the political allegations that the middleman in the deal was Ottavio Quattrocchi, an Italian business executive based in Delhi who was close to Rajiv's family.

Rajiv lost the elections in 1989 largely because of the controversy surrounding the corruption in the Bofors deal. Moments after V.P. Singh stepped into the prime ministerial post, Rajiv summed up his own five years in office thus, 'I think India has never had the sort of development and progress and international standing that it has gained in these five years.'

As a politician's boast, it was justifiable. However, critics contest this claim to assert that this was merely a rhetorical flourish, and that the actual performance was a mixed bag. But to be fair, he was sincere in his effort to put India in the technological stream that was sweeping the world. And he successfully presented an image of India that was persuasive, modern-minded and free of opportunism. Like many others, he may not have delivered entirely what he had promised, but he was certainly not cast in the standard mould of the Indian politician; he was more of a prince charming, suave of manner and sophisticated in his conduct. Alas, this reluctant politician was outwitted by the professional ones.

Almost all through, Rajiv was living a charmed life, but the danger to him was just a terrorist's bullet away. An intelligence assessment made by the CIA in January 1986 said categorically that there were even chances of Rajiv being assassinated before the end of his term in 1989! It listed the terrorists from Kashmir or Punjab as the likely suspects for carrying out an attack on him. The CIA report also went on to speculate on the effect that the assassination could have on India and its external relations, besides introducing instability in Indian politics. A change in leadership could introduce an element of uncertainty in the relations with the US, which had begun to warm up under him. The assassination could also cause a shift in South Asian relations, with a deleterious effect on the US's interests, the report added darkly.[19]

This CIA report was remarkably prescient regarding the danger to Rajiv's life. It is a small quibble that he was killed in a terrorist attack in

1991, after he had demitted office, and that the attack was by LTTE, not a terrorist from Kashmir or Punjab. However, despite investigations by the government, there is still no definite word on whether LTTE was acting by itself or had the encouragement and support of a foreign intelligence agency. And like Rajiv Gandhi's assassination, that of Indira Gandhi as well continues to raise questions. Was it just the security guards who pumped bullets of outrage into her, or was some bigger force behind the act? A well-regarded former officer of the Research and Analysis Wing (R&AW), B. Raman, writes,

> It would be incorrect to characterize his [Rajiv Gandhi] operational policy towards Pakistan as a carbon copy of the policy followed by Indira Gandhi. There were nuances, which differed from those of his mother. Indira Gandhi came to office with a strong dislike and distrust of Gen. Zia-ul-Haq, which continued till her death. She was convinced in her mind that Zia was not a genuine person and that his expression of warmth and bonhomie towards Indians was contrived...Rajiv Gandhi did not inherit his mother's anti-Zia prejudices. He was fully aware of the role played by the ISI in supporting terrorism in Punjab. The suspicion that the ISI under Zia might have been behind the assassination of Indira Gandhi by her security guards was never proved, but it kept haunting the minds of some persons (including me) during the 1980s.[20]

Raman's suspicion regarding the ISI connection to Indira's assassination could also apply to the bomb blast that took Rajiv's life. The direct accused in both killings were known immediately, but the darkest of the dark forces that authorized them remain unrevealed. Meanwhile, one should reflect on the cruel irony that of the two monsters whom Indira Gandhi helped create—Jarnail Singh Bhindranwale in Punjab and Velupillai Prabhakaran in Sri Lanka—the former's followers claimed her life and the latter's cadre her son's.

Overall, Rajiv Gandhi is remembered as a well-meaning, decent inheritor of the Nehru–Gandhi name. Though he did shine brightly on the international landscape with his gracious and open manner, the successes that he notched up were limited in scope. It was perhaps in the domestic affairs that Rajiv has left a larger mark. His encouragement of modern technology and the introduction, in an ambitious way, of telecom and IT, have been transformative for India.

He gave a big push to the modernization of equipment in the defence sector as well. Among the major purchases during his time, the more important included Mirage-2000 fighter aircrafts from France besides the Milan and Matra missiles, Bofors guns from Sweden, and Type-209 submarines from Germany. There were purchases too of the MiG-25, TU-142s, IL-76 heavy-lift and AN-32 medium-transport aircraft. He strengthened the navy, too, with purchases of Kilo-class submarines, and took a nuclear submarine on lease from the Soviet Union. Another aspect that has not received adequate acknowledgement is the fact that during Rajiv's time, the defence budget was allocated at about 4.5 per cent of the GDP, compared to around 2 per cent today.

This degree of involvement in shaping a new India was quite remarkable for a man known to be a loner from his school days; who felt more comfortable soaring in an aircraft than in the hurly-burly of politics. Not long after he became the prime minister, Rajiv was asked whether he missed the life of a pilot. 'I sometimes get into the cockpit all alone and close the door,' he replied. 'Even if I cannot fly, at least I can temporarily shut myself off from the outside world.'[21] The question that bemused critics, reflexively asked, was: Can such a man long rule a nation so vast, so complex and riven by multiple problems at home and abroad? It did not take long for these cynics to rethink and reconsider. His record provided the verdict. Rajiv is admired generally for his modern outlook and an honest desire to make a difference for the better in the national destiny.

5

NARASIMHA RAO: THE REAL CHANAKYA?

At the end of many lives, the man of vision comes to me.
'God is all' this great man says.
Such a spirit sublime, how rarely is he found.

—BHAGAVAD GITA

A succession of weak governments followed that of Rajiv Gandhi. At a time when India needed direction, it was rudderless economically, politically and strategically. The economy, in particular, was in critical shape, while the world around it was changing rapidly.

At this uncertain phase, P.V. Narasimha Rao was a spent force in politics. He had been denied the ticket by Rajiv to contest elections in May 1991, virtually retiring him from politics. Rao knew this was an unceremonious send-off into the political wilderness. He noted in his diary, '26-4-91. At 3.00 PM today, a gap has appeared in my legislative career for the first time in 34 years. I am feeling extremely dejected.'[1]

Consequently, he was only marginally involved in the general election campaign of 1991, issuing the occasional statement. No one paid any attention to him and his statements. In any case, he was a reluctant speaker; he used one word where two might do. He believed that some things should be left unsaid. But he was astute. It was said that if Nehru had a temper, Rao had a temperament.

As he himself acknowledged in his diary entry, the denial of the party ticket had hurt because he had a long record in politics and had been loyal to Indira Gandhi all through. He was Chief Minister of Andhra Pradesh from 1971–3, where his record is generally seen as weak. After moving to Delhi, he held a series of major portfolios in the 1980s, including External Affairs, Home Affairs, Defence, and Human Resource Development.

But after the rebuff from his party, he had made up his mind to retire from politics and go back to Hyderabad. He was just waiting for the right moment to make his intent public. In this state of despondency, he had forgotten all about his family lore—when he was born, a Sufi pir had come up to his father and said, 'Your son will be a badshah (king).'

Sometimes fate intervenes most unexpectedly, and in this case, it struck to make Narasimha Rao truly the first accidental Prime Minister of India. Natwar Singh gives this first-hand account of how it happened:

> On May 21, 1991 Rajiv Gandhi was devastatingly cut down… For his funeral, many world leaders arrived… After the Kings and Captains had departed, intense political activity became evident. The aspirants included the late Arjun Singh, N.D. Tiwari, Sharad Pawar and Madhav Rao Scindia… I told her [Sonia Gandhi] that the time had come to indicate her preference for Congress president. He would naturally become Prime Minister. I suggested she ask P.N. Haksar for advice. Haksar's advice was to offer the post to Vice-President Shankar Dayal Sharma… Shankar Dayal Sharma gave us a patient hearing. He then said… 'The prime ministership of India is a full time job. My age and health would not let me to do justice to the most important office.' Once again she turned to P.N. Haksar, who advised her to send for P.V. Narasimha Rao.[2]

THE SPHINX-LIKE ENIGMA RISES

That call to meet Sonia was political resurrection for Rao, who had resigned himself to a period of quiet retirement filled with hours of listening to classical music. In fact, on the night of 21 May 1991, Rao was packing up his library in his New Delhi home in preparation for retirement in Hyderabad. All that changed with the news that Rajiv had been killed in an explosion while campaigning in the southern town of Sriperumbudur. With the leader dead, Congress was rife with rumours spread by the competing factions within the party. This competition worked to the advantage of Rao. By a process of elimination of the more powerful, he emerged as the consensus candidate to 'carry forward' Rajiv's legacy. Ironically though, Rao had only recently published an article under a pseudonym, denouncing Rajiv as a brash, insecure and self-destructive politician.

His senior colleagues did not expect him to last long in the job. They considered him a 'sphinx-like enigma', who was fluent in 12 languages but spoke his mind in none. They were not wide of the mark, because Rao was an unlikely pragmatist; at 70 he was physically frail, having undergone a recent triple-bypass surgery. He was a career politician, but he had no political constituency of his own. His elevation to the premiership surprised and disappointed his peers in equal measure. Yet this elevation was only the beginning of many surprises; his term in office was going to be one of the most invigorating phases for India. If Jawaharlal Nehru 'discovered' India, and if Indira Gandhi made it 'proud', Narasimha Rao 'transformed' it.

But there were tests of fire that awaited him and the country that he had been asked to lead. For an omen-conscious polyglot who could read and speak a dozen languages, there were bad tidings to be read all over when he took over as the Prime Minister of India on 21 June 1991. The Indian economy was in a pitiable state, separatism was simmering in Punjab, and the secessionist movement in Kashmir was peaking. Externally, India's reliable friend, the USSR, was lurching towards disintegration. Visiting India at this time, the writer Ved Mehta felt 'a sense of dread about the economic, political and religious direction of the country which I don't remember encountering in any of my other visits over the past 25 years.'[3]

India had been troubled economically earlier too; in 1960s, in the 1970s, and again during Rajiv's premiership in the 1980s. But by mid-1991, India was facing its worst economic crises: A large fiscal bill with a rising current account deficit and low foreign currency reserves. Since countries were reluctant to lend it money and the global confidence in India's economy was low, India was forced to pledge and even sell gold for the first time since Independence. In fact, the gold had to be transported from Mumbai to London as collateral in order to get loan. The first placing of 20 tonnes of gold to the investment bank UBS took place on 30 May to secure a $240 million loan, before Rao took over as PM. Then, after Rao took over, India pledged gold three more times, shipping 46.8 million tonnes of the yellow metal to secure $400 million in loans from the Bank of England and the Bank of Japan. Psychologically speaking, this blow to the national pride may not have been comparable to the military humiliation of 1962, but it was bad enough. However, all this gold was repurchased by December that year.

There were other challenges too, but the list above should suffice as an indication of the odds facing him. To cope with them, Rao, the ninth Prime Minister of India, was an unlikely head of government for the world's biggest democracy. A withdrawn, enigmatic figure with no great skill at rabble-rousing or in any form of public speaking, he had inherited the leadership of a bitterly divided Congress party at a time when India needed a leader who could inspire and unite.

Rao was a complex personality who was at the centre of two of the three most violent events of India after 1947: The anti-Sikh violence of November 1984 and the destruction of the Babri Masjid in December 1992. During the 1984 carnage, Rao was the Home Minister of India and did nothing to save the Sikhs. In 1992, as prime minister, he was in his puja room when the reports started reaching him about the demolition of the Babri structure.

Given this background of inaction, Rao presents a remarkably agile picture of a leader determined to move mountains in the economic sphere. This resolve by itself was an amazing turnaround in a man who was, till then, a socialist by conviction.

As prime minister, he was quick to shed his socialist chains; not so much because of a change in his conviction but out of pragmatic compulsion. India was then at the point of an economic meltdown; just about a billion dollars separated the country from bankruptcy. The foreign exchange reserves were just enough to cover two weeks' worth of imports. Rao was told by his newly appointed finance minister, Manmohan Singh, that the petrol pumps would run dry after that. Further, its industrial production was stagnant, and there was hardly ever any news of foreign or domestic investment that could lift the gloom somewhat.

In this dire setting, nothing dramatic was expected from the mild-mannered Rao. The opinion of those who mattered in Delhi's social circles was that he would let events take their course and even be overwhelmed by them. As a wit put it, when in doubt he would pout, and judging by his perpetual pout he seemed constantly in doubt. But in assessing him a lightweight, his critics were making a gross error of judgment.

EMBARKING ON A ONE-WAY STREET

Rao surprised the doubters when he boldly devalued the rupee on 1 July 1991. Within 48 hours, he devalued it still further. He then went on national television to deliver one of the most consequential speeches of modern India.

'Desperate maladies call for drastic remedies,' Rao warned the people as he revealed his austerity programme. 'This is the beginning. A further set of far-reaching changes and reforms is on the way...we believe the nation, as well as the government, must learn to live within its means... there is much fat in government expenditure. This can, and will, be cut.'

The plan that he announced would substantially deregulate industry and liberalize the private sector, pull down the barriers to foreign investment and provide tax concessions to private corporations, slash subsidies to farmers and curb labour activism. The transition from the Nehruvian idea of the economy had begun. 1991 became the year when the socialist shackles started being reduced. Private banks came up, as did private airlines. Indian capital markets were liberalized with limited entry for foreign institutional investors (FIIs). Television went from two state-owned channels to 20 private ones. The telecom revolution, ushered in by Rajiv Gandhi, got a further push.

Among the more prominent of reforms introduced on 24 July 1991 were the privatization of some government companies, the reduction of import duties and incentives for foreign investment. These measures, along with the budget that year, are credited with the economic regeneration of the country. Though Rao was the prime minister, and it was he who took the responsibility if things went wrong, Manmohan Singh as the finance minister received most of the credit for reforms.

At first, Rao's party colleagues reacted negatively to his reforms. Long used to the socialist path set by Nehru and followed largely by Shastri, Indira and Rajiv, they were alarmed by this radical and abrupt shift from a tried and tested economic formula. To them, the slow and steady Hindu rate of growth of economy had kept the country stable, and them and their party in power. That cosy arrangement risked being derailed now. The party leaders rose up against him and beseeched Sonia Gandhi to take over the Congress party and rescue the country. *The National Herald*, the Congress party's newspaper, said that Rao's programme was designed to give 'the middle-class Indian crispier cornflakes or fizzier aerated drinks.' That, the paper insisted, 'could never have been the vision of the founding fathers of our nation.'[4]

Rao's response came in quickly and it was firm. 'Reversing the policy options is not available to this government anymore. It is a one-way street and on all sides I have red lights.'[5]

It did not take long for the results to show up. The turnaround of the Indian economy within two years was the fastest positive change in the history of the International Monetary Fund (IMF). Less than three years later, in 1994, India's GDP was galloping along at 6.7 per cent a year and the profits of private companies had increased by 84 per cent. Foreign exchange reserves had increased by more than 15 times. The first private radio stations and airlines had begun operations.

One result of the economy beginning to take an upturn was that the New Year card for 1992 sent out by the PM had this inscription: 'Change is the only constant.' Accompanying it was the sketch of a spinning wheel gradually transforming into a mechanical gear. It was symbolic of the evolution of tradition, not its abandonment.

But Rao was not content in conveying his reading of change through just a New Year card. That would only have reached the elite, as a turn-of-the-year ritual. He wanted the young and the old of this ancient country also to understand and to be in sync with what he meant by change and how he was bringing it about. Once, while speaking at a public forum, he explained, 'We have this great tradition of interpretation, the Bhashyakara... Nehru took the text from Gandhiji. He moulded it, interpreted it, so as to be in continuity with Gandhiji and still different from what he started with.'[6]

This message was as much to his detractors in the Congress party as to the masses. The former ignored it, and for the latter it was obtuse. But those who did care for the substance were quick to absorb the significance of what he had conveyed. The ones whom he wanted to address and appease ignored it. His challenge from party veterans like N.D. Tiwari and Arjun Singh was so enormous that it was getting difficult for him to run the government. Yet, in his understated manner, he carried on.

The Guardian commented with a kind pen, 'He inherited the leadership of a bitterly divided Congress party, at a time when India was in the throes of communal and caste conflict, and in the grip of economic crisis. Nevertheless, PV Narasimha Rao...became the first non-member of the Gandhi dynasty to last a full five-year term as prime minister.'[7]

CONTINUITY WITH COURSE CORRECTIONS

It was against the resistance from within that Rao had to push through his ambitious undertaking. In the end, it was his steadiness that made the economic reforms politically tenable. A related move that is not often talked about was the manner in which he astutely linked economic policy with foreign policy by reaching out to the US. This was a sound way of conveying that India would need the West's support if the economic reforms were to succeed. Significantly, this would steadily chip away at the otherwise jaundiced view that many in the Indian establishment had of warming up to the West.

There were other moves that had been unthinkable before. He established full diplomatic ties with Israel in 1992. Given India's dependence on remittances of a fairly substantial $2.10 billion in 1991 from the non-resident Indian (NRI) population in the Gulf States, it required considerable courage on his part to establish these ties. A year later, in September 1993, he went to Tehran, becoming the first Indian prime minister to do so since the 1979 revolution.

That's not all. He was conscious that the economic fulcrum of the world was fast shifting east. In recognition of this new reality, Rao was the initiator of the 'Look East' policy, hoping thereby to link India to the booming economies in East Asia. For instance, the breakthrough in relations with South Korea came about with Rao's visit there in 1993. He met the chairmen of the top Korean chaebols (conglomerates) and invited them to take advantage of the ongoing liberalisation of the economy. It was largely as a result of this initiative that investments by

Samsung, Lucky-Goldstar (LG) and Hyundai Motors followed. But it wasn't just economy and trade that made him turn east; he was keen that this move should give the countries in Southeast Asia the possibility of a counterweight to China within Asia.

In yet another example of his ability to keep many balls in the air, Rao sought détente with China to pursue his economic agenda at home. His visit there in 1993 led to the signing of the agreement for 'Maintenance of Peace and Tranquillity along the Line of Actual Control (LAC) in the India-China Border Areas'—an agreement that has largely ensured calm at the border ever since.

But there are dissenting voices as well about this agreement. One such maintains,

> The Rao Government fell for the Chinese ploy... With a stroke of the pen, the entire disputed border was renamed the Line of Actual Control. Hitherto, the LAC had meant a mere 320 kms from Daulat Beg Oldi (DBO) to Demchok in Ladakh (Western Sector)... In the Eastern Sector, India continued to refer to the border as the McMahon Line, a colonial term unacceptable to China...after the signing of the Agreement, the disputed border acquired three lines: The border as perceived by China; the border as understood by India; and the line of Actual Control as agreed by both.[8]

Down south, regarding relations with Sri Lanka, time has testified to the validity of his views. Rao was opposed to Indira Gandhi's decision to give political and material support to the Sri Lankan Tamil militant groups. Later, serving as foreign minister in the Rajiv Gandhi government, he had reservations about India signing an agreement with Sri Lanka in July 1987 regarding a solution to the Tamil–Sinhala ethnic conflict. He was of the view that India had rushed into taking that responsibility. He believed that Sri Lanka's Tamils should have been direct parties to the agreement with India, acting as an external guarantor. In this, his was a prescient view, because one of the principal conditions of the accord was the surrender of arms by Sri Lankan rebels. Now, how do you guarantee that, if the rebels themselves are not a party to the agreement? His fears came true when they refused to surrender their arms. Rao also had reservations about the Indian armed forces being sent into Sri Lanka.

If the security situation in the south was fraught, the conditions within were worrying too. On 6 December 1992, the controversial Babri Masjid was demolished by a mob. In the post-event analysis, there were accusations that Rao had not taken preventive steps. Moreover, the riots that followed in Bombay, and later the ISI-supported and Dawood Ibrahim-sponsored serial bomb blasts that shook the city, were reactions to the Babri demolition.

The incidents of terror became steadily bolder and more frequent—so much so, that by 1994, these had peaked enough for the Indian political parties to send a joint message. As a warning to Pakistan, the two houses of the Indian parliament unanimously passed a resolution on 22 February 1994 demanding that Pakistan cease its support to terror against India. The resolution also affirmed the Indian demand that Pakistan vacate the J&K territory occupied by it:

(a) The State of Jammu & Kashmir has been, is and shall be an integral part of India and any attempts to separate it from the rest of the country will be resisted by all necessary means;

(b) India has the will and capacity to firmly counter all designs against its unity, sovereignty and territorial integrity; and demands that,

(c) Pakistan must vacate the areas of the Indian State of J&K, which they have occupied through aggression...[9]

But Pakistan showed no sign of letting up on its terror activities. In his Independence Day address in 1994, Rao used uncharacteristically blunt language to warn Pakistan. He said, 'With you, without you, in spite of you, Kashmir will remain an integral part of India.' For good measure, he added, 'The one unfinished task is that Pakistan vacate its occupation of those areas of Kashmir which are under its control and should form part of India.' Gradually, the situation began to improve and the Indian security forces got a handle on terrorism in Punjab, as also the Kashmir insurgency, during his term in office.

There were many who understood the great change that he was trying to usher in. They appreciated that his understated style was, at that time, the need of the country. *The Financial Times* chose him along with Deng Xiaoping as 'Man of the Year'. German Chancellor Helmut Kohl considered him less flamboyant than Rajiv Gandhi, but a leader who was the need of the hour: 'Perhaps the country needs more substance than style at this moment.'[10]

Rao moulded India's foreign policy in the manner of *Bhashyakara*. It largely represented continuity with Nehru; there were subtle adjustments of course. If he was radically bold in opening up to Israel, he adopted a conciliatory yet guarded approach towards China. And in his quiet, unobtrusive way, he had begun preparations for a nuclear test. As former President A.P.J. Abdul Kalam recounted at the 7th R.N. Kao Memorial Lecture, 'I still remember a scene during May 1996. It was 9 p.m. I got a call from the then PM's house that I should meet the Prime Minister P.V. Narasimha Rao immediately. I met him just two days before the announcement of the general election's results. He told me, "Kalam, be ready with the Department of Atomic Energy and your team for the nuclear test and I am going to Tirupati. You wait for my authorization to go ahead with the test. DRDO-DAE teams must be ready for action."'[11]

However, that was not to be, for two reasons. In the elections that were held two days later, the Congress party lost. Second, the Americans had found out about the hectic activity that had started in Pokhran. So a disappointed Rao was thwarted—but he had prepared the ground for his successor.

Three days after Rao's death, Vajpayee, on 26 December 2004, made an important disclosure crediting Narasimha Rao as the 'true father' of India's nuclear programme:

> Vajpayee revealed that when he assumed the Prime Minister's office in 1996 [the 13-day stint], he received a paper from his predecessor, urging him to continue the country's nuclear programme. 'Rao had asked me not to make it public. But today when he is dead and gone, I wish to set the record straight... Rao told me that the bomb is ready. I exploded it. I did not miss the opportunity.'[12]

That single statement by Vajpayee sums up the man and the irony of his stars. Rao, probably more than any other prime minister, had faced enormous internal challenges. He had overcome them steadily, calmly and in the face of considerable scepticism from within the party.

THE IRONY OF HIS STARS

Yet, he was not given due recognition by his own, nor trusted by them. *The Guardian* summed up his relationship with the Sonia Gandhi family in this single sentence—'His only crime was loyalty.'[13]

The distrust against him became so personal that when he died, his body was not allowed to be placed in Congress headquarters, as was the custom till then for the party's leaders. Rao had earned Sonia Gandhi's opprobrium because of his achievements and because he was perceived as having become an independent power centre, whereas Manmohan Singh, the man he led in the initiation of economic reforms, walked into India's hall of fame for those reforms and became Sonia Gandhi's man of trust.

Dispassionately viewed, though, Narasimha Rao made profound changes in foreign policy as well, with a quiet, unobtrusive touch. From an economic basket case, India began to be viewed by the world as a country on the rise. He proved himself to be a man of conviction, who left his country with a new direction. As the journalist Sunanda Datta-Ray put it, 'He brought to governance a mind that was supple and subtle. Calling himself "a lover of obscurity", Narasimha Rao said he had never had a visiting card. Silence was a reply, he believed, inaction a form of action. Soon, people were calling him Chanakya.'[14]

This largely sums up Rao, the man. But as a leader, was he truly a Chanakya? That label is not a fair verdict on a politician who believed that the answer to the problems of democracy lay in more, not less, democracy. It might be more accurate to describe Rao as a good approximation of the great man, but not his spitting image, because Narasimha was only human. Sadly, by the end he began to cut a sorry figure, as an air of sleaze surrounded him. Though he was still regarded as personally incorruptable, no party would have anything to do with him. The Congress shunned him while he fought a jail sentence in a corruption case.

Yet, Rao continues to be a compelling reminder of a critical phase in independent India's journey. He provided truly transformational leadership at a most precarious time in India's economic history, and that will remain his calling card for the nation.

6

ATAL BIHARI VAJPAYEE: POET, POLITICIAN, PATRIOT

In this world there are two roads of perfection, as I told thee before,
O prince without sin: Jnana Yoga, the path of wisdom of the Sankhyas, and
Karma Yoga, the path of action of the Yogis.

—BHAGAVAD GITA

Close to four years after Atal Bihari Vajpayee had taken over as prime minister for a full term, the international media increasingly began to carry reports sceptical of his ability to put in long hours at the desk. Or, for that matter, put in any time at all in his office at South Block. Most official business, these doubting voices alleged, was leisurely transacted at the Prime Ministerial residence at 7, Race Course Road. Speculating on this state of affairs, *Time* magazine carried an article on 10 June 2002 titled 'Asleep at the Wheel?'

Had that article been written four years earlier, in 1998, the magazine would have chosen an entirely different title. Something like, 'Alert at the Wheel'. Had the copy editor fancied a slightly more provocative title, he might have modified it to 'Alert at Wheel, while Washington Sleeps'. It would have been most apt, too.

On 10 May 1998, when Washington was approaching midnight, a new day had already dawned in India. As usual, the summer desert in Pokhran, Rajasthan was awash in bright sunlight. While Washington slept, there was hectic activity in the heat-baked Pokhran to put the final, frantic touches to a bold enterprise.

At 10.13 a.m. on 11 May, the first of the three nuclear explosions was set off. Two more explosions were to follow on 13 May. As in 1974, it was once again on Buddha Purnima day that India had detonated the nuclear devices in Pokhran. And, as in 1974, this time too India had managed to hoodwink the US.

When Washington woke up the next morning, it seemed to be an unremarkable, normal workday for the White House, the State Department and at the CIA headquarters in Langley. Strobe Talbott, the deputy secretary of state, started that morning with a senior staff meeting at 8 a.m. It was mostly routine stuff, after which he turned to take a quick look at *The New York Times*. He speed-read some articles about Arab-Israeli tensions but skipped a feature about India. Explaining that decision, he writes in the book, *Engaging India: Diplomacy, Democracy, and the Bomb*:

> In Government, it is often said, the urgent drives out the merely important. India—the world's second most populous country, its largest democracy, and the most powerful country in a region that is home to nearly a quarter of humanity—seemed permanently stuck in the latter category.[1]

All that was about to change and India was soon going to grab the urgent attention of Talbott and everyone else who mattered, in Washington and in the other world capitals. It was a CNN report that shook Washington almost 12 hours after the event. The CNN and the newswire traffic soon began to pile up to tell the mightiest empire on earth that it had missed a big story—an earth-shaking story, literally.

Then, all hell broke loose. Washington was rattled, and it stayed very angry with India and Vajpayee for weeks and months after that. Its bitterness was personal: That it had been conned into believing all was well, even as India was preparing this package of nasty surprise. The US reacted quickly. Just hours after the Pokhran tests, President Bill Clinton made the announcement outside the Sanssouci Palace in Potsdam, after a meeting with the German Chancellor Helmut Kohl, 'I believe they (the nuclear tests) were unjustified. They clearly create a dangerous new instability in their region and, as a result, in accordance with U.S. law, I have decided to impose economic sanctions against India.'

Fearing that Pakistan would follow suit, he despatched Talbott to Islamabad to try and convince Prime Minister Nawaz Sharif that he should show restraint. Clinton urged 'Pakistan not to follow the dangerous path India has taken.'[2] Later, in a telephone conversation with Sharif, he offered economic inducements, including aid of up to $5 billion. But none of it worked, and Pakistan tested six nuclear devices in the mountains of Balochistan by the end of the month. Clinton's warning from Potsdam had not worked on India either, which went ahead to test two further devices on 13 May.

In India there was great jubilation. Vajpayee told an ecstatic Parliament, 'We do not intend to use these weapons for aggression or for mounting threats against any country, these are weapons of self-defence, to ensure that India is not subjected to nuclear threats or coercion.'[3]

But a fawning India did not impress the frowning West. Britain voiced its 'dismay', while Germany called it 'a slap in the face'. Even the Russians voiced their displeasure. India's relations with Japan, free otherwise of ideological, cultural or territorial disputes, were far more severely affected by the Pokhran-II tests. The Japanese Ambassador to India was recalled temporarily and Prime Minister Ryutaro Hashimoto made a statement on 29 May that he had done his best to place the issue of Kashmir on the Security Council agenda.[4]

As in 1974, this second time too, India's curious mix of demonstrations of strength and declarations of restraint puzzled and frustrated strategic experts. Yet, as on the previous occasion, this time as well its assertively painted portrait of a principled, responsible nuclear power was ultimately persuasive. The India–US civil nuclear deal of 2007 was a final admission that for all practical purposes, India's nuclear trespasses were only a forceful assertion that it had arrived in the big league. Nicholas Burns, the US Undersecretary of State for Political Affairs (2005-2008), described India as 'a largely responsible steward of its nuclear material that had played by the rules of a system to which it did not belong.'[5]

However, that sigh of satisfaction took many years to come. For long after the noise from the bombs had died down, the West continued to hold it as a black mark against India. It was not convinced that carrying out the nuclear explosions was a wise decision for the country, for its own sake and that of the region. In support, the critics cited the multiple retaliatory explosions that Pakistan soon carried out at Chagai in Balochistan. They argued that India's actions gave Pakistan the opportunity it had long sought, setting it free from the fear that it might be found out for possessing the forbidden. But for the blasts at Pokhran, Pakistan's nuclear programme would have remained under wraps and as before, it would have hesitated to flaunt it as its deterrent. Pokhran, the critics argued, was a self-goal for India, immobilizing it strategically from military action against its enemy.

If that was the substance of the West's complaint, then India had good reason to go in for the tests. It had watched warily as Pakistan pursued a covert nuclear weapons programme, aided by China. By the late 1980s, India knew Pakistan had acquired nuclear weapons, blunting India's conventional military superiority against Pakistan and making the latter more brazen in its use of terrorism against India. New reports suggested that based on the North Korean missile No Dong 1's design, Pakistan had perfected the delivery system for its nuclear arsenal. This was the little known but interesting sidelight to Vajpayee's decision to go in for nuclear tests soon after taking over as prime minister in March 1998.

There was Narasimha Rao's invocation, of course, and the desire to avoid American pressure against the test by springing a surprise on it. But there was a third element too. This was introduced by Pakistan when it test-fired the nuclear payload-capable Ghauri–I missile on 6 April 1998 from the Tilla Test Range. It could carry a payload of 700 kg to a range of 1,500 km, which was enough to reach most, if not all, of India. This was supposedly one of the reasons why India decided to rush in for its nuclear tests; a message had to be sent to Islamabad in response. When India delivered this message, it did not know that the first Ghauri missile fired by Pakistan was flawed. Its frontal conic nose section material had burned on re-entry.

But it wasn't just Pakistan's capabilities that India was concerned about. China, to its north, was multiplying its nuclear arsenal alarmingly. And at that point, neither the US nor Russia was in China's atomic crosshairs. That left just India as the target. Therefore, even if the West was petulantly upset, India had reason to believe that the blasts were necessary not just as technical tests but also as an announcement that this capability was necessary for its survival in a tough neighbourhood.

Prime Minister Vajpayee proclaimed South Asia's new bombs to be 'weapons of peace', implying therefore that possessing them had made war an impossibility in the region. It was a clever bureaucratic feint with words, but it failed to convince the world. In any case, this proposition was soon mercilessly exposed by the Kargil war, during which Pakistan was readying itself for use of the nuclear option.

PAK PERFIDY AND PROVOCATIONS

At Lahore

Before receiving the shock at Kargil, Vajpayee himself sprang a surprise. Even as the Pakistani soldiers were making themselves at home in Kargil, he decided to visit Lahore on 20–21 February 1999. The visit was high on optics all the way through. Vajpayee's speech at the Lahore Fort reception touched emotive chords on both sides of the border, and reflecting the sentiment of the moment, Nawaz Sharif quipped, '*Vajpayee sahab ab toh Pakistan mein bhi election jeet sakte hain* (Mr Vajpayee can now win elections even in Pakistan).'

But it didn't take long for disillusionment to set in; some critics maintain that though well intentioned, the visit was not adequately thought through:

> Vajpayee went to Lahore, without any preparation. The Lahore Declaration he signed with Sharif on February 21, 1999, mentioned the U.N. Charter as well as the Simla Agreement (in 2001, the draft Agra Declaration omitted mention of both). The two Prime Ministers agreed 'to intensify their efforts to resolve all issues, including the issue of J&K'. This was the only issue that was specifically mentioned (in the Lahore declaration).[6]

The point here being: Why did Vajpayee concede so much so readily on the Kashmir issue in Lahore when, for a never fully explained reason, he was going to scuttle the Agra Summit for much less?

This contradiction was bad enough, but it was worse still that Vajpayee should have forgotten his own statement castigating Indira Gandhi for faltering at Simla and agreeing to make Kashmir the subject of negotiation.

Speaking in a Lok Sabha discussion regarding the Simla agreement on 31 July 1972, Vajpayee had lamented the decision that gave away at the negotiating table, the gains that were made on the military front. He regretted that India should have scored a self-goal on the Kashmir issue:

> Has the Kashmir issue been resolved at Simla? Far from it, it has been reopened anew. The portion of Kashmir that is with us has also been a subject of dispute at Simla. So far we have been saying that Kashmir is a part of India, that its accession to India is final... Was Kashmir not made a subject of dispute at Simla? What is meant by a 'final settlement of J&K'? We have undone all that we have been advocating at the United Nations...We had said (at UN) that Pakistan is an aggressor in Kashmir, that it has no locus standi in Kashmir that it must vacate aggression and go...We had said at the UN that our sovereignty, our rights in Kashmir were not negotiable. How did then Kashmir become a subject of negotiations? What is the meaning of a 'final settlement of J&K'?[7]

At Kargil

Yet the same Vajpayee, as the prime minister, was now endorsing what he had railed against as an opposition leader in 1972. Critics alleged that following the Lahore Bus diplomacy, Vajpayee went a step further and the Pakistani Army's business units were given considerable contracts to supply sugar to India.[8] What India got in return was Kargil.

Though they were not connected, a series of Pakistan-related events followed each other in quick succession after the Pokhran tests. Every one of them was potent enough to leave a long-term mark on the region and beyond. Fortunately, none were to prove fatal in the long-term, but the Pakistani intention was clearly to deeply wound India.

The intrusion in Kargil started in February 1999, and the total area occupied by the Pakistani soldiers by May was over 130 sq kms. Some of the mountain peaks they occupied were located 10 to 12 kms inside Indian territory. From the Pakistani viewpoint, it was meant to be the first step that would eventually lead it to the Valley itself.

Because the Indian security had failed to see them and their hectic activity, the Pakistani soldiers became steadily more brazen, so much so that their Army Chief General Pervez Musharraf spent a night each, on at least two occasions, at the heights captured by them. In one such instance on 28 March 1999, Musharraf flew across the LoC in a helicopter and travelled 11 km into the Indian side to spend a night there.[9] Yet, all the activity that precedes and accompanies an army chief's visit went unnoticed on the Indian side. Nor did the noise of the helicopter raise any alarm in that barren landscape, where the slightest sound travels far! For that matter, it also escaped the attention of the Indian personnel posted in Kargil that crows or other birds were highly unusual at those heights. In the days following the Pakistani intrusion, the birds had begun to appear regularly because they were looking for the leftover food thrown out by the Pakistani soldiers!

Later, post-event, there were claims and counter-claims as to whose fault it was that an intrusion on so large a scale had gone undetected. Eventually, the blame was conveniently pinned on the intelligence agencies. But was that fair? What was the army doing when such a large-scale enemy intrusion was taking place in plain sight and so deep into Indian territory? And why did the various authorities not see red when one intelligence report after another trickled in, warning of just this type of intrusion? Why were no preventive measures taken by those in Kargil? The prime minister himself had been informed of this possibility, yet it did not affect his plan to take the bus to Lahore:

> In the months preceding the intrusion, the intelligence agencies circulated several reports indicating the possibility of increased artillery shelling and infiltration in the Kargil sector. As early as June 1998, the IB reported 'increased activities at the border and continuing endeavour to infiltrate a large group of foreign mercenaries.' It also reported 'increased movement' of Pakistan Army opposite the Kargil sector. Importantly, this report...was sent directly to the prime minister and the home minister as well as the director general of military operations... In October, R&AW reported that 'Pakistan appeared hell-bent on interdicting our Dras-Kargil highway' by means of increased shelling. The report also observed that 'A limited swift offensive threat with possible support of alliance partners cannot be ruled out.'...The following month, the IB reported that Pakistan

was providing military training to Taliban, who were likely to be infiltrated into Kargil area in April 1999…[10]

A far more specific piece of information was given by Shyamal Dutta, the director of the Intelligence Bureau (IB) at that time. Ajit Doval, who was later to become the national security adviser (NSA), talked about it in an interview in 2010:

> There was a definite intelligence about it. There was a definite communication sent to the people concerned… The fact that the Pakistanis planned it, the fact that people had come, that people were being trained and positioned in Kargil area for an offensive was known well in advance, on June 2 [1998]. Nine months before, it was alerted…. The communication was signed personally by the then director Shyamal Dutta. Directors of the IB don't sign unless it's something extremely important. It is signed by much junior officers. It is something extremely important when they sign it. In this case, it was signed personally by the Director, Intelligence Bureau. It was sent by him to the Defence Minister, to the Director General Military Intelligence (DGMI) and various officers… That letter is so specific. It talks about Kargil, Tiger Hill and other features. Every word is well chosen.[11]

At last, as the euphoria surrounding the Lahore visit subsided somewhat, the scales started to fall from the Indian eyes. Even in May 1999, when the country finally woke up in alarm at the enormity of the Pakistani dare in Kargil, some went about their business as usual. If on a foreign tour, the visit was completed as sanctioned. This is not the only criticism levelled against some of the senior generals. As a news report commented:

> In an unprecedented order, the Armed Forces Tribunal raised serious questions on the military leadership in the 1999 Kargil war…(the) Army reacted cautiously to the Tribunal's order backing claims that top commanders had fudged accounts of the 1999 Kargil war, particularly of battles waged in the Batalik sector.[12]

However, the bravery, leadership and sacrifice of the younger officers came in for all-round praise. It was these officers and their men who successfully fought an entrenched enemy at 20,000 feet above sea level. Besides this, the Indian diplomatic effort to sensitize the world against Pakistan's perfidy began to bear fruit. Consequently, the global public opinion began to pile up against Pakistan. That, and Pakistan's reverses on the military front, slowly sent its political and military leadership into the panic mode:

> ...as adversity struck, with military pressure mounting on Pakistani troops, Commander Force Command Northern Areas (FCNA) lost his nerve... In a meeting, lieutenant-general Javed Hasan implored the others: for God's sake, forgive me. I have made a big mistake. Now is the time for prayers. This Napoleon was one of the four architects of Operation Koh Paima, commonly known as the Kargil operation.[13]

The US started making efforts in early June to defuse the situation and get the Pakistanis to agree to withdraw their forces behind the LoC. In late June, Clinton called Sharif to stress that the US saw Pakistan as the aggressor. Hoping for comfort from China, Sharif went to Beijing, but he came back without any assurance.

Eventually, Sharif rushed to Washington. There, on 4 July, he pleaded with Clinton to resolve the issue. In their internal meetings prior to Sharif's arrival, his aides had given enough information to convince Clinton that South Asia was at the brink of a nuclear war. He feared that unlike Kennedy and Khrushchev in 1962, Vajpayee and Sharif did not realize how close they were to it.

On the morning of 4 July 1999, the CIA wrote in its top-secret Daily Brief to the President that:

> Pakistan was preparing its nuclear weapons for deployment and possible use. The intelligence was very compelling... [NSA Sandy Berger] urged Clinton to hear out Sharif, but to be firm. Pakistan started this crisis and it must end it without any compensation. The president needed to make clear to the prime minister that only a Pakistani withdrawal could avert further escalation.[14]

All this, while Washington was getting a sense from Delhi that it 'would grow weary of attacking uphill...into well-dug Pakistani positions. The casualties the Indian forces were taking were mounting. New Delhi could easily decide to open another front elsewhere along the LoC to ease its burden and force the Pakistanis to fight on territory favourable to India.'[15]

When Clinton spoke telephonically to Vajpayee in end-June, the latter was adamant that withdrawal to the LoC was essential and that he would not negotiate under the threat of aggression. Clinton assured him that the US would not countenance Pakistani aggression, nor reward them for violating the LoC, and that direct talks between India and Pakistan were the only solution to Kashmir, not third-party intervention. Simultaneously, the US had introduced other cards into play. The British Prime Minister Tony Blair too advised Sharif on the need for withdrawal from Kargil.

When the PIA commercial flight carrying Sharif approached Washington, it was diverted from its usual landing site at JFK to Dulles Airport. No one from the US side was there to receive Sharif. Instead, at the US's request, the Saudi Ambassador to the US, Prince Bandar bin Sultan, was waiting to have a chat with him. The impression the Prince gathered then was that Sharif was 'distraught, deeply worried about the direction the crisis was going toward disaster, but equally worried about his own hold on power and the threat from his military chiefs who were pressing for a tough stand.'[16] Such was the level of Sharif's anxiety that he had brought along his family, just in case he was unable to return to Pakistan because of the army.

On 4 July, Clinton did not meet Sharif at the White House to avoid giving the impression that the US was somehow sympathetic towards Pakistan's position. Instead, he chose to go across to the Blair House. There, the meeting with Sharif had moments of high drama.

Clinton said bluntly that '[I]f Sharif refused to withdraw, the United States would...shift its historic alliance with Pakistan publicly towards India... For hours, Sharif's delegation invented trick language to suggest that Clinton somehow blessed a Pakistani withdrawal... Or that Pakistan itself need not withdraw, because the fighters...were really mujahideen fighters disguised as soldiers...'[17]

Annoyed by this, Clinton asked aides on both sides to leave and then met Sharif alone. An angry Clinton told Sharif that 'Kargil was not a border skirmish; it had the potential to set off a nuclear war. When the Cuban missile crisis occurred, the US and the Soviet Union had more information about each other's nuclear arsenal than India and Pakistan had in 1999. Your brinkmanship...could set off nuclear exchanges.'[18]

But Sharif would not budge. Surrender, he told Clinton, was worse for him than war. 'He could either order a nuclear war...or risk being overthrown by...General Musharraf... He could yield to Clinton only by baring his neck to Musharraf.'[19]

'So be it,' Clinton said.

Clinton was later to recall that 'their argument....was his most ferocious encounter in politics—bar none.'[20]

This was the turning point. Clinton just had to push Sharif to a point where he wasn't seen to be humiliated. It was equally important that he should leave Washington with the clear understanding that the LoC had to be respected and that the Pakistani forces would have to withdraw to their side of it.

For Vajpayee, this episode represented a major turnaround. Earlier when he had just taken up charge as PM, cross-border terrorism was rampant, yet no major power in the world was willing to support India's contention that Pakistan was sponsoring terrorism from across the border. The big change came during the Kargil war. This time, the world had seen through Pakistan's deception, and India's persistence in meticulously presenting its case had paid off.

However, it did not take long for Pakistan to bounce back to its familiar ways. Despite its humiliation at Kargil, the Pakistani mischief did not end.

At Kandahar

Barely five months later, on 24 December 1999, an Indian Airlines flight, IC 814 from Kathmandu to New Delhi, was hijacked by the Pakistan-based terror group Harkat-ul-Mujahideen. The hijacking, lasting seven days, touched four countries and ended in Kandahar on the eve of the new millennium when the Vajpayee government released three terrorists: Maulana Masood Azhar, Ahmed Omar Saeed Sheikh and Mushtaq Ahmed Zargar.

This incident has since become a textbook example of how a hijacking situation should not be handled. It was a series of blunders at every level, which ended in total capitulation to the demands of terrorists at Kandahar. It should suffice to recount just the first two of these: 'The hijackers took advantage of Kathmandu airport's allegedly poor security to board flight IC-814, carrying guns and grenades. Four boarding cards, it is said, were issued under a single name!'[21]

A.S. Dulat, the then chief of R&AW, recalls what happened when the plane landed at Amritsar:

> ...the Crisis Management Group (CMG) 'goofed up' the entire case by not immobilising the plane when it had landed in Amritsar... No one was willing to take a decision...no instructions were passed on to Punjab Police, which had moved in its personnel. They carried on debating and the plane flew off.[22]

The government's excuse, that it was able to save the lives of 170 passengers, is countered robustly by its critics, who say that the terrorists whom it released in Kandahar have since been responsible for major acts of violence resulting in thousands of deaths. For instance, Masood Azhar went on to establish the Jaish-e-Mohammad (JeM) in 2000. This group has undertaken a series of major terror strikes against India, starting with the attack in 2001 on the Indian Parliament to the one in Pulwama in 2019. Omar Sheikh played a role in planning the 9/11 terror attacks and in the killing of the journalist Daniel Pearl.

At Agra

Yet, within a year of the Kargil conflict and six months after the humiliating Kandahar hijacking episode, the Vajpayee government decided to give peacemaking yet another chance. What brought about the summit at Agra despite the series of setbacks that Vajpayee's efforts had suffered already? There is no single trigger point, but it says a lot about Vajpayee's magnanimity that a day after the Kandahar hijacking ended, he should already be thinking of the next effort towards Indo-Pak peace. In his Kumarakom musings on New Year's Day 2001, Vajpayee wrote, 'India is willing and ready to seek a lasting solution to the Kashmir problem...we are prepared to re-commence talks with Pakistan at any level, including the highest level, provided Islamabad gives sufficient proof of its preparedness to create a conducive atmosphere...'

There was no special sign in the Indo-Pak tea leaves to warrant this optimism. Still, it was decided to invite President Musharraf for a summit meeting in Agra to resolve the bilateral issues.

When countries plan a summit meeting, it should be preceded by weeks and even months of careful preparation. What is achievable, and what pitfalls are to be avoided, should be methodically thought through. Even the text of the statement or declaration that could come out at the conclusion of a summit is more or less fleshed out by the officials and sometimes the foreign ministers of either side before the summit. This is the standard drill followed everywhere, and it is even more important in the Indo-Pak context, where every meeting is prone to nasty surprises and each summit becomes a contest in one-upmanship. However, when impulse overtakes prudence and the desire to do something out of the box overtakes counsels for careful preparation, upsets are inevitable.

The Agra Summit lasted from 14–16 July 2001. Musharraf did some grandstanding with the Indian media. But for that, there was nothing exceptional, nor did the draft declaration go beyond what had already been agreed to by the Indian side in Lahore. Yet Vajpayee gave in to pressure from some of his aides and the summit was curtailed rather shabbily.

In the final analysis, there was not a single, readily identifiable cause for the failure of the summit at Agra. Broadly, however, in addition to the doubt planters within the Indian camp, the blame could be apportioned to the following points: 'The first souring of the mood began with Musharraf's aggressive posture in his interaction with the Indian media on the morning of July 16. It was followed by his insistence that Kashmir was a "core issue", and his refusal "to address cross-border terrorism".'[23]

Vajpayee would certainly have been disappointed that yet another of his efforts to seek peace had been scuttled. Perhaps in anguish as much as in hope, he wrote in the visitor's book of Jaypee Palace Hotel, where he had stayed during the summit, 'I carry back with me memories of my excellent talks with His Excellency General Pervez Musharraf, the President of Pakistan. I am confident and I sincerely pray that the Agra Summit will ultimately prove to be useful milestone along the high road to peace and normalization of relations between India and Pakistan.'[24]

Before the end of that eventful year there was even more unpleasantness in store. On 13 December 2001, five terrorists drove into the Parliament House complex with the intention of killing the parliamentarians. However, they were challenged by the security staff, who suffered nine casualties in the gunfight that followed. Still, this attack shook up the political establishment. Had the terrorists succeeded in killing some parliamentarians, the implications would have been horrendous. The very fount of Indian sovereignty was the target, and an outraged government responded with a military build-up.

Codenamed 'Operation Parakram,' this was the first full-scale military build-up by India after the 1971 war. Begun on 20 December, a week after the attack on Parliament, India went on to mobilize around 500,000 troops and three armoured divisions on Pakistan's border. After some initial nervousness, Pakistan responded similarly, deploying around 300,000 troops. The stalemate lasted ten months till October 2002, when a tired Indian government told its bewildered soldiers that they could go back to doing what they were doing before the start of the ill-conceived operation.

The soldiers had spent the intervening ten months contemplating the border that they weren't authorized to cross. Meanwhile, the losses of men and material in the searing heat and icy cold continued to mount up; about 2,000 Indian soldiers died, 1.5 lakh civilians were displaced and the cost of Operation Parakram was over $3 billion.

Later, analysts pointed out the many drawbacks in this episode. It was hastily conceived and poorly planned and executed. It took nearly one month for the army to mobilize its troops; in the process, the element of surprise was lost. Moreover, it should have been clear from the beginning that the international environment was not in favour of a war. The attack on the Indian Parliament was preceded by the 9/11. It should therefore have been obvious to the planners of Operation Parakram that the US would not want any distraction while it was trying to seek Pakistani cooperation in its war against the Taliban in Afghanistan. As one commentator wrote,

> ... [The] government's October 16 decision to pull back troops from the western frontier marks an end to arguably the most ill-conceived manoeuvre in Indian military history. Intended to signal India's willingness to go to war if Pakistan continued to aid cross-border terrorism, Operation Parakram ended as an ignominious retreat after having failed to secure even its minimum objectives. But the

worst is maybe yet to come. Pakistan has called India's cards, and discovered that its much-hyped hand contains no aces...[25]

Therefore, if India had gained in prestige for the valour of its soldiers during the Kargil conflict, it had nothing to show by way of results after Operation Parakram. Rather, the resulting stalemate has continued to haunt the strategic planners ever since; would India be able to overwhelm Pakistan in the next one?

FROM LOVE TO HATE TO ONLY BUSINESS

The relatively short period from 1998 to 2002 was full of surprises in India's relations with Pakistan, some of them rather nasty. Did we acquit ourselves with quotable aplomb in these? Did we fully take into account the long-term consequences of our decisions? Perhaps not. Just to give one example, during Operation Parakram, India decided to ban Pakistani planes from flying over its territory for their journey east. Pakistan grabbed this chance and banned Indian planes from overflying its territory on their journeys west. In the process, Indian airlines and their passengers were the sufferers, because while Pakistani traffic to the east was meagre, the substantial Indian air traffic west now meant a long detour involving higher fuel cost and longer travel time. Pakistan used this ploy again recently after the Balakot attack.

It wasn't just this issue; Vajpayee's policy on Pakistan was full of unexpected U-turns. Yet the surprises that he sprang on people were accepted as normal in what was advocated as changed circumstances. And after every disappointment, Vajpayee tried again. He took a great gamble by taking the bus to Lahore, capped it with a visit to Minar-e-Pakistan, and spoke to Pakistan from his heart. These gestures won him appreciation in India, Pakistan and the world. But when the euphoria ebbed, Indians made the unpleasant discovery that Pakistani soldiers had occupied the heights at Kargil. Yet no one pointed fingers at Vajpayee for undertaking the visit to Lahore and waxing eloquent there about the stability of Pakistan, while at that very moment India's own integrity was being spliced by its soldiers. Instead, the blame was passed on to intelligence agencies. Nor was it considered necessary to question the planners of the

Lahore visit as to why they did not take the warnings about Pakistani incursions into account before giving the clearance for the visit.

If any further warnings were needed about Pakistan's designs, they were provided by the Kandahar hijacking. But it did not deter the government from hosting the summit at Agra.

Around the time when Operation Parakram was called off, the international media had begun to view Vajpayee's performance in office with a less kindly eye. *Time* epitomized this in its assessment:

> He drank heavily in his prime and still enjoys a nightly whiskey or two at 74. India's leader takes painkillers for his knees...and has trouble with his bladder, liver and his one remaining kidney. A taste for fried food and fatty sweets plays havoc with his cholesterol. He takes a three-hour snooze every afternoon on doctor's orders and is given to interminable silences, indecipherable ramblings and, not infrequently, falling asleep in meetings. Atal Behari Vajpayee, then, would be an unusual candidate to control a nuclear arsenal.[26]

This article's doubtful combination of personal health with governance was frowned upon by Vajpayee's admirers, who continued to see him as bereft of warts. In taking an unduly harsh swipe at his ability to control a nuclear arsenal, this assessment made a fundamental misjudgement. It ignored the patience and balance with which Vajpayee handled the many provocations from Pakistan.

Still, the criticism against him was muted. The reality was that it would have been considered blasphemous to question Vajpayee. He was a grand creator of moods. When he wanted friendship with Pakistan, Indians joined him in his jhappis (hugs). When warring with that neighbour, Indians warred with him. Vajpayee's relationship with Pakistan meandered from love to hate to 'only business', and at each turn he found people standing by his side. He spurned Musharraf at the Agra Summit, but people were not any wiser as to what the offending word was in the joint text that made him do so. Yet, they applauded him for standing firm and giving Musharraf a talking-to.

Whatever his personal foibles, there is no doubt that Vajpayee was a major Indian statesman, admired for his speech and action at home and abroad. His message in Kashmir in 2003 that '...we wish to resolve all issues, both domestic and external, through talks…that the gun can solve no problem, brotherhood can. Issues can be resolved if we move forward guided by the three principles of *Insaniyat, Jamhooriyat aur Kashmiriyat* (humanity, democracy and Kashmiri unity)' electrified Kashmir. And his words '*insaniyat ke daire mein* (within the ambit of humanity)' continue to resonate there.

ARCHITECT OF THE CHINA POLICY

Though Pakistan frustrated him repeatedly, the record shows that he did not give up the hope that one day, all could be well between India and Pakistan. In some measure, his approach to China too reflected the gloss that a poet contemplates. But his first official visit to China was not propitious.

As foreign minister, Vajpayee was on a fence-mending visit to China in February 1979 when reports came in that Chinese forces had launched an attack against Vietnam. In Delhi, Prime Minister Morarji Desai expressed 'profound shock and distress' over China's invasion and called for the immediate withdrawal of its forces. In China, Vajpayee had to abruptly break off his stay in Canton after conveying India's protest to the Chinese Ambassador to India, Chen Chao Yuan, who was accompanying him. Vajpayee took a hydrofoil to Hong Kong, where he boarded a flight for India.

Though ill-starred in this respect, Vajpayee's visit continued to be in Deng's mind. In December 1982, a delegation from the Indian Council of Social Sciences Research had called on him in Beijing. Recalling his meeting with Vajpayee, Deng said:

> When I met your former foreign minister in 1979, I put forward a 'package solution' to the problem. If both countries make some concessions, it will be settled… The problem between China and India is not a serious one… The problem we have is simply about the border. Both countries should make an effort to restore the friendship that existed between them in the 1950s. As long as we go about it in a reasonable way, I think it will be easy for us to settle our border question. Because this question has a long history, you have to take

into account the feelings of your people, and we also have to take into account the feelings of our people. But if the two sides agree to the 'package solution', they should be able to convince their people.[27]

His visit to China as foreign minister may have ended on a sour note, but this was not the case for his visit to that country as prime minister in 2003. Though even in this case, some critics bemoan the fact that Vajpayee controversially agreed to India recognizing the Tibet Autonomous Region as an integral part of the People's Republic of China (PRC). It was small consolation that during this visit, China had also, for the first time, referred to Sikkim as a state of the Indian union. The critics were not assuaged. They felt that India had given up its Tibet card. Among these criticisms, and there were many who were not enthused, was this comment:

> Seeking to placate China, its long-time rival, India has shifted its stand on Tibet to recognize the Chinese annexation… Insecure about its hold and unsure of the validity of its claim on a territory that was mostly independent in history, China sees New Delhi as the key to its continued control of Tibet, whose traditional cultural and trade links were southward to India. By handing Beijing the formulation it wanted, India has opened itself to more Chinese pressure, especially because it is home to the Dalai Lama and more than 100,000 of his followers. China could in the future demand that New Delhi live up to the new formulation and disband the Tibetan government-in-exile headquartered in Dharamsala…[28]

However, looking back at Vajpayee's strategic record, it becomes evident that his was a good mixture of resolve and restraint; a focus on hard capabilities tempered by the possible. All along, he was also conscious of the fact that the world respects the strong. Seen as such, his record with respect to the economy has much to be admired.

A VISIONARY

Vajpayee's was the first truly right-wing government in India, and it showed in his policies. There was privatization of government companies via strategic sales, foreign exchange rules were made friendlier, there was rationalization of taxes, reforms were initiated in the capital markets and the insurance sector was liberalized. Infrastructure projects like the Golden Quadrilateral (GQ) were important by themselves; they were also boosts for industry and employment. All told, the push given through these policies led to India's GDP growth rate reaching a respectable 8 per cent from 2003 onwards.

Like Nehru, whom he admired, Vajpayee had a grand vision. It may not have been as all-embracing as Nehru's, nor did it create a diversity of institutions and centres of excellence on a Nehruvian scale. But in terms of ambition and impact, his projects were impressive. The GQ and the Pradhan Mantri Gram Sadak Yojana (PMGSY) were arguably the most audacious infrastructure projects undertaken in the country. They connected not just India's metropolises and big cities but its hinterlands as well.

Politically, too, his was an enviable record. In fact, it would be hard to find a phase in his political career where he could be faulted. Vajpayee's gift with words and poetry, topped by a cultivated ambiguity about ideology, added up to a picture of a liberal with a large heart. But he was not this liberal that he came to be known as through his years as prime minister. What he really had was a chameleon-like ability to change with the mood and edit and modify his stated views, emerging none the worse for it. To the public, his flip-flops acquired qualities of flexibility and tolerance.

Opinions differ on how effective Vajpayee's policy on the two persistent and critical foreign policy concerns for India was. It is claimed that:

> The foundation of India's present weak-kneed foreign policy was laid between 1999 and 2004 by Atal Bihari Vajpayee, who executed more policy U-turns than probably any other prime minister since independence. Vajpayee's roller-coaster policy on Pakistan exacted a major toll on institutionalized policy-making, exposing India's glaring inadequacy to set and unwaveringly pursue clear goals. Under Vajpayee—who also surrendered India's Tibet card in a 2003 Beijing visit—personal rather than professional characteristics defined India's foreign policy.[29]

There was no shortage of questioning voices abroad as well. In its final words on him, *The Guardian* wrote, 'Vajpayee had a gift for ambiguity. Nobody could be completely sure whether he was a lone liberal among Hindu fundamentalists or simply a plausible salesman for religious nationalism.'[30]

As if anticipating an obituary like the one above, *Time* wrote this in praise of Vajpayee in 2004:

> Vajpayee's greatest trick—and the one that places him among the world's most significant figures—is his pursuit of peace with Pakistan while heading the Bharatiya Janata Party (Indian People's Party), which rose to power in the 1990s on a wave of Hindu chauvinism. In January the Hindu Vajpayee met Pakistan's Muslim President Pervez Musharraf in Islamabad and agreed on talks to try to end a half-century of war and hostility. Anwar Sadat's 1977 mission to Jerusalem is the only other journey in modern history that bears comparison.

The article goes on to describe Vajpayee's effort at peace with Pakistan in these superlative terms:

> Critics claim it is an old man's obsession with legacy that was the true spur for his trip to Islamabad. Whatever the motive, after three wars with Pakistan in 57 years, the greatest gift any Indian leader can bequeath his people is peace. That the man who exploded the subcontinent's first atom bomb may also lead his nation out of war has both an inconsistency and a karmic symmetry that is pure Vajpayee and pure India.[31]

Incidentally Alex Perry, the writer of this accolade, had two years earlier chosen to characterize Vajpayee's performance as a leader 'asleep at wheel.'

Often at meetings, Vajpayee did give the impression of somnolence, but mostly he was engaged in deep thought behind those shut eyes, as startled visitors found by the profundity of his replies. This kindly man was in the ultimate sense a patriot, who did not hesitate to praise his opponents. He was lavish in his praise of Nehru and Indira when their actions, or the occasion, so demanded. He agreed readily when Narasimha Rao asked him in 1994 to lead India's response against Pakistani allegations about Kashmir at the UN Human Rights conference in Geneva. But in an aside, he also told Rao prophetically, '*Yeh masla aap nahin suljha payenge. Yeh kaam hamari party karegi* (You will not be able to resolve this matter. It will be done by our party).'

In personal dealings, he was a gentleman who bore no grudges. As a politician, he fought hard with his opponents but gave them the respect that was their due.

When Vajpayee first entered his office in South Block as external affairs minister in 1977, he noticed a blank spot in one of the walls. He turned to one of his officials and said, 'This is where Panditji's portrait used to be. I remember it from my earlier visit. Where has it gone? I want it back.'[32]

The admiration was not one sided. In 1957, after listening to Vajpayee's speech in Parliament, Jawaharlal Nehru had predicted: 'This young man one day will become the country's Prime Minister.'[33]

It will not be just to compare the two visionaries, but suffice it to say that had Nehru been alive, he would have been proud to see that Vajpayee had lived up to his expectations in almost every respect. As a lifelong politician, Vajpayee knew the pulse of the people, and equally importantly, the pulse of the moment. In office as prime minister, he was a statesman who escaped successfully the clutter of details.

7

MANMOHAN SINGH:
WILL HISTORY BE KINDER?

When wisdom is thine, Arjuna, never more shalt thou be in confusion: for thou shalt see all things in thy heart, and thou shalt see thy heart in me.

—BHAGAVAD GITA

A little before he was to demit office in 2014 at the end of two terms as prime minister, Dr Manmohan Singh confided sorrowfully to an aide, 'I have done nothing wrong, I want to go as an honourable man.'[1]

Did he really have cause for concern?

Long after he has left office, no one has yet accused him personally of any wrongdoing. Then why was he worried that his record might be sullied? One explanation could be his background as an academic. An economist by training, he taught in Punjab University prior to moving to Delhi and taking up government jobs, subsequently holding ministerial positions and eventually becoming the prime minister. He was the country's first prime minister to hold a doctorate.

A quiet, cerebral man who maintained a simple life, he was far less comfortable in the hurly-burly of politics than most of his predecessors. He was not a politician in the classical mode: He had no mass base among people, nor did he have the support of the party cadre. One evidence of this was the fact that he never won an election. Manmohan Singh was acutely aware of these shortcomings. That's probably why he once said, 'It is nice to be a statesman, but in order to be a statesman in a democracy you first have to win elections.'[2]

Winning elections was not an essential requirement when Narasimha Rao appointed him as the Finance Minister of India in the middle of 1991. This appointment had taken most by surprise, because he was not Rao's first choice. It was I.G. Patel, who had been Manmohan's predecessor as Governor of RBI. Since he could not take up the job, Rao turned to Manmohan Singh.

India was at the point of bankruptcy then. Its economic situation was desperate. Wasteful fiscal policies had exhausted the country's foreign exchange reserves, obliging New Delhi to dispatch nearly 50 tons of gold to the Bank of England to serve as collateral for a loan. *The Economist* likened the transaction to 'an indigent household pawning the family jewels.'[3]

In such humiliating circumstances, status quo was no longer tenable. So India changed course and Manmohan Singh drew up reforms that liberalized the economy. As he later explained, 'There were no foreign lenders willing to finance our current-account deficit. Our foreign exchange had disappeared.'[4] Singh's message to Narasimha Rao was both bleak and honest: 'I said to him that we are on the verge of collapse... We must convert this crisis into an opportunity to build a new India.'[5]

In 1991, when he rose in the Parliament to present the Budget, it was against this backdrop of the Indian economy plumbing the depths of desperation. 'We shall make the future happen,' Manmohan Singh said bravely in the Parliament, announcing a series of liberalising measures, 'Let the whole world hear it loud and clear—India is now wide awake.'[6]

He was later hailed as the man who saved India, though in large measure the credit was due also to Narasimha Rao who, as the prime minister, provided the steering vision for the reforms.

It is important here to recall a barely known fact about him. The general perception maintains that Manmohan Singh came to the notice of the Congress leadership when he was appointed as finance minister. That is largely true, but the political class first took note of him after the Bangladesh war. Manmohan Singh describes it thus:

When I came to the Finance Ministry in 1971, I wrote a paper called 'What To Do With Victory' (that was when Indira Gandhi's popularity was at its peak). I had written at that time that all these controls in the name of socialism would not lead to growth but would strangle the impulses for growth. I had said that these controls would not reduce inequalities but increase them. I have not been timid. I have spoken my mind freely and frankly. But I've also served as a faithful civil servant. Even if I have been overruled, I have carried out the orders of my political masters.[7]

This was an interesting interview, more so because it was given at a time in 1991 when he was new to Delhi's political ways. The candidness of his remark about being a faithful civil servant is particularly noteworthy. In the same interview, Thakurta asked Manmohan Singh in what manner his economic views had changed over the years. He said:

I used to be in favour of gradual change. But I look around the world and realize that time is not on our side. There has been a complete collapse of the command economies of Eastern Europe. This country will be marginalized if we don't move forward at a breath-taking pace. I'm convinced that if there has to be structural change, it must be done quickly. That's how my views have changed.[8]

This comment and his earlier remark about controls in the name of socialism are revealing. They are proof that the budget of 1991 was not merely a knee-jerk reaction to a panic situation or a sudden stroke of inspiration. Instead, it was the maturing of a deeply-held conviction that was first articulated in his 1971 paper. On the whole, Manmohan Singh defied ideological labels. If anything, he could only be called moderately left-of-centre. In a large way, he made liberalisation appear acceptable.

When Narasimha Rao's government completed its term in office in 1996, it was expected that Manmohan Singh would fade away to a life of quiet reflection and participation in seminars on economic issues. However, that was not entirely the case. Out of the government, he was not at a loose end, because the Congress sponsored him as a member of the Rajya Sabha. Since he was not comfortable with the struggles of being a politician in the Opposition, he was dutiful as a parliamentarian but remained aloof otherwise. Therefore, in the period after 1996, he was mainly leading a quiet life. He did contest once in his political life for a Lok Sabha seat from South Delhi. This was in 1999, and the loss then put him off the political struggles of campaigns forever.

He may not have been active in party matters like the other politicians, but all through, he remained in obsequious touch with the President of the Congress Party, Sonia Gandhi. He also had the lucky stars on his side. However, even he may not have expected that he, rather than Sonia herself, would be asked to take up the top job after the party's alliance emerged victorious in the 2004 general elections. Manmohan Singh was therefore both excited and disbelievingly nervous when he was actually handed the job:

> ...when the Congress...made it to office [in 2004], Sonia turned to Manmohan... I remember watching him go to 10 Janpath, eyes gleaming with excitement, hands trembling with anticipation, eager to become Sonia's nominee for the job. But the Congress was not ready. Congressmen and women wept and begged Sonia to reconsider. She refused point-blank. Manmohan Singh was her choice, she said, and she would not be swayed...nobody in the Congress had any enthusiasm for a Manmohan Singh prime ministership. He was...seen as a creation of the hated Narasimha Rao and hard-core politicians had contempt for his lack of political skills.[9]

Sonia's will prevailed and Manmohan became the prime minister. However, it soon became clear that Sonia had assigned for herself and her close confidants the role of the backseat driver. When she made her mind known on a particular policy or issue, the government machinery cranked itself to super-speed to carry out her wishes. This dichotomy of power affected governance in a debilitating manner. The party members, taking the cue from her, looked at the Congress headquarters for favours and political directions: 'For Congress MPs, the leader to please was always Sonia [Gandhi]. They did not see loyalty to the PM as a political necessity, nor did Dr Singh seek loyalty in the way in which Sonia and her aides sought it.' It was also alleged that '...a prominent bureaucrat in Mr Singh's office, at the behest of Sonia Gandhi, had regular, almost daily meetings with Sonia at which he was said to brief her on the key policy issues of the day and seek her instructions on important files to be cleared by the PM.'[10]

As a result, after an initial spurt, the economy did not show spectacular results. Some ascribe the slide that started in 2010 to the global slowdown. But there was more to the Indian economic deceleration than ill winds from the foreign markets. Gradually, the reports of massive corruption, policy paralysis and general inefficiency began to trickle out. A government led by a man who was once admired for transforming the economy as finance minister, was failing to deliver when, technically speaking, the buck stopped with him.

PAKISTAN—FOUR STEPS AND MISSTEPS

But to his credit, it must be said that the economy had shown a healthy growth during his first term, reaching a thriving 10 per cent by the end of it. However, it is difficult to see too many bright spots in Singh's foreign policy during his tenure. The deteriorating situation at the LoC, where soldiers were being beheaded by the Pakistani army, the gaffe about Balochistan at Sharm-el-Sheikh and the regular Chinese incursions into Indian territory did not show him in good light as a leader.

Fortunately for India, some higher force must have come to its aid, otherwise Manmohan Singh seemed to have been ready to take India to the point of no return on Kashmir. Soon after assuming office in 2004, he asserted rather boldly to an American journalist, 'Short of secession, short of re-drawing boundaries, the Indian establishment can live with anything. Meanwhile, we need soft borders—then borders are not so important. People on both sides of the border should be able to move freely.'[11]

In making this statement, he was already revealing all his cards, or the lack of them, to Pakistan. Did he not consider for a moment the disaster that was waiting to happen if his assurance that people on both sides of the border would be able to move freely actually turned into reality? Infiltrators would have had a field day and the Pakistani army would have grabbed this as an open invitation to repeat Kargil on a vast scale!

It is also claimed that India did well by building a 746 km-long-fence across the LoC in 2004–5. The advocates of the fence also cite the reduced numbers of terror incidents as a direct result of this barrier. But they err grievously. The fence has become India's Maginot Line, turning the army to the issues of counter-insurgency in Kashmir. As experts attest, this type of fortification introduces a false sense of security, stifling the offensive instinct.

Then there is the claim that the understanding with Pakistan had reduced the terror incidents in Kashmir. This was indeed so, but it was done by Pakistan for tactical reasons. It was preoccupied in the post-9/11 phase with the developments in Afghanistan and at that stage, when its focus was to weaken the American operations there, it did not want to keep the Kashmir pot boiling, thereby opening a second front for its agencies. However, this did not mean the end of terror travails for India. It simply meant that the terror attacks had shifted to the hinterland, where the Pakistani link would take time to establish. Soon, Pakistan's terror operations became bolder and bigger. Some of the most lethal terror incidents in Pune, Mumbai and Delhi took place in the period after 2004, the deadly 2006 terror attacks killing over 200 in seven trains in Mumbai being the goriest of such incidents. All the training, planning and preparation for the 26/11 attack were completed during this period. Despite Musharraf's assurance that Pakistan's territory would not be used for setting up terror activities in India, the facts on the ground presented a different picture. Yet, we were lavish in our praise of Musharraf's word, because it was convenient politically to tout it as a foreign policy success.

Besides this, Musharraf also had reason to feel encouraged by Manmohan's 2004 statement in favour of soft borders. After all, what he had failed to achieve in Kargil could now be within reach, as the bigger prize of Kashmir. As army chief, he had employed stealth in Kargil; now, as president, he was depending on subterfuge. It was therefore natural that he should have followed this up with the infamous four-point formula on Kashmir.

It involved the following:

1. Demilitarization or phased withdrawal of troops;
2. No change of borders of Kashmir. However, people of J&K would be allowed to move freely across the LoC;
3. Self-governance without independence; and
4. A joint supervision mechanism in J&K

According to reports circulating then, the Indian government reacted enthusiastically, as it was expected to, because it was virtually a co-author. But in doing so, India was disregarding the fact that the four-point formula was merely a repackaging of an old proposal. It was put together first by the US–UK combine and articulated by Zulfikar Ali Bhutto at the Indo-Pak meeting on Kashmir in January 1963.

Though the details of it have been mentioned earlier in the book, still it is worth repeating a section of it briefly to show how Musharraf had resuscitated an old idea and advanced it as his own: '…[in January 1963] Bhutto was leading a Pakistani delegation for a second round of talks in Delhi. It was here that the "soft borders" approach was broached. The idea was floated first in a document prepared by Roger Hilsman and it involved an undivided J&K jointly administered by India and Pakistan.' Actually, in the run-up to the second round, US officials had considered various possibilities including 'an undivided state of J&K jointly administered and jointly defended by India and Pakistan.'[12] There were other variations of this theme, and the pressure on the recently defeated India was great, but Nehru held firm. This, despite the fact that India was vulnerable economically. And after its humiliation in 1962, it was in urgent need of British-American benevolence, defence wise. Still, India managed to ward off the UK-US combine on the Kashmir issue.

But that was then, at a point when we were weak and despondent. Since then, India has risen and the situation has turned vastly different in this millennium. India was no longer vulnerable economically nor in need of urgent American assistance for defence equipment. If in 1963, India was recovering from the trauma of defeat, in the first decade of this millennium, it was exulting in the humiliation it had inflicted on Pakistan in Kargil. Despite being in a position of relative strength, it is unfortunate that we should have almost succumbed when Pakistan dusted off this old proposal, modified it a bit, and presented it as Musharraf's four-point formula.

The big difference from the 1963 negotiation was the support given to the proposal by the Indian side. Earlier, the Pakistani push had been stymied by the 'ifs and buts' of the Indian negotiators. This time the Indians were so passionately involved in this enterprise that this four-point formula became known as the Musharraf–Manmohan four-point formula.

By early 2007, the back-channel talks on Kashmir had become 'so advanced that we'd come to semicolons,' Musharraf's Foreign Minister (Khurshid) Kasuri recalled... Pakistan's NSA (Tariq) Aziz and Manmohan's Special Envoy (Satinder) Lambah were negotiating the details for a visit to Pakistan by the Indian Prime Minister during which, they hoped, the principles underlying the Kashmir agreement would be announced...[13]

The Manmohan–Musharraf formula for Kashmir, if implemented, would have resulted in India's control over Kashmir slipping steadily. To give just one argument—if India finds it hard to control J&K with nearly 600,000 soldiers, how will it do so when most of its army has been withdrawn in favour of joint control by India and Pakistan?

The question that must be asked is this: Do we not learn from history? Seemingly not, otherwise why should we have risen to Musharraf's four-point bait with our eyes wide open? Was Manmohan Singh not advised by his aides that an almost identical proposal had been rejected by Nehru nearly half a century earlier?

Equally alarmingly, the four-point formula had been kept a great secret from the Indian people. Fortunately for India, the plans for Manmohan Singh's 2007 visit had to be abandoned because the agitation by lawyers against Musharraf had gathered steam in Pakistan. In India, too, the hints that a questionable exercise called the four-point formula was underway had set off alarms in the media against this enterprise. Had the gods not been by India's side and if Manmohan Singh had actually gone to Islamabad in 2007 to set his prime ministerial seal on Musharraf's formula, it is doubtful that the verdict of history would have been kind to him.

There were murmurs that Manmohan Singh was obsessed with his legacy. Some of the more uncharitable comments alleged that his obsessive quest for peace with Pakistan was driven by his desire for the Nobel Peace Prize. It may be unfair to ascribe his efforts at achieving peace with Pakistan to his quest for legacy or some prize, but there is no doubt that his policies towards Pakistan were seen by people as bordering on appeasement. His decisions—whether at Sharm-el-Sheikh or the inaction after 26/11—were not only enough to blot his record, but reinforced the impression that for some inexplicable reason, he was bending over backwards to propitiate Pakistan.

In this list of negatives, 26/11 rankles the most. In the months leading up to it, the CIA had warned the Indian intelligence agencies of planned attacks on Mumbai's major landmarks, including its high-end hotels. There was also intelligence information that the terrorists might choose the unconventional sea route to arrive.

The attack took place as warned. On 26 November 2008, ten Lashkar-e-Taiba (LeT) terrorists began the coordinated shooting and bombing attacks on 12 locations, lasting four days. By 29 November, when the attack ended, at least 174 people had been killed—including 9 attackers—and more than 300 had been wounded.

For those 72 hours, a non-stop drama of gore was played out live on millions of television screens across the world. The masterminds of the terror, based in Pakistan, were also glued to their television screens, profiting from the latest information from Mumbai. As for the counter-terror efforts then, it is hard to find any supportive voice: '…sheer paralysis gripped the top levels of government. Confusing signals emanated from different power centres: the PMO, the home ministry and the security establishment.'[14]

To give just one instance of how inapt the response was, this comment should be sufficient: 'The naval officers in charge of the MARCOS—India's equivalent to the US Navy SEALS—hesitated to send them, fearing that they were "the wrong dog for the fight". Eventually, in the early hours of Thursday, fewer than twenty MARCOS out of a team of 1000 arrived.'[15]

Insofar as lessons learnt are concerned, the diagnosis is not encouraging at all:

> …only lip-service would be paid to understanding how the world's fourth-largest city could so easily be brought to its knees… Scott-Clark and Levy observe that 26/11… "received only a cursory grilling from the Pradhan Commission, a two-man panel formed in Mumbai on 30 December 2008 to explore the 'war-like' attacks on the city," compared to the many months of exhaustive probing into 9/11 and London's 7/7 attacks.[16]

The government did take up the issue with Pakistan and made strong representations against it in the world capitals. But the public anger was not assuaged. The question that people kept asking of the government was: Would your dossiers be enough to deter the ISI and its terrorists from launching attacks in future? There were also questions as to why the government did not consider a punitive response.

Further, the timing of some of the actions by the government seemed to be insensitive to the victims of 26/11. For instance, within a few months of the attack, when the anger among people was still red hot, Manmohan agreed to put India on par with Pakistan on terror, in the Indo-Pak joint statement at Sharm-el-Sheikh. One Indian journalist felt sufficiently provoked to comment:

> Through this act of utter foolhardiness, the Indian prime minister had transformed the Balochistan problem from being a festering wound of Islamabad's own creation to one caused by alleged Indian meddling. He also managed to put the issue in international focus. It is a mistake India will rue in the days to come. Most Indians know nothing about Balochistan. It was never on their radar screen. It had no reason to be.[17]

The blunder at Sharm-el Sheikh was widely condemned as among the most disastrous in many years of Indian diplomacy. Its immediate impact psychologically was that Pakistan felt free to squeeze itself out of the guilty corner that 26/11 had pushed it into. After Sharm-el-Sheikh, the Pakistani responses to Indian requests for action against the perpetrators of 26/11 became steadily more brazen. Salman Bashir, its high commissioner in Delhi, dismissed the copious dossiers that India had given on the Mumbai attack as pieces of fiction. Overall, the feeling of frustration among people at the government's handling of the terror issue kept mounting. Another commentator wrote:

> Singh's fixation on quasi-failed Pakistan has paralleled Vajpayee's quest to make peace with that implacable enemy... In 2006 at Havana, he equated the exporter of terrorism with the victim of its terrorism, setting up the infamous and now-defunct joint anti-terror mechanism. Three years later at Sharm el-Sheikh, Singh included Baluchistan in

the agenda—grist for the Pakistani propaganda mill that India was fomenting the insurrection there. This blunder allowed Pakistan to externalize the Baluch problem by turning…India, into the principal accused.[18]

The comments quoted above are representative of the general tenor of national anguish with his Pakistan policy. This feeling of frustration was compounded by the fact that neither in office nor later has Manmohan Singh given his version of why he pursued peace with Pakistan in the manner that he did. Rather, the occasional attempt at an explanation made by some of his former aides reinforces the feeling that he went the extra mile in vain. Another leader, in some other part of the world, may not have shown the same degree of restraint that he exercised despite the extreme provocation of 26/11.

TREADING CAUTIOUSLY WITH BEIJING

Manmohan's government could never properly explain why India was being trifled with at will by Pakistan. Some also add China to this list.

However, it will not be fair to describe it only in unfavourable terms. Objectively viewed, Sino-Indian relations were then in a phase of trust building, though with intermittent setbacks due to Chinese incursions. In the cloud of anger over these, it is sometimes not adequately appreciated that it was during Manmohan's tenure that agreements in 2005, 2012 and 2013 added new procedures and mechanisms to shore up the regime of mutual military restraint along the border. Most significantly, in 2005, the Indian and Chinese Special Representatives arrived at an understanding on the political parameters and guiding principles for settling the boundary question.

During Manmohan's visit to China in October 2013, the joint statement on a strategic and cooperative partnership included calls to resolve the border issue, pursue defence exchanges and cultivate enhanced economic ties. The Sino-Indian Border Defence Cooperation Agreement was also finalized during the visit, aiming, in theory, to minimize the chances of conflict arising from unexpected movements in the contested areas.

Yet China was and will be both an opportunity and a danger for India. It could be strategically helpful to India by reining in Islamabad, by helping Afghanistan develop and stabilize, and by reminding the Americans that India has other options. It had already become India's biggest trading partner, the bilateral trade having grown by a factor of 67 between 1998 and 2012. More accurately, the bilateral trade, skewed heavily in China's favour, had grown from just $13.6 billion in 2004 at the start of Manmohan's two terms to some $65.5 billion annually, with the Indian deficit touching $31.4 billion.

Despite this, China could be a potential danger, too. The LAC witnessed military confrontations of an unusually large number in 2013 and 2014. In April 2013, the two came close to adding a fourth to the list of their previous confrontations, which included the Indo-Chinese war of 1962, the 1967 Chola incident and a 1987 skirmish. This latest incident happened when a PLA platoon set up camp 30 km south of Daulat Beg Oldi in Ladakh, in a previously uncontested area. It involved the most serious accusations by India in 25 years. At first, Indian officials underplayed the alleged incursion. The prime minister called it a 'localized' problem and said his government did not want to 'accentuate' it. Foreign Minister Salman Khurshid described the dispute, in a much pilloried statement, as 'acne' that could be addressed 'by simply applying an ointment'!

But Khurshid's efforts did not succeed. The Chinese platoon withdrew only after India agreed to the Chinese demands to destroy its bunkers in the Chumar sector. Throughout the entire incident, China denied India's charge that the PLA had camped out in 'India proper' as delineated by the LAC. It maintained that it had never crossed into Indian territory.

As a result of the increased number of incursions, Manmohan has sometimes been criticized for following a policy of least resistance in relations with China, especially on the vexing boundary issue. But viewed fairly, was he the only leader to tread cautiously on the border dispute? Perhaps it might be more reasonable to say that like those before him, he too tried to muddle through, neither surrendering to Beijing nor confronting it. The effort was to compartmentalize and quarantine the stagnant parts of the relationship from the more productive parts.

But at least on one occasion Manmohan broke free from the mould of hesitation. Since 1949, India had been supporting the 'One China Policy'.

This formulation required countries to acknowledge that Taiwan and Tibet were part of China's mainland. India felt aggrieved by China's consistently unfavourable attitude on the J&K issue, in which it has been siding with Pakistan. Despite this, India continued to reaffirm its adherence to the 'One China Policy' in all joint statements with China till the end of 2009. Then, for the first time, it declined to reiterate the 'One China Policy' in a joint statement that was issued after a meeting between Manmohan Singh and the visiting Chinese Premier Wen Jiabao in New Delhi in December 2010. The immediate provocation was the new practice that China had initiated of issuing stapled visas to the residents of J&K. The Indian government viewed this as a Chinese ruse to question India's claim over J&K.

While his government seemed helpless in drawing the red line over Chinese incursions, the fact that there was steady progress in increasing understanding is often overlooked.

LANDMARK DEAL DELIVERS LITTLE

The high point of Manmohan's two terms was not on the economic side, but a civil nuclear deal with the US, which ended New Delhi's status as a nuclear pariah.

During his visit to the US in July 2005, Manmohan and George W. Bush agreed to enter into a civil nuclear agreement. This landmark agreement was preceded by acrimonious debate in the Indian Parliament, where it saw an unusual combination of two differing shades of political opinion—the BJP and the Communist parties getting together to oppose the deal. Their objections were on the ground that India's strategic autonomy, its nuclear programme, and the attendant issues of reprocessing and future nuclear tests would be compromised.

The deal was opposed in the US, too, with the doubters wondering 'whether US is compromising its non-proliferation policy? Is this agreement damaging the Non Proliferation Treaty (NPT)? Is India gaining too much with little or no advantage to the US?'[19]

In this background, the negotiations between the two delegations were bitter and prolonged, till the two leaders stepped in to put their seal to it. The signing of the deal marked the end of 30-year-old sanctions imposed by the US after the 1974 nuclear test by India. This shift also meant an implicit recognition of India as a nuclear weapons power.

But India also had to make the commitment that it would

- place civilian nuclear facilities under the International Atomic Energy Agency (IAEA) safeguards,
- sign an Additional Protocol which allows more intrusive IAEA inspections of its civilian facilities,
- continue its moratorium on nuclear weapons testing,
- strengthen the security of its nuclear arsenals.

The US, for its part, agreed to work towards full civil nuclear cooperation with India, including granting India a waiver from the Nuclear Suppliers Group (NSG), which would allow members to trade nuclear material with India even though it was not a part of the NPT.

This last part was critical, because India's supply of yellow cake, which is the basic feed material for the nuclear power plants, was running dangerously low, and the countries capable of supplying this material were hesitant to do so till the agreement with the US had been sealed and the critical element of signing the Additional Protocol had been agreed to by India.

This deal certainly marked a significant personal success for Manmohan, one at which he could look back with considerable satisfaction. He had stood firm both in Parliament and with the US when its team of negotiators was toughening its stand to an unreasonable pitch.

However, even after this, the malign stars seemed to have cursed the Indo-US relationship. The ties with Washington sank into a rough period after the controversial arrest of an Indian diplomat in New York. Besides, there was a growing list of irritants in bilateral ties, including disagreements over intellectual property rights, pharmaceuticals and trade. Moreover, on issues ranging from climate change to the crisis in Syria, the Indian foreign policy under Singh was often too cautious and timid.

ELEPHANT FLAILS ABOUT HELPLESSLY

About 18 months before Manmohan Singh's term was due to end, *The Washington Post* wrote dismissively, '...Singh was a major force behind his country's rapprochement with the United States and is a respected figure on the world stage. President Obama's aides used to boast of his tremendous rapport and friendship with Singh. But the image of the scrupulously honorable, humble and intellectual technocrat has slowly given way to a completely different one: a dithering, ineffectual bureaucrat presiding over a deeply corrupt government.' It went on to assert, '[the] 79-year-old is in danger of going down in history as a failure.'[20]

This assessment by Simon Denyer reflected the prevailing mood of the people. They were increasingly angry and resentful that the government had failed to deliver, especially in its second term. The general resentment with his government found expression in scathing media debates and people's protests in Delhi. The opinion in the country was steadily more scornful of him and his government as scam after scam tumbled out; 2G, Coalgate, Commonwealth Games and the Adarsh housing society in Mumbai being some of them. Moreover, dismal news about the economy was beginning to accumulate, caught as it was in the vicious trap of high inflation and low growth. Staving these negatives off and surviving for yet another day became a daily struggle for the government.

Once the bad news starts multiplying domestically for a government, it also has an impact on its image abroad. Still, Singh tried to showcase his government's achievements abroad, calling the India–US nuclear deal his most satisfying moment. Speaking in the parliament in August 2013, he talked of the high regard the world had for him, 'I command certain status, certain prestige, certain respect in the council of the Group of 20.'

However, his opinion of himself was not matched by the negative verdict that observers had already started giving about him. By 2012, his government was virtually immobilized by corruption scandals concerning his colleagues and the shine was beginning to wear off. In April that year, *Time* magazine had placed Manmohan Singh as nineteenth in its list of 100 most influential world figures. But perceptions change fast and three months later in July, the same magazine splashed the front cover of its Asia edition with a forlorn image of Manmohan Singh and the headline 'The Underachiever'.

'India is stalling,' the magazine declared. 'To turn it around, Prime Minister Manmohan Singh must emerge from his private and political gloom.'

There were other missteps, but the Sharm-el-Sheikh statement can be called the beginning of the phase of knee-jerk decision-making in Indian foreign policy. Since that was early on in his ten-year stay as Prime Minister, he never recovered from that slip. The mistakes kept on accumulating and to cover them up, his aides conjured up fancy new terms.

Rehashing the old theory that had outlived its sell-by date in 1991, New Delhi unveiled non-alignment 2.0 to a disinterested world. It was presented as a newborn with promise. Alas, this was an ill thoughtout recommendation that ran against the tide of international affairs, and though a few half-hearted efforts were made to wave it to the world, it died an unlamented death. In the post-Cold War age, a deep flaw in non-alignment as a grand strategy was its premise that refusing to align with other great powers preserves the strategic autonomy of its member states. This attempt to equate non-alignment with preventing loss of sovereignty confused ends and means.

In any case, the flexibility of not allying with any great power was no longer a practical option for India. Its threats from Pakistan and China, individually or in concert, were alive and growing. And in future, India would of necessity have to ally with America, not formally but in spirit and in deed. In addition, it may have to form protective partnerships with a select group of other countries like Japan, France, Germany and Russia, who may share concerns of a somewhat similar nature.

But Manmohan's advisors were not disheartened. After non-alignment 2.0, India swung to the other extreme. Its invocation of the so-called 'strategic autonomy' was without a firm foundation. Big words like 'strategic autonomy' should be bandied about when a country has a solid economic base and a self-sufficient defence industry. In the absence of these basics, the claims of strategic autonomy end up being thin air.

Alas, the desire that surface appearances should be wrinkle-free meant that much of what was wrong with the results was brushed out of sight. The emphasis was to create the impression that India's foreign policy was doing well. Behind this camouflage of major partnerships looking steady and joint declarations proclaiming convergence of interests was the reality that all was not well on this front.

India's foreign policy then lacked solid strategic moorings of the kind where a partner would readily stand by your side if things got rough with a neighbour. In fact, India's major relationships began to suffer, as questions were being asked in Washington as to whether India's advertised rise was for real. In Moscow, there was concern that India was leaning excessively towards the West. In Southeast Asia, there were doubting voices suggesting that, despite the intention to look east, India's lethargy on the ground did not give the confidence that it could be a credible balancer to China. This impression of the elephant flailing about helplessly was noted with satisfaction by the observers in Beijing and Islamabad.

MUTED APPLAUSE

It is still too early to determine whether Singh's accomplishments outweigh his failures. Though he was never implicated himself, Singh stood as a mute witness to the wave of corruption scandals that engulfed his government. There were many reasons for the sharp decline in his image, and in his approval ratings, during the second term in office. But corruption must be placed at the top of any such list. Alongside, there was a general feeling of ennui—as if the government machinery had stopped functioning, terrified by the enormity of its misdeeds.

Some critics maintain that he never grew past the status of a finance minister, because economics was where he felt at home. He had excelled there, and he should have continued there. He was not at ease in politics nor comfortable with the rough and tumble that Indian politicians are so adept at. He was far too soft-spoken to outshout the other politicians, and too gentle to say no to his party even when his instincts told him that the course being suggested would make for bad policy. But he could stand his ground on issues that he considered vital. He did that with both the Bush administration as also his political opponents at home when negotiations for the nuclear deal were at the final, critical stages.

The country, at large, deservedly applauded him for getting the deal through. He was also sought by the world leaders for advice when the 2008 financial crisis threatened to overwhelm the banking systems and the global markets. President Barack Obama and Prime Minister Tony Blair were lavish in their praise for his wisdom at that time.

Yet, he faltered where it mattered. The frustrations at home kept on increasing largely because corruption scandals kept leaping out of the newspapers with sickening regularity. The popular frustration and the intensity of public disillusionment with Manmohan Singh and his government were reflected in the immediate verdict of the people in 2014.

His disappointing performance could be attributed in part to his timidity, bordering on obsequiousness, towards Sonia Gandhi. However, throughout those ten years in office, Manmohan continued to be favoured by the stars. Even when critics came out in hordes during his second term as prime minister, many passed on the blame for the ills of the government to Sonia Gandhi. Yet, at the end, Manmohan Singh sadly remained isolated, marginalized by his party, mocked by the Opposition and hounded by the media. In his place, a shrewd politician like Narasimha Rao would have navigated the complexities of the situation better.

Viewed in retrospect, it is hard to imagine why Manmohan Singh's achievements were overshadowed by his failures. During his decade-long tenure, over 137 million people were lifted out of poverty, yet he was considered a disappointing failure. His approval ratings, after completing two tenures in office, hovered at about 5 per cent. He displayed a remarkable absence of flourish while in office, and left it in a manner that was as understated as his personality.

However, to be fair, it must be noted that history does not award points for flamboyance while recording its judgment. It will remember his striking boldness in putting India on a radically new economic path in 1991. He will also be given credit for guiding India safely through the global financial crisis of 2008. The ten-year period up to 2014 saw the Indian economy register an average annual growth of 7.6 per cent. Despite some missteps in dealing with Pakistan, he will also be remembered for the skill with which he guided India's nuclear deal with the US.

These are not insignificant achievements. Yet, the applause for him continues to be muted. Manmohan Singh himself seemed to be conscious of it, and close to the end of his ten-year tenure as prime minister, he said in a moment of self-doubt, 'I have done the best I could under the circumstances. It will be for the historians to judge how successful it was.'[21]

Disappointed and embittered politicians often say words to this effect. But Manmohan Singh may be judged kindly by history because his most important work was done not as prime minister, but as finance minister. Moreover, it will be a mistake to condemn Manmohan Singh as a weak leader. He was not always the helpless man that he was made out to be by friend and foe alike. He could hit back when driven to the wall. Even then, for the friend he reserved a slight smile, but he could be very sharp with a foe. When L.K. Advani charged in Parliament in 2009 that Singh was a weak leader, Manmohan shot back, wounding not just Advani but Modi as well, who was then the Chief Minister of Gujarat, 'Unlike the NDA's prime ministerial candidate, I will not be found in a corner while hoodlums tear down a centuries-old mosque. Nor will I be found wringing my hands in frustration while one of my chief ministers condones a pogrom targeted at minorities.'

8

NARENDRA MODI:
THE RULE MAKER

*It is better to live your own destiny imperfectly than to live
an imitation of somebody else's life with perfection.*

—BHAGAVAD GITA

Almost a year before Narendra Modi was to move to Delhi
from Gujarat, two books were published about him and the
political style that he had cultivated.[1] The books were written by
experienced journalists and the impression that came through clearly was
that this man was destined for Delhi, come what may. In their assessment,
Modi made a conscious effort to project a larger-than-life persona of an
austere workaholic, an alpha-male passionately striving for the protection
and betterment of his flock. It was also clear that despite his avowals
about not wanting the chief minister's or the prime minister's post, he
was determined to get there, because Modi is a full-time and consummate
politician. As Nag recalls in his book, 'One of his ministers remarked,
"Every waking moment of his day is spent thinking and strategising
power play"...when Modi was appointed chief minister little did the party
leaders realise that they were unleashing a chief minister who would,
within just a year, become so powerful that he would care for just about
nobody in the party.'

The election campaign in 2014 had pitched Modi, rather than his
party, against the ruling NDA. This was not a new political strategy. After
all, the BJP had projected Atal Bihari Vajpayee similarly in 1998 with its

slogan, '*Abki bari Atal Bihari* (this time around, it's Atal Bihari).' But Modi's election juggernaut at the 2014 Lok Sabha polls was an example of a marketing and branding campaign. Modi addressed nearly 200 meetings in just about two months and ran a high-adrenalin, tech-savvy campaign that dazzled and engaged voters directly through social media. There was simply no escaping Modi for the voter. His image and in-your-face messaging overshadowed all other parties and all other leaders; including those in his own party.

Expectedly, he became the prime minister. But Modi, the state-level politician, was new to the subtle play of world affairs. He could have waited to let events unfold for on-the-job tutorials, or stormed the world stage in his own fashion. He chose the latter course. There, on the policy front, he faced three choices. He could reverse the policy of the previous governments, stay the course the Congress had charted, or take it to altogether new levels.

He opted for course correction; seeking change while not abandoning the past in any major way. Ram Madhav captures the essence of Modi's strategy in these words:

> Modi is a shrewd learner. He didn't hesitate to follow Napoleon, whom historian Eric Hobsbawm described as the 'secular deity', in some of his tactics. Napoleon had mastered the art of using propaganda. He ran a government newspaper, *Le Moniteur Universel* that regularly informed the French public about his military heroics and war successes. 'What counts is what the people think as true', Napoleon used to say. Narendra Modi is seen by the people of India as not just another prime minister, but as a 'transformative leader'.[2]

The first transformation was conceptual. The earliest to go were the hesitations of the past that had restricted India to the negatives of a do-nothing, take-no-risk approach of non-alignment. To that extent, three streams merged to form his strategy—personal ambition, the desire to transform India in his fashion and the conviction that he could make a difference in world affairs.

Modi's personal ambition required grand optics and a scheme that could not wait for the fruits of patient diplomacy. Accordingly, from the very beginning, he revelled in swashbuckling personal diplomacy. Under that veneer lay profound ambition, both for himself as a world statesman and the recognition of India as a global power, with a desire to drive a foreign policy focused on national interests.

In a sense, he was a shade of Nehru, but without the latter's idealism. And like Nehru, he too did not have the cushion of adequate support; his foreign minister during the first term, Sushma Swaraj, was keeping indifferent health and the bureaucratic recommendations took time to adjust to his frantic style. But that is where the similarity ends, because unlike Nehru's reflective and sometimes ponderous pace, Modi was a practical man in a hurry. From whirlwind visits around the globe to stadium-packed appearances abroad, he seemed to be everywhere. By his selfies and bear hugs with world leaders, he soon left a distinctive mark on the international stage. But he was also amenable to suggestions, and that's why, after initially stomping the arenas of New York, London and Dubai in rock star fashion, he slowed down. He still likes to dazzle full stadiums in distant lands, but these events are organized more selectively now. They are not a de rigueur for all his visits. Nor does he surprise other leaders any longer with hugs. There are exceptions, of course— for example with Trump—but they prove the rule that hugs are to be avoided.

Modi, therefore, has adjusted to the international setting as needed, but has his hectic schedule resulted in a transformative role for India? For instance, India under Nehru was routinely labelled as 'the leader of the developing world'. However, it is hard to apply that label to Modi. On a narrower plane, and till the beginning of this millennium, India and China were held as competing models, where the Western bet was on India. It was hoped that the democratic model of India would prevail over China's communist and closed economy. It was also said that an India that turns its back on liberal values will also be weaker internationally.

These seemingly disparate, yet intrinsically connected, strands must have worked on his mind as he maneuvered to find for India, in his own way, a place in the world. In fact, soon after taking over as prime minister, Modi urged senior Indian diplomats 'to help India position itself in a leading role, rather than as just a balancing force, globally.'[3]

This ambitiously framed goal was a departure from the placid pace of the erstwhile take-no-risks policy. For long years, the country had been led to believe that remaining non-aligned was the ideal way to navigate safely in an uncertain world. This was also the prudent choice of most in the developing world, because the US and the Soviet Union seemed to mostly be in a confrontational mode. But after the Cold War ended, questioning eyebrows were raised about the continued relevance of non-alignment as a national policy. Yet some who were bred on its eternal validity were nonplussed. In a bid at retrieval, they advocated non-alignment 2.0, which received only a quick dismissive glance from the Modi government. It had put its faith in selective alignment depending on the issue and the cause. In Modi's lexicon, non-alignment was neutral and passive, whereas his approach, as in the case of domestic politics, was to confront the issue head on. Overall, the panache with which Modi interpreted the foreign policy fundamentals of the past is striking.

EXPECT THE UNEXPECTED

In addition to dispensing with India's didactic commitment to non-alignment, Modi, at the beginning of his first term in 2014, had hoped to transform relations with China and Pakistan and extend Indian influence in South and Southeast Asia.

It isn't as if the previous Indian governments had neglected the neighbourhood and beyond. They too had tried, but Modi's manner was sudden in execution and dramatic in effect. He decided boldly to invite Pakistan's Prime Minister Nawaz Sharif to his inauguration in May 2014. There were other invitees from the SAARC region, but the invitation to Pakistan took the domestic conservative establishment, and many in the wider world, too, by surprise. With that, Modi also announced to the sceptical strategic community that it should get used to expecting the unexpected from him.

By and large, people welcomed this gesture towards India's neighbours. There was hope that even with Pakistan, it could be the start of the first baby steps towards normalization. All seemed to be going well at first, but for some inexplicable reason, and even as Sharif was busy holding farewell meetings with his Indian guests at his hotel suite in New Delhi, the Indian foreign secretary decided to hold a press conference. This misconceived initiative to pre-empt Pakistan soured instantly all that Modi had hoped to achieve by inviting Sharif. For all practical purposes, the relations went back to their familiar chill.

It wasn't just with this important neighbour that Modi's plans didn't work out the way he had hoped. Some of the other early initiatives that he took were poorly executed by his aides. He had reason to be disappointed with the way even the basics of his trip to Germany in July 2014 were planned. This was to have been a brief but important first stop to meet with a major Western leader, Germany's chancellor, Angela Merkel. He was making this visit within weeks of being sworn in as the Prime Minister of India, and his entourage was impressively large.

On 13 July, when his 21-luxury-car convoy streamed out of the airport towards the hotel, some members of the delegation were struck by the fact that the bustle they usually found on Berlin's streets was missing. It seemed as if the entire population of the capital had gone on a mass vacation. Even the lobby of their grand hotel was eerily empty except for a few staff at the reception desk.

But the delegation didn't give it more than an amused passing thought; after all, the purpose of their trip was a meeting with Merkel. In the meanwhile, they made themselves comfortable in the hotel lobby to watch the FIFA World Cup Final, which was about to start in Brazil. It was then that they saw Merkel sitting at the Maracanã Stadium in Rio de Janeiro, watching Germany play Argentina in the football final.

Despite these initial gaffes by his officials, Modi's leap into the international arena was unconventional and unanticipated. The world had hardly expected a departure from the usual pattern of somewhat elderly and even staid Indian leaders prone to repeating the tested policy line. It was still rubbing its eyes in disbelief when it realized that Modi's foreign policy style was different and dizzying.

A BOLD DEPARTURE FROM THE PAST

Modi also made a bold departure from the past by engaging with the Gulf countries, especially Saudi Arabia and the UAE, because their interests overlap with those of India in important areas. The size of the Indian community settled in the Gulf states, the expertise that it provides, its responsible, law-abiding conduct, the impressive volume of bilateral trade, the security and intelligence cooperation—these are all factors that benefit both the Gulf states and India significantly. Some recent large-scale investments by these states in Indian companies have added further substance to this bond. While most ingredients for a warm relationship with this region were long there, India had not gone out of its way to inject adrenalin into it. Modi has certainly brought in that difference with his 'Look Gulf' outreach. In turn, their response to Modi's initiative has been encouraging—one need only look at how both Saudi Arabia and the UAE (besides the US) engaged India and Pakistan almost equally to help manage the post-Pulwama crisis.

Besides the welcome that his Gulf initiative received, Modi also succeeded in establishing a warm personal relationship with the leaders of Japan, Israel, and to some extent China and the US. However, Modi's hopes of making a major mark on the global stage were stumped by India's continued inability to gain entry into the NSG and to secure a permanent seat on the UNSC. As one observer put it:

> Modi has run an egocentric approach to foreign policy since he became prime minister nearly five years ago. He has successfully expanded India's image abroad, but aggressive Hindu nationalism has become a negative driver of policy on Pakistan. He has made himself the government's only significant player on international affairs, and has revelled in the personal exposure he has gained by visiting over 60 countries and attending high-profile and frequently choreographed meetings with world leaders...[4]

All through, Modi kept up a blistering pace of travel in a high-energy effort at showing the Indian flag. Some have criticized it as too haphazard to be effective at anything more than giving temporary cheer. Still, as prime minister, Modi visited 92 nations in a little less than five years, while Manmohan Singh travelled to 93 nations in ten years.[5]

WORRY LINES SET IN

A greater concern has been the lack of warmth in relations with the countries in the neighbourhood. India's relations with its South Asian neighbours may not have been at their warmest in 2014 when Modi became prime minister, but they were not worrisome. If 'neighbourhood first' was the declared mantra of the Modi foreign policy when he was sworn into office, it did not take long for the worry lines about its direction to set in. Modi's counterparts in South Asia were sometimes left wondering who his real messengers were. Were they the robed priests or the professional diplomats?

In the months and years since then, India's relations with almost all its neighbours have dipped to an all-time low. The unnecessary blockade of goods to Nepal for several months in 2015 and 2016 served no other purpose than to annoy all sections of Nepalese society. Even the otherwise well-disposed Bangladesh was taken aback by being picked as one of three countries that, in India's view, was the object of the Citizenship Amendment Act (CAA). And Sri Lanka has been playing its China card with dexterity. With its South Asian diplomacy caught between the party's political agenda and the need to serve the country's national interests, Modi's foreign policy seemed to have hollowed out.

By 2016, the neighbourhood was not forgotten but the shine had worn off. Sounding a note of caution, *The Hindu* wrote, 'If we are unable to maintain strategic ties with our neighbours by catering to their economic and infrastructure requirements, let's at least not alienate them with our undiplomatic and bullying behaviour.'[6]

Within months of that newspaper comment, Modi startled Pakistan by his reference to Balochistan from the ramparts of the Lal Qila on 15 August 2016: 'I want to speak a bit about the people in Balochistan, Gilgit, Baltistan, and Pakistan-occupied Kashmir. The world is watching. People of Balochistan, Gilgit and Pakistan-occupied Kashmir have thanked me a lot in the past few days. I am grateful to them.' Since then, there has been no significant effort to take up the issue of human rights violations in Balochistan at the world forums and make it an issue demanding international attention. This lack of concrete follow-up can be counterproductive. The tested and prudent formula that statecraft has followed for ages is this: If you want to stir trouble, be sure you have already put in place all the ingredients necessary for it.

Overall, India's relations with its neighbours remain in a state of sulk, though this is not due to lack of effort on Modi's part. He has certainly exerted himself in making a difference, but despite his efforts, there has not been any great change.

FLIP-FLOPS ON PAKISTAN

Modi has added many other features to the instant remix that foreign policy seems to have become during recent years. It is true that sometimes the unexpected works wonders in international relations. A touch of spontaneity can break the ice, and a well-chosen remark delivered on the right occasion can be a game-changer. But it isn't always so. The Pakistan policy, in particular, has been the cause of much surprise, bewilderment and disappointment. People have sought to find a method in it, and many have tried to put a label to it, the term 'flip-flop' being used most often.

In a relationship as crisis prone as that between India and Pakistan, anything out of the ordinary is viewed with suspicion. A gesture of friendship by an Indian towards a Pakistani politician can be a kiss of death for him. But how was Modi to know all this when he was relatively new in his tenure? These intricacies are passed on to leaders by and by as the need arises; because it is not possible to flood the new leader with all the details at once and expect him to absorb them in one go. Moreover, each situation requires its own special response. That's why patience has its rewards in the world of diplomacy.

But even the officials accompanying him to Kabul seem to have been taken by surprise on the morning of 25 December 2015. The Indian delegation was busy packing to fly back to New Delhi when Modi decided to surprise Nawaz Sharif by visiting him in Lahore on his birthday. He may have been emulating Vajpayee, who too had travelled to Lahore to meet Sharif. However, there was a big difference in the two situations, because Vajpayee's visit had been worked out in advance by both sides. Despite that, Vajpayee's visit was to set in motion a chain of events that eventually led to Musharraf's coup against Sharif. Ironically, in a case of history repeating itself, Sharif's political stars began to change for the worse after Modi's surprise visit. In this case, the suddenness of it gave rise to multiple conspiracy theories in Pakistan, all of them working against Sharif.

Essentially, the Pakistani army refuses to take kindly any gesture by India; it suspects anti-Pakistan conspiracy lurking behind every such move.

And it holds any Pakistani participant in such gestures to be equally a partner in what it suspects is another devious Indian plan. Yet, if the account below is to be believed, Sharif too had been taken by surprise when Modi rang him up from Kabul to say that he was going to visit him that afternoon. Nawaz Sharif's close aide and special advisor Tariq Fatemi confirmed that Sharif was taken 'totally by surprise' when he received a call from Modi that December in 2015:

> (He) told my PM (Nawaz Sharif) that he had finished his official visit in Afghanistan and was flying back from Kabul to Delhi and wanted to stop over and have a cup of coffee. The PM said great, wonderful, we would be delighted. But he pointed out that he was not in Islamabad (but) in Lahore for the wedding of his granddaughter.
>
> And Mr Modi said well that's fine, we do visit our friends when they are celebrating these occasions.[7]

As in the case of Vajpayee's bus journey to Lahore, this time as well the Pakistani establishment did not take long to deliver its message. On 2 January 2016, within a week of Modi's Lahore visit, a heavily armed Pakistani terrorist group, belonging to JeM, attacked the Pathankot Air Force Station. The security forces battled the terrorists till 5 January, when the fifth terrorist was declared shot dead. Seven Indian security personnel were martyred during the operation, but the airbase itself escaped any major damage. However, the very fact that the terrorists could travel for over 150 kms inside Indian territory, without being detected or challenged, was alarming enough. It should have been equally worrying that Pakistan was able to mount such an audacious operation at a week's notice.

There was worse to come. This time it was a challenge to the Indian army's might at Uri. In 2016, a group of four Pakistani terrorists attacked the camp in the early morning on 18 September, killing 27 Indian soldiers. This was an extreme provocation and India chose to retaliate. On 29 September, it attacked the terror launch pads in POK, in what was later termed as a 'surgical strike'. There were conflicting reports from both sides on the effectiveness, or lack of it, of the surgical strike. But the point had been made that India would not hesitate to cross the LoC to administer justice.

Punitive raids by the Indian army inside the POK had been undertaken earlier as well. But they were done discretely, with no follow-up publicity. The big difference this time was the publicity given to the 'surgical strike'.

Given the possibility of nuclear escalation, it was till then not clear if an Indian prime minister would easily order a cross-border retaliatory strike and have it announced as such to the world. Successful deterrence relies on being able to demonstrate a military threat that is credible and realistic. This was the largely held conventional wisdom; that the rubicon must not be crossed, otherwise Pakistan's nuclear card would come into play. Modi had crossed the rubicon. The possibility that the nuclear card could come into play was very much in the air. But this time, it wasn't just Pakistan giving that dare.

South Asia's nuclear tipping point has been balanced on a razor's edge for at least two decades. The risk that a confrontation might deteriorate into a nuclear exchange has been there from the time of the Kargil conflict (1999) to the attack on the Indian Parliament (2001), followed by the terror attacks in Mumbai (2008). While the world has admired India's restraint on each occasion, within India the inability to inflict punitive punishment on Pakistan has been criticized as a sign of weakness; and worse still, as indicative of cowardice in the face of Pakistan's nuclear challenge. The provocation for this complaint may be the long simmering resentment in the Indian people, and among the security forces, that they are being used as reaction-less punching bags by the Pakistani terrorists.

So far, except for the rare exceptions cited above, the fear of crossing the border or the LOC and provoking a nuclear response from Pakistan had been holding India back. But that restraint buckled in February 2019. A caravan of buses carrying over 2,500 CRPF security men was attacked in Pulwama, J&K, by a suicide bomber who managed to ram his car into one of the buses. Forty-four Indian security personnel were killed in the mayhem that followed. That the Pakistani signature was writ large in the planning and execution of that attack became obvious quickly, through human intelligence and communication intercepts. The gaps, if any, were soon filled by the terrorist organization JeM itself, which stepped forward gleefully to take responsibility for the attack.

Had it just been a solo foray, or had the casualties been lesser, the situation may still not have spiralled out of control. But the scale and the brazenness of the attack was a challenge made worse by the fact that the JeM had been responsible for some of the most audacious terror attacks in the past—the 2001 Parliament attack and the Pathankot airbase attack. Even then, the situation might not have approached dangerous levels but for the fact that Imran Khan, the Prime Minister of Pakistan, neither condemned the attack in Pulwama nor expressed any regret for the loss of Indian lives till it was very late.

The enormity of the loss of life in the Pulwama attack had shocked the nation. The Indian government, under pressure from a nationwide cry for revenge and with an eye on the approaching national elections, decided to overcome the hesitations that had stayed its hand in the past. It sent its Mirage fighter aircrafts across the border into Pakistan to attack a terror training camp of the JeM in Balakot.

The mission was successful and Pakistan, in turn, felt provoked that its sovereignty had been violated. Its response followed a day later, on 27 February, when it sent 24 of its strike aircraft to target an Indian army ammunition dump and a brigade headquarters. The Indian air force fighter planes were quick to scramble in response, to challenge the Pakistani aircraft. In the dog fight that ensued, both sides lost an aircraft each, but in their hurry to withdraw, the Pakistani bombs missed their targets and fell harmlessly on vacant ground. Nevertheless, the enormity of the potential damage that a successful bomb attack may have caused on the intended targets set in motion events that alarmed the world.

The situation became even more worrying with the reports that missiles were being readied by both sides for attack. This would have seriously escalated matters. The danger in the use of missiles is the fact that, so far, there is no known technology that can distinguish between an ordinary and a nuclear weapon-carrying missile. So the country under attack has to decide instantly on the degree of its retaliation. To make matters worse, Pakistan army's publicity wing abandoned restraint to say repeatedly that it was prepared for full-spectrum nuclear war. This was an irresponsible statement coming from an army general. He would have surely known the alarm his statement was going to cause not just in the two countries, but in the wider world as well. However, it was precisely for this effect that this statement was made.

Was the nuclear option closest to actual use on the night of 27 February 2019? Perhaps it was, because the slide into that mode was just one mistaken decision away.

One effect of this episode was the coming into prominence of the Saudi and UAE crown princes and their countries as factors in the regional power play. A side-effect of their conciliatory role was the dilution of suspicion in the Indian mind that the two countries would lean in favour of Islamic Pakistan in a contest with India.

DEALING WITH TRUMP

Another factor in play during the post-Pulwama attack crisis was the US President, Donald Trump. Speaking at a press conference in Hanoi after a summit with North Korean leader Kim Jong Un, Trump said he had 'reasonably attractive news from Pakistan and India'. The US had been 'involved in trying to have them stop,' he told reporters.

Crisis management of the post-Pulwama type is different from the conflict resolution of the Kashmir issue. One is a temporary need after a sudden eruption, the other is a balm that may or may not work. In most cases, only a thin line separates the two. So, there is a risk that one may lead to the other if you involve a third party in managing your crisis. The problem with involving others is that sooner or later, it is payback time. And at that point, the ones you went to for help determine the type, and the extent, of the payback.

So far, New Delhi has resisted foreign mediation in its long-standing conflict with Pakistan on the Kashmir issue. Still, it has had to pay the price one way or another due to the intrusive interest from the US, which has all along been prodded by Pakistan to take a mediatory role in the matter.

An instance from the past is worth recalling. Starting in the late 1950s, when the US began to see great strategic merit in Pakistan being its partner, it was keen to somehow resolve the Kashmir issue to Pakistan's satisfaction. Since India was proving to be obdurate in the matter, it switched focus to the Indus waters issue. The US found an opportunity to pressurize India because it was passing through economic difficulties. The rest was accomplished by the World Bank, which was appointed to act, on paper at least, as an honest broker. It came up with the 1960 Indus Waters Treaty, which continues to remain the most generous water treaty in the world ever signed by an upper riparian state.

By the words engraved in this treaty, India gave 80 per cent of the waters of the six rivers to Pakistan. But what has not been realized so far is the sleight of hand by which the six rivers were apportioned between the two countries. India was given the control over waters flowing in the three 'eastern' rivers of India: the Beas, the Ravi and the Sutlej. These are Punjab-based rivers. Pakistan was given control over the waters flowing in three 'western' rivers that pass through Kashmir: the Indus, the Chenab and the Jhelum.

Is it any surprise that Pakistan got control over the rivers flowing through Kashmir? The US, the puppeteer behind the World Bank's decision, had engineered this to strengthen Pakistan's political claim over Kashmir. Sadly, the Indian side did not see through this deceit and did not protest. Nor has this mischief been remarked upon in the public domain so far. And it is a greater pity that India has made no move yet to fully claim the waters assigned to it.

The point in recounting this episode here is to stress that there is seldom an honest broker. And that the concession you make in a moment of weakness haunts the country for a long time.

Kargil and the post–Pulwama military standoff are the recent instances of American mediation. But as and when we ponder over the next one, it might be worthwhile recalling that once, in an introspective mood, Henry Kissinger had confessed, 'It may be dangerous to be America's enemy, but to be America's friend is fatal.'[8]

To illustrate this point in the present context, every move in dealings with the outside world must pass the test of 'America First'. To that extent, there is a non-negotiable and unchanging fundamental of national interest that determines the conduct of the US under Trump. For instance, when commerce becomes the lens that the US sees the world through, India and China look similar; to Trump, both are trying to extract benefits from it. Trump pressurizes Modi for trade concessions every time they meet, though India's surplus was only $24 billion in a total trade turnover of $88 billion in 2018. In contrast, India's trade deficit with China in 2018 was a whopping $60 billion, in a total trade turnover of $76 billion.

Yet, we do not make any great noise about it to the Chinese, or if we do, it has not had the desired effect because the deficit has only kept increasing. Our hesitation could be a part of the larger concern—that the bilateral boat must not be rocked at this stage.

At a time when the economy is growing at its slowest rate in five years and unemployment is at a 45-year high, India needs stability of external conditions, especially with regard to the security of oil supply and its pricing. At this stage, America's heavy-handed tactics have driven up India's oil import bill by stopping it from buying at concessional rates from next-door Iran. The US actions also risk undermining India's relationship with Tehran, which is about more than just oil. The transportation corridor to Afghanistan that India is building via Chabahar in Iran, bypassing Pakistan, may be at risk. That would also snap the hopes that were building up of a route further north, to the Central Asian countries.

Despite this, Modi is likely to sustain the momentum in the Indo-US relationship in view of a complex international situation. The threats now are numerous, complex and dynamic. They are being charged by technological advances that will work in ways no one can fully comprehend.

But the road ahead is even more difficult because of Trump's mercurial nature and limited interest in global affairs. As the book *A Very Stable Genius* reveals, 'Trump seemed to alarm Indian Prime Minister Narendra Modi and his aides by saying India doesn't share a border with China.' 'It's not like you've got China on your border,' he said, and Modi's eyes 'bulged out in surprise... Modi's expression gradually shifted, from shock and concern to resignation.'[9]

Still, Modi has been indulgent towards Trump, who has been getting his way so far. Sometimes, Trump seems to dismiss India's security interests as secondary to US determination. Almost all through, Modi has been accommodative, but pushed beyond a point, the strongman in him puts up a wall, as in the case of the contract with Russia for supply of the anti-missile defence S-400 system.

That's why being a friend of Iran and the US at the same time is getting more and more difficult. But what side will India take if US–Iran relations deteriorate further and Trump returns to the Bush motto of 'with us or against us'? That it could happen is almost a given. Whether it happens soon or at some point in the future remains to be seen, because the US experience in wars in the Gulf has not been congratulatory. None of them have produced the results that had been hoped for initially.

However, the situation in the region is uncertain. Even if one crisis is somehow tided over, the differences between Iran and the Gulf Arabs are deep rooted; they could bubble over again. As in the past, this next time too, the US could get involved directly or indirectly. And in all likelihood this would have ill effects on other countries like India; the American whims about sanctions at that point of time would determine the extent of damage it could do to the economies of these other countries. Therefore, a situation where fighting breaks out between them would add further to India's dilemma of 'with us or against us'. A war or warlike situation in the Gulf region would put not just its oil and gas supply at risk, but also the welfare of millions of Indians working in the region.

WOOING BACK RUSSIA

There are other challenges that constrain Modi. Four decades of superpower rivalry during the Cold War saw steady growth of international law and even greater faith in rules-based order. Unfortunately, the current form in international affairs is characterized by the lack of multilateral cooperation. This puts India in a quandary because its experience, post-independence, of multi-ethnic, multilinguistic and multireligious nation-building has made it comfortable with plurality in the global system. That multipolar aspect offers possibilities for the aspirations of a country like India, which is seeking a more prominent place in the world. It also suits Modi, because being pragmatic, he can then pick and choose ideas and ideologies to serve domestic interests.

But he is not pragmatic in the way the term is generally used, in the sense of sidestepping ideologies. Instead, to him, nimble-footedness in policy means the ability to turn and make course corrections—for instance, India's reflexive response to Beijing's rise has been to move closer to the US. It also means shedding inhibitions to reverse a previous course deviation in order to woo back a trusted partner like Russia.

At their meeting in Goa at the India–Russia annual summit in October 2016, Modi quoted a Russian proverb to Russian President Vladimir Putin: 'An old friend is better than two new ones.' Observers maintained that Modi's reference was to Russia's new friends China and Pakistan; ironically, though, the former had been promoted by the US as a counterweight against the Soviet Union and the latter had helped the US defeat the Soviet Union in Afghanistan.

Changed times change perception and policy, and a new set of circumstances create new allies. But to blame only Russia for seeking new friends would be unfair. Russia could very well complain that the fault lay with India and its neglect of Russia in the last five years or so. Its unstated complaint was that India was swayed by the possibility that it could finally be the sole American ally in South Asia. So abandoning all caution and a trusted partner of many years and multiple trials like Russia, it decided to put all its policy eggs in the American basket. Disillusionment with America did not take long to set in for India, as it warily eyed Trump's wayward ways. However, in the hiatus that had been created in the meanwhile, Russia had begun to find new comfort in the charms of China and Pakistan.

KEEPING CHINA ENGAGED

If these three were to engage actively on strategic issues and have a coincidence of interests on matters relating to Afghanistan and South Asia, it would be the stuff that nightmares are made of. Our recent neglect of Russia would in some measure be the cause of it. The impression that India finds comfort in America's desire that it be the counterweight to China could also have triggered increased Chinese bellicosity.

In mid-June 2017, a PLA unit of around 70 personnel, with a dozen bulldozers, was building a motorable road from Doklam to Zompelri near the Bhutanese post. This would have brought them close to the Siliguri corridor—the narrow strip of land connecting mainland India with its northeastern region. The Chinese activity was aimed at advancing Chinese security interests vis-à-vis India, weakening India's privileged relationship with Bhutan and the settlement of the Sino-Bhutan border.

While Doklam is of strategic significance to India, it has no claim over the area, unlike the contested claims between China and Bhutan. However, India is committed under a 1949 treaty—the Treaty of Friendship and Cooperation—to guide Bhutan's diplomatic and defence affairs. It was because of a combination of its own strategic interests, and the treaty obligation, that on 18 June 2017 about 270 Indian troops, armed with weapons and two bulldozers, crossed the Sikkim border into Doklam to stop the Chinese troops from constructing the road.

Over the next two months, the world watched anxiously as the two armies faced each other hostilely. Finally, following diplomatic efforts, the two sides announced on 28 August that they had withdrawn all their troops from the face-off site in Doklam.

But this hasn't stopped China from needling India. It has repeatedly blocked, since 2016, India's bid to become a member of the 48-nation NSG, which regulates the global trade in nuclear material. As if this was not enough, China pointedly pressed the UNSC on two occasions in 2019 to discuss the issue of Kashmir. Though Modi and Xi Jinping had a candid discussion at the October 2019 Mamallapuram informal summit, Beijing has not yielded on any of its core interests. Rather, it tried a third time in January 2020 to raise the Kashmir issue at the UNSC.

Even more worrying are the trend lines in the India-China military equation, which are broadly negative for India. Up in the north, on the Himalayan frontier, the state of play is mixed. The Indian army has an advantage in localized military strength, but China has made significant infrastructure improvements in Tibet to enhance the PLA's mobility. India has not stood still either. To counter a potential PLA attack, India has been speeding up its infrastructure, modifying its command, control and communications systems, and has improved its air defence to ensure a more punitive deterrence posture. Yet, all this may not be enough to keep pace with the tremendous military power that China has stationed across the mountain passes.

Deep south, in the Indian ocean, the Chinese naval presence has become formidable, surpassing in some respects Indian capabilities—for example in the number of diesel-electric attack submarines, of which China operates 16 compared to India's 15. India's fears of maritime encirclement by China have further increased with the formal opening of a large Chinese military facility in Djibouti, its repossession of

Hambantota Port in Sri Lanka, and its virtual control over the deep-sea port of Gwadar in Pakistan. All these have amplified longstanding Indian fears of maritime encirclement.

Modi's ability to keep China engaged has been amply in evidence in the two summits with Xi at Wuhan and Mamallapuram, but whether that has made China less hostile is doubtful. Some say that China, more than Pakistan, should occupy the Indian strategic mind in the coming years. In a reflection of this, and four years into his first term, Modi said in 2018 while addressing the Shangri La dialogue, 'Asia and the world will have a better future when India and China work together with trust and confidence.'[10]

MASTER OF SURPRISES

Besides the above, there were other areas where the successes were not as complete as first thought.

A strategy needs to be consistent and for that to work, the policy that defines the strategy needs to be clear. Media management cannot be passed off as strategy. That's why the manner in which the surgical strikes have been advertised to the public has raised more questions than it has answered. Or, to take another recent example, the Indian establishment was loud in its boasts that it had the upper hand in the confrontation with the Chinese forces at Doklam. But later events do not fully support that claim.

The point, therefore, is that chest thumping might be good in the short term to score points in internal political battles, but it does not reverberate as success for long in the wider world. Strategy works well when the idea of it is consistent with the results. Contrarily, boasts about imagined capability can be disastrous. Uniquely, for some time a senior cabinet minister insisted that India would respond to Pakistan's terror with terror ('*Kante se kanta nikalenge*'). Such a boast, without having the capability of doing so, can be self-defeating. And a claim of intent like this, without any actual involvement in acts of terror in Pakistan, only gives Pakistan a propaganda handle and makes India complicit.

A certain amount of ambiguity is par for the course in foreign affairs, and sometimes even the '*kante se kanta*' type statements can be of use. But these have to be carefully thought through before use. That's why guidance from a foreign office becomes so important for a politician, even more so when the government is new and needs careful immersion in the big and complicated world of foreign affairs.

India's External Affairs Ministry has performed ably, but it is overstretched. The routine and the urgent combine to overwhelm the limited human resources it has, leaving it little time to plan policy. It tries to cope as best as it can, but the task becomes doubly difficult when a leader in a hurry seeks lightning-fast reactions. Therefore, the question of who makes policy becomes that much more difficult to respond to. When India's foreign secretary asked senior officials who, within the government, does the thinking about overall foreign policy, he was met with an embarrassed silence, according to a Brookings Institution study of Modi's foreign policy.[11]

On the economic side, if there is one overwhelming image that defines his first term, it is that of demonetization. The economy was ticking along well till then—the industry was in a buoyant mood and there was hope of even better times to come. But the announcement that delegitimized the national currency in one go changed the national mood, too, in one go. Ever since, the economy continues to splutter, as *The Guardian* wrote morosely:

> Modi is determined not to concede the folly of demonetization, which cost 100 lives, at least 1.5m jobs and left 150 million people without pay for weeks... Modi claims to be a religious man. That perhaps explains why his belief in this wrong-headed policy has never wavered...Democracy's conceit is that governments are accountable while in power. Mr Modi exposes this as hollow: he ducks arguments rather than faces them... India's economic credibility has been dented...[12]

However, he remains confident that India is headed in the right direction and that all the pieces will fall in place soon.

> Questioned about the pace of his reform drive, Modi points to the change in the economic mood from the glum months leading up to last year's election, 'You will actually see that internationally the world is, once again, excited and enthusiastic about India and the opportunities that India represents.'[13]

Alas, after every major mistake, the government tries bravely to put a positive spin on it. All of a sudden, claims begin to be made confidently that a new dawn is around the corner. Many times in the past, the world too has responded enthusiastically to these promises. It becomes excited all over again about India and its perennially untapped potential. Invariably in the past, that burst of positive energy did not last long. And every time, the world turned away in disappointment when the performance fell short of the hype.

Apart from the state of the economy, there were many others troubles at home that kept preoccupying Modi even as he maintained a hectic pace of travel abroad. This was especially the case regarding the situation in Kashmir.

Initially, Modi took a muscular take-no-prisoners approach towards the terrorism in J&K. But this hard-line approach did not succeed, as popular support for the insurgents grew with every encounter between the security forces and the terrorists.

Over time, though, a glimmer of hope began to shine through. The number of terror incidents showed a declining trend and terrorists themselves did not venture out as brazenly as they had been doing till the beginning of 2019. But this phase did not last long.

Characteristically, a few weeks after a spectacular win in the 2019 elections, Modi sprang another surprise. On 5 August 2019, the government abolished Articles 370 and 35A of the constitution that gave special status to J&K. It also announced the bifurcation of the state into two separate union territories of J&K and Ladakh.

The move was bold by any standards. Almost all national leaders, starting with Nehru, who had brought in these provisions, felt that the two articles needed to be repealed for the full integration of the people of that state with the rest of the country and for its overall development. But they hesitated in taking that step because of the fear of the internal and external blowback that it could generate. Modi decided to take the plunge, which has been widely appreciated in the country and understood by many outside.

Though the revocation of Article 370 was a much-needed step, the government is being faulted for not fully anticipating the Pakistani moves against it. Pakistan has been vocal in its protests, and Imran Khan has taken up the issue with a missionary zeal. Tackling this would have been task enough, but it was made tougher still by the move to introduce the CAA, which pointedly excludes Muslims from its ambit. The protests against the CAA in India have given Pakistan an additional case in its point that India's actions should be a matter of wider concern. Pakistan's propaganda machine has successfully turned the global attention to what it alleges are human rights issues. It has had a favourable response from the Western media, and many leaders across the world have been sympathetic to Imran's lament.

It is possible that once the restrictions on movement in Kashmir are lifted, there may be protests and even acts of violence. But that is unlikely to have any long-term effect on this decision. Rather, by repealing boldly the two articles and by reorganizing the state into two union territories, the government may have set the stage for a major transformation of the country and the region. The big 'if' here is whether Pakistan is willing to give up its old, bad ways. Grimmer tests in Kashmir may lie ahead, but as long as the Indian Army remains focused on counterinsurgency functions, its capability to fight a conventional war gets diminished by that much.

It was expected that a leader who lays such great emphasis on hard power would reform India's lumbering military bureaucracy. Yet, that still remains just a hope. However, some steps are now being taken in that direction. A chief of defence staff (CDS), a precondition to jointness among the military's three branches, is finally a reality. When the Modi government set out to reform the country's national security architecture in 2018, it did so though a series of workarounds that diminished the role of his cabinet and concomitantly emphasized his own office and that of the NSA.

It seems that economic woes internally and China and Pakistan externally will preoccupy Modi in his second term. This combination, to a greater or lesser extent, had also kept the previous governments busy, but this time the issue is more complex, and like Modi did by removing Article 370, the powers hostile to India may want to emulate his ways in forcing an outcome that benefits them.

VERDICT ON INDIA'S STRONGMAN

If we were to bifurcate his first term from the second, it might be fair to say that Modi's achievements do not match up to the image he had portrayed, and the expectations that had been raised at first with his vigorous style.

This vigorous diplomacy naturally seeks a greater global footprint. In this quest, Modi is guided by a nationalism that has cultural and economic components. And he is not shy of emphasizing the nation's soft power attributes, from yoga to the diaspora. Along the way, he has long shed any diffidence about India's great-power aspirations. This transition has sometimes led Indian foreign policy into taking the uncharted path. He has, undoubtedly, challenged some of the assumptions that had governed India's foreign policy engagements. India is no longer the cautious power. There is a certain amount of risk-taking now, unlike the risk aversion of the past. It is seemingly nimble and willing to take on a larger global role.

During the first term, Modi tried to transform India from being one of the important players in the global order into one that wants to participate in defining the priorities of the international system. That has not happened, and India is not a game changer in world affairs. On the other hand, for an entirely different set of reasons, it remains wooed by America, and continues to be confronted by Pakistan and constrained by China.

As the elections approached and the prospects of Modi getting a second term increased, the outside world adjusted quickly to the possibility. A new assessment began to take hold, which framed as distant memories his missteps like the demonetization and the poor implementation of the GST. In its place, the strongman image began to overwhelm the awe that the victory numbers had brought in. Anticipating this change, *The Financial Times* was laudatory; but it also held out a red flag:

> A second general election victory in 2019 would cement Mr Modi's position as one of the leading political figures in the world. But it would not end the anxieties about his political project. As the cases of Messrs Putin and Erdogan have demonstrated, strongman leaders have a tendency to become steadily more autocratic the longer they stay in office.[14]

A word of caution would be necessary here. The problem with being a strongman is that while it works internally—for some time at least—it is difficult to bend those outside to your will. For instance, the otherwise self-willed and strong Trump is seen cajoling North Korea's Kim Jong Un, just to get him to agree to meet. Moreover, between them, strongmen seldom make stable friends. Instead, chances are that they might engage in one-upmanship. When Trump interceded to defuse the crisis after the Indian air-strike at Balakot, it was he, not Modi, who announced the India–Pakistan de-escalation on 28 February 2019.

But Modi is not cast in the same autocracy-democracy mould as Putin, Erdogan or Duterte. And he is subject to far more checks and balances than Xi. Besides, he is a committed economic reformer with a real popular touch. Despite the setbacks in his first term, from demonetization to large-scale unemployment, most people believe that the Indian dream is here to stay.

EPILOGUE
The More It Changes the More It Remains the Same

As an argumentative people in a noisy and somewhat chaotic democracy, Indians have been fortunate in having a good number of leaders who have steered the national ship reasonably well. It is true that in the fierce passion of the present, we tend to be overly critical of them. This is only natural in a large country with multiple issues, which are often complex. Since no single leader can tackle them all to national satisfaction, it is easier to recount the negatives, because gossip finds ready audience. As Mark Antony said, 'The evil that men do lives after them.'

As in the past, so too in future, it will be unrealistic to expect that there could be a leader without flaws, or one who is never touched by failure. If we accept the proposition that leaders too are mortal—of flesh and blood like the rest of us—then it will be reasonable to conclude that the leaders in our list have largely been good for the country.

If we look back dispassionately, the prime ministers listed in the preceding chapters have each made significant contributions to the country. Their achievements must be viewed in context; they were not leading a prosperous country at the top of the development ladder. A somewhat fractious and large society like ours constantly passes through many internal and external trials.

All that should concern us is whether the leader was able to deliver what he had promised, and if at the end of his innings he has left behind a plan of his country's interests that is persuasive and doable. India's voyage is long and the quality of the people who steer it may be varied. But as of now, our list of eight has done well enough to illuminate the path ahead.

Chronologically put, we start once again with Nehru in this brief recap below. His secularism, idealism and commitment to building modern temples of development gave a solid start to the nation. But just as these were grand, equally monumental were the slips he made. India still looks back with anguish at his error of judgment on the Kashmir issue.

His successor, Shastri, did not live long enough to leave a large mark. Still, he is remembered for the grit he showed in countering Pakistan in the war of 1965. But he is also blamed for losing at Tashkent what the soldiers won in the battlefield.

Indira Gandhi's name is synonymous with the victory over Pakistan in 1971, leading to the birth of a new nation. She is also remembered for her 'Garibi Hatao' pro-poor policies, and alas, also painfully for the Emergency she imposed on India besides the Operation Bluestar at the Golden Temple.

Her son Rajiv Gandhi introduced computers to India and initiated the revolution in the telecom sector. But he is also remembered for the Bofors corruption scandal.

P.V. Narasimha Rao came in at a time when bankruptcy stared India in the face. He guided the country safely out of the crisis. He is remembered for ushering in the age of economic liberalisation, but also for not doing enough to stop the demolition of the Babri structure.

Vajpayee began his tenure with the nuclear test at Pokhran. Like Nehru, his too was a larger-than-life persona. He too dreamed big for India and led it sagaciously. But there were many false steps with Pakistan in his tenure.

Manmohan Singh led India wisely to double-digit growth. But he did not act decisively against the corruption that marred almost the entire tenure of his second term.

Modi's is a continuing story, but already his distinctive contribution is writ large on the global stage. During his first term, he figured among the front ranks of the global leaders. If demonetization set back the country economically, his single act of repealing Articles 370 and 35A earned him a place in history. By that one stroke, he has set the nation free from the restrictions it had imposed on itself for long years. Alas, this was followed soon by the CAA, to countrywide protests and condemnation abroad. As a leader, he has brushed aside criticism to lead the country repeatedly into and through stormy times.

By and large, therefore, the eight prime ministers on our list have done well by India. It might be in order now to carry our enquiry further and ask what sets these leaders apart from others. If they are a cut above the rest, then do these leaders share some characteristics in common? Was it just chance that they occupied the high office, or would they have taken the lead position even in a different age and circumstance? It is true that the mask of celebrity hides the real face from public view; still, it can be said that a common trait defining them is their ability to stand up to challenges. To beat the occasional failure, there is of course their silver tongue and their sharp elbows. Outward humility marks, generally, their conduct with the constituents. Invariably, a visitor to them comes away with the impression that the leader gave them a fair hearing and full attention, bringing out the best in them.

As creatures of flesh and blood they too get angry, as Nehru often did. Even these flashes of temper have added to their legend. There are exceptions, of course: Shastri was extraordinarily humble and self-effacing, so on these two counts, he was different from others. But like the rest, he too was ambitious; otherwise he would not have reached the very top.

Another aspect that sets these eight leaders apart from others is their ability as communicators. With one or possibly two exceptions, the rest have been great communicators. Each has had a distinct style, and every generation has had its own unique set of tools for communication; from radio in the 1950s to television in the 1970s and social media now. The medium has varied, but the message has been direct and simple in every case. Therefore, while each of them excelled in their age, they would have fitted in and adjusted to a different time and its practices with equal ease.

A question that could be asked as a follow-up is this: Were their qualities of leadership, confidence, communication skills and determination enough? All these may have carried them to the top, but could they have notched up successes in the job all on their own?

Well, many leaders like to think that they had scored those successes all by themselves. But history has shown that they were wrong in that assumption. Luck, pluck, intuition and hard work, individually or in combination, do play an amazing part in a leader's success. But all that cannot move the bureaucracy. That's why a leader needs support. Able ministerial and sound bureaucratic advisors are essential to a leader's success. But standards have varied, and it is often said that the bureaucracy is no longer the same—that the dedication of purpose is lacking. This is not true as a general rule, because there are many who would still qualify as able and dedicated; but the perception of decline in standards is bad enough. A feeling has gained ground that unlike in the first decades of India's independence, the bureaucrat has gradually become an impression of his political master or, in other cases, an entrepreneur of some businessman's fancies.

Therefore, as in the past, in future too, a leader would need an able team to support him. He would need to have advisors around him who can show him the mirror of truth and point him towards the right course. Otherwise, the achievements that are claimed during his term in office would turn out to be ephemeral after he has left office.

A leader's success, however, is dependent on many more factors than the ones we have listed so far. Beyond internal stability, a peaceful external environment and able advisers, he needs lucky stars too, because matters as diverse as climate change and hostile powers can undo all his good work.

Let's turn the crystal ball a bit and consider the state of the country under a future prime minister. Will it be any different from what it is today, or what it was in the past? What powers, hostile or otherwise, would an Indian leader have to contend with in the coming years?

It can be said with a fair amount of confidence that the basic political structure of the country that he leads would largely be the same. While India's democracy has its flaws and is far from perfect, it is also a fact universally acknowledged that democracy makes tough demands that need compromise and diversity. This is even more necessary in today's interconnected world. The government has the responsibility to shape the imagination of the people about their place in the world. But, for too long, Indian policymakers have allowed 'strategic ambiguity' to guide foreign policy choices. In a rapidly fluctuating world order, this is bound to confuse the country itself as well as others. A future leader must make clear what role he seeks for India in the international order. The task does not end there: He must then decide upon the means to achieve that role, and pursue the task determinedly, because the world is impatient with those who spin slogans merely for effect.

Sometimes one gets the feeling that to be a leader of India is a complex, contradictory business, and that the contradictions will get more acute in the years ahead. The country has a thousand-year-long history of enslavement, yet there is a strange pride in it. It glorifies religion, yet disowns the very idea of religion. Its social mores go back thousands of years, yet it makes desperate efforts to erase them all. It is all so contradictory, yet so profound. Perhaps that's what makes India so unique, and its journey so enduring, as a nation.

In 1882, French philosopher Ernest Renan delivered a speech titled, 'What is a Nation'. In it, he made the suggestion that historical amnesia is an essential part of nation-building—that nations need to forget the horrible price they have paid in the distant past for their unity. He was right, of course, because it is futile to remain a prisoner of the past. But what if that past refuses to fade away, as in India's case? In its recent past is its amputation by the departing British, carved deep into the national psyche. This was quickly followed by the horrors of the Partition and the unruly neighbour India inherited. In its past is also the humiliation in the battlefield by China. These hurts continue to splutter, haunting our present. They hover like a shadow over India, affecting its actions and reactions.

There is another, deeper past too. After all, India's engagement with the world started when through the Maha Upanishad it declared, '*Vasudhaiva Kutumbakam* (The World Is One Family).' Ever since, it has been a participant on the global stage; by trading silk and spice with the Roman Empire, by spreading its word and reach in Angkor Wat, by its people transforming the marshlands of faraway Guyana and Mauritius, and more recently, through the nobility of its struggle for freedom. At no time, post-Independence, was India too wrapped up in itself to bother with foreigners. India has had a presence in, and its own idea of, the world from the beginning. Its past was indeed one of the referral points in post-Independence India's foreign policy. Whether it will remain a standard to measure our tomorrows remains to be seen. To that extent, both these streams—the one that began with ancient India and the other post-Independence—represent continuity in the Indian foreign policy regardless of the complexion of the government. There might be a difference in nuance—some slight shift occasionally to suit a particular circumstance.

Otherwise, the fear of China continues to cramp our policy space. And Pakistan has consistently set the hostile tone and then bemusedly waited for us to react. Pakistan being the cat in this cat and mouse game, it devises the terms of our acrimonious engagement. This fundamental is not going to change in the foreseeable future. So, besides leading a complex country, our leader of tomorrow will also have to contend with a fractious neighbourhood.

A NATURAL PARTNER

It need not have been this way had the South Asian region been more integrated. With a combined population just short of the two billion mark, it could have provided a market cushion for the occasional policy hiccups at the national level. That is how it was before 1947. Before Partition, the economic synergy across different parts of the subcontinent was a historical reality. After Partition, by the mid-50s, the sealed borders had slammed shut the free flow of goods. Connectivity crumbled, and it created massive dysfunction as the economies of scale and production chains were disrupted.

It could be argued that India is big enough to sustain industries and the market for their products on its own. That is so, but only to a limited extent. The distance from Amritsar to Chennai is far greater than the former's distance from the cities across the border in Pakistan. The savings in transportation costs alone would justify more trade between Amritsar and Lahore. Besides, there is also the question of taste; consumer preferences in Amritsar do not overlap with those in Chennai to the same degree as in the neighbouring Lahore.

The size of a population may help an industry's economy of scale. But that cannot be the entire argument. China's is a bigger population than India's, yet it seeks foreign markets aggressively. This is a major part of its quest via the Belt and Road Initiative (BRI). It is also the logic of globalization, despite some ill-founded efforts by Trump to the contrary. In sum therefore, India's market needs cannot, and should not, be limited to its borders. However, it needs to do far more to make this happen.

According to a 2018 World Bank study, India's trade in South Asia amounted to $19.1 billion, which is just about 3 per cent of its total global trade at $637.4 billion. Taken to its potential, the study maintains that India's regional trade could easily reach $65 billion. But that needs a strong political will among all the regional partners. Of the many other negatives standing in the way of greater trade, there is also the issue of high tariffs. The average tariffs in South Asia during 2016 stood at 13.6 per cent, as against the global average tariff of 6.3 per cent.

To take another example, while the trade between India and Pakistan presently stands at around $2 billion, without any trade barriers this figure could go up to $37 billion, which will far exceed India's current total trade with the rest of the South Asian countries. However, Pakistan would rather cut its nose than let this happen.

Beyond trade, there are other opportunities that await the region. Our shared history, culture and tradition all point to immense possibilities if the locks that constrain us are broken open. Already, Bollywood and cricket provide us with two common languages. Some of the major hospitals in India present a picture of South Asian diversity in terms of the patients of different nationalities that they treat. This logic can be expanded to other areas, especially tourism.

By its size and location, India should be a natural partner in every respect for the South Asian countries. India and Nepal share an open border; India signed its first free trade agreement (FTA) with Sri Lanka in 1998; India and Bhutan have mutually beneficial economic interlinkages and India has been a major economic partner to Bangladesh.

Yet, this is not enough, and the interchange is far below its potential. As a result, the South Asian region is one of the least economically integrated regions in the world. Ideally, South Asia should be a project for social justice, to be achieved through economic rationalization, subregional interactions and open borders like that between Nepal and India. Yet, that is unlikely as long as Pakistan and India remain entangled in differences.

In our present obsession with somehow wishing Pakistan away from us, we tend to overlook the historical record. It suggests that for long in its history, India has experienced invaders or plunderers from across its western borders. In contrast, India's main trading and cultural partners in history were the countries to its east. Despite wide acknowledgement of this reality, the former continues to preoccupy us while the latter relationship bears signs of neglect.

Further, India's internal performance is unlikely to take it to the peak of glory. As Singapore's leader Lee Kuan Yew had noted perceptively, 'With slow economic but high population growth, India is not about to be a wealthy nation for some time. It has to solve its economic and social problems before it can play a major role in southeast Asia.'[1]

Let's look at the issue in the framework of regional mechanisms. Practically viewed, SAARC boxes India in a narrow, artificial framework limited to the Indian subcontinent. On the other hand, the east-oriented Bay of Bengal Initiative for Multi-Sectoral Technical and Economic Cooperation (BIMSTEC) seeks to realign India along its historical axis. In this effort to act east, it will need Bangladesh and Myanmar as active and willing partners; a task that demands liberal movement across borders. Unfortunately, that cooperation could become a victim of the acrimony surrounding India's efforts to push back the migrants from these countries, especially Bangladesh. Alas, decisions motivated by domestic political considerations sometimes do not anticipate their external fallout.

This is a great pity because the neighbourhood, no matter how we describe it, can be a great opportunity. On the other hand, it could also be a complex challenge. It becomes even more so when the neighbouring countries are significantly smaller in size; then their sensitivity increases in inverse proportion. Deft political management can smoothen some of the wrinkles, but crisis control does not bridge the entire gulf. Translating India's natural weight in the region into influence was easier in a pre-globalized world, especially before China emerged in its assertive incarnation. Since then, every Indian action has been subject to a counter challenge.

CHINA: A POTENTIAL FRANKENSTEIN?

This red marker may feature more prominently in the times to come, because China's domination of the east is enormous and India's promises do not match its performance. Moreover, India does not yet have the economic or strategic heft to undertake, in a substantial way, commitment towards an entire region. Its focus, and its engagement, will have to be country-specific and limited to a few countries. But for the time being, it is far too distracted by Pakistan to device a coherent scheme of economic engagement with a thriving east.

A new opportunity had beckoned India after the US-China trade friction started. Besides looking to replace some of the items that China had so far exported to the US, it could have also positioned itself aggressively as the alternate market for investment by American and other global companies wishing to move their manufacturing activities out of China. But India's investor-unfriendly budget in 2019 and its stringent tax regime became formidable disincentives.

Be it on the economic side or on the diplomatic front, Pakistan, China, the US and Russia will remain the key to India's strategic plans. These relationships are also tied to the evolving global order, where India's place would be determined not by what it thinks of itself but by how the world views us. We are, of course, entitled to an exalted view of ourselves and our capabilities. But the outside world, especially China, does not see us through the same rose-tinted glasses. As Strobe Talbott writes in his book *Engaging India*, 'There's China, which treats India with total contempt…'[2]

China's contempt for India is not of recent origin. If anything, it has increased further, as China outdistances India in every sphere of nation-building. Therefore, in the times to come, the inherent relationship between China and India will be one of tension, whether in the economic, energy, nuclear, strategic or security sphere. In absence of careful attention by both parties to mitigate them, these tensions are likely to increase, as both India and China try to take the leadership roles in Asia. However, despite its large landmass and expanding markets, Asia is not big enough to accommodate, at the top, both an acknowledged global power and one with ambition.

The desire to be alone at the top is grounded in the Chinese conviction that its foreign relations should be hierarchic and non-egalitarian. In pursuance of this logic, the Chinese leadership, through the ages, has seen China and its civilization as the centre of all meaningful human activity. As for others, it should suffice to quote Confucius: 'Know thy place.'

It is this message of 'know thy place' that has been conveyed repeatedly to India through China's 'string of pearls' strategy, by the China-Pakistan Economic Corridor (CPEC) and via China's military support to Pakistan.

Over the years, Chinese troops have also been testing the limits of Indian fortitude along the Sino-Indian border. Despite denials by India, experts insist that the transgressions across the LAC are almost always one-way—from the Chinese side. The Indian troops, having learnt their lessons from Nehru's Forward Policy, are wary of crossing the LAC.

On two occasions in the past, India had pushed forward. In the 1950s, India attempted to increase its military capacity along the border where China had made deep incursions in Aksai Chin. China reacted by invading, which resulted in the border war of 1962 and the humiliation of India. The second time, in the 1980s, a confrontation on the border led more or less to a stalemate militarily, and somewhat unexpectedly to a defreezing of the relations.

Fortunately for both sides, the territorial intrusions by Chinese soldiers into Indian territory have not led to active hostilities. But suspicions linger, and what is worse, in the long-term view, is the fact that there is hardly any people-to-people contact between the two. As a result, knowledge of the other is next to negligible. This knowledge, so essential to empathy or even a minimum understanding of the other, is shallow even among the political elite and professionals. Just about a handful of scholars in the two countries can claim expertise beyond foreign policy into areas like the language, culture and history of their large neighbour. This state of ignorance is harmful to both because when misunderstandings crop up, chances are that the situation could turn uglier than it should.

Even if there have not been active hostilities, there are areas of concern that crop up regularly. These tensions along the northern border are bound to linger till the border issue is resolved, but a greater source of concern in future could be the Chinese activities in the Indian Ocean. For long, India had viewed this ocean as its lake, its preserve. In the last few years, China has begun to challenge that assumption. Gradually, the chain of Chinese bases is assuming a formidable strategic shape. It is doing so ostensibly for the security of its oil imports from the Gulf, but they could equally be a check on oil imports by other countries. India's trade in oil and other commodities could be choked by the Chinese vessels based in Gwadar as and when its next conflict with China or Pakistan breaks out. And China does not fight shy of making its intentions clear, either down here or up in the north.

As Chinese scholar Yang Xiaoping points out, India can no longer take for granted the security cushion that Nepal and Bhutan had traditionally provided as buffer states. China has steadily increased its presence in Nepal, which in turn has actively welcomed this development. Bhutan, too, may not be able to resist the Chinese advances for long. Yang's reading of the situation holds out a warning for India:

> To some extent, India's mindset limits its imagination and ability to accept China's inevitable advances into these areas. Even if the temporary creation of buffer space works on land, it will be more difficult in the maritime domain.[3]

Another lament that is heard in India is about the opaqueness with which the China policy is handled. It is not as if the Indian people expect to be consulted in the formulation or the implementation of it, but they resent being kept in the dark about where we stand in relation to China. For instance, has China sliced off further portions of Indian territory since 1962? If Doklam was such a success for us, why did the prime minister have to rush to Wuhan? It is easy to obfuscate or explain away an issue through a faithful section of the media. But the truth has a habit of popping out uncomfortably, sooner or later.

It is not only at land and in sea that India and China will engage regularly in future, sometimes precariously. They will also be watching each other warily in the international arena, as had happened in August 2019 and January 2020 at the UNSC over Kashmir. China is now a multilateral diplomatic activist. And its activism goes over and above the conference halls to launching diplomatic initiatives beyond its own immediate sphere of strategic interest. This new activism on China's part, plus its ambitious global agenda, limits India's space.

Moreover, China's strategic interests are pulling it in a direction away from America towards Russia and Iran. This and the strong policy overlap it has with Pakistan do not bode well for the India-China relationship. Yet, even if the relations remain fraught, it does not mean that they would, or should, slip into open hostility. Rather, they could continue to maintain a 'new normal' through crisis management.

However, 'crisis control' too has a limited shelf life. At some point or the other, the patience of one of the parties might wear thin and the long-suppressed angst may bubble over. This is a real possibility given the fact that so far, China has had its way. India's buffer space via smaller neighbours is no longer a zone of comfort for it. And as the Doklam incident has shown, China may agree to soften somewhat without conceding substantively.

Another change from the past is in the economic domain. Once China's economic interests began to cover much of the world, it followed that Beijing should try and secure them by spreading its military reach. Add to this the age-old truth that flag follows trade. It was partly in acknowledgement of this that the Pentagon's annual report for 2018 mentioned that 'China's advancement of projects such as the "One Belt, One Road" Initiative (OBOR) will probably drive military overseas basing through a perceived need to provide security for OBOR projects.'

This is one explanation why China is increasing its bases abroad. However, other experts insist that a prime objective of OBOR is strategic. It is through this imprint that China plans to spread its influence and control over other countries and their people. India is a late starter in this field, and a lazy one at that. It has an air base at Aini in Tajikistan, which it has neglected to put to effective use despite its strategic location. On the other hand, it ended up in a wild goose chase in 2018, seeking a base in the faraway Seychelles.

For China and India to compete for military bases abroad is an extension of their overall rivalry. It also marks a decisive phase in their evolution as modern states.

With its hyperactivity abroad, is China's goal to put its military footprint over the rest of Asia? Or is it China's aim to ensure that the international environment in which it operates makes it richer and more secure? China does not need to become an empire to do these things; instead, it can pursue a hegemonic rather than a direct, imperial form of control. But it would inevitably mean crossed wires when a rival rising power like India seeks to spread its shadow over that same area.

Today's reality—and that for the foreseeable future—is that containing China is impossible; balancing it on India's terms is going to be extremely difficult. In fact, India's concern should relate to the other extreme. China had remained largely neutral in both the previous India-Pakistan wars and during the Kargil conflict, but it may not remain so in the next one.

For India in particular, and for China's neighbours in general, it might be worthwhile reminding themselves ever so often that nearing the end of his life, Nixon confided in his friend William Safire, 'We may have created [by helping China] a Frankenstein.'[4]

DEALING WITH THE WORLD'S ENFANT TERRIBLE

If China is a potential Frankenstein, Pakistan is a practising one. Indeed, it has been so from its very beginning. That's why it has been called every negative term known to man, from a 'failed state' to 'terroristan'.

But India–Pakistan is not the only bitter and long-lasting feud that the world has witnessed in its long history. There was the war between Greece and Persia before the Christian calendar started. In recent centuries, Germany and France have battled hard before calming down and being nice to each other. The lesson of these bitter rivalries is that unless you are aiming for a fight to the finish, a way out of feuding must be found.

It is wise to ensure that bickering does not degenerate into a war that drains you economically. But successful exercise of deterrence doesn't just mean threatening an adversary with punitive action. It must shape the adversary's perceptions, i.e., force the adversary to change its behaviour by estimating that it has options other than aggression, which are more cost-effective. However, that secret formula continues to elude India, and in the meanwhile, Pakistan finds it cost effective to pursue the proxy war.

If at all the theory of karma were ever to apply to nations, then for all the mayhem it has sponsored in India, Afghanistan and beyond, Pakistan should suffer the horrors of hell for generations to come. Instead, it merrily keeps celebrating its fresh misadventures. Obviously then, God has failed to deliver retribution, and taking a cue from the higher forces even man seems to have given up. Rather than having to atone for its sins, Pakistan is rewarded repeatedly for its strategic location. At best, someone or the other tries to reason with it that it should keep some sort of a lid on its mischief. At this, Pakistan nods placatingly and says the right things to get a new promise of aid, then carries on doing all the wrong things as before. In this background, India's goal of moving past Pakistan is smart, but the means to do so remain out of its reach. For instance, despite India's consistent efforts to de-hyphenate its relationship with Pakistan, it has not been able to escape Pakistan. Instead, Pakistan has been successful in dragging every issue into an Indo-Pak framework.

Quite simply, Pakistan revels in its role as the enfant terrible of the world. Still, its wickedness could be checked, were it not for the limitations imposed by India's righteousness. It is a rarely acknowledged fact that the Indian leaders have been fatalistically drawn to Pakistan and its promises of good behaviour. This faith that Pakistan, like the prodigal son, would one day mend its ways and live in peace with India is misplaced. Nothing in Pakistan's behaviour so far suggests that it will abandon the formula it has perfected over the years of using proxy wars as a matter of state policy. This conclusion has been drawn repeatedly by strategists and politicians the world over. The exhaustive Kargil Committee report, too, had warned:

> The Pakistani establishment has a long and consistent history of misreading India's will and world opinion. In 1947, it did not anticipate the swift Indian military intervention in Kashmir when it planned its raid with a mix of army personnel, ex-servicemen and tribals... In 1965, it took Zulfikar Ali Bhutto's advice that India would not cross the international border to deal with Pakistan's offensive in the Akhnur sector. In 1971, it developed...totally unwarranted expectations about the likelihood of US-Chinese intervention on its behalf. The same pattern of behaviour was evident this time too... It has obviously been a victim of its own propaganda.[5]

Sometimes, the argument is made that it is the military that is the source of all troubles in Pakistan. This is facile reading of a complex situation. In some measure, it also reflects the reality that Pakistan is a closed state to a foreign observer; access to the inner functioning of its society being severely restricted. That's why it is often not realized that on strategic concerns, there is surprisingly little difference between Pakistan's civilian regimes and its military ones. On issues like religion and policy towards India, Afghanistan, US and China, both the army and its politicians think and act alike. As Michael Morell, a former acting CIA director, says, 'Pakistan is the most dangerous country in the world—not this year, not next year, but certainly down the road.'

Expanding further on this theme, Morell adds:

> Pakistan has the world's 5th largest population, 5th largest military and 6th largest nuclear arsenal. The danger begins with a dysfunctional economy and a rapidly growing population of young people without education or job prospects. Add to that a military that continues to call the shots as though war could break out at any moment.[6]

That Pakistan's army is an omnipresent control freak in every aspect of the country's life is bad enough; it is worse still that it considers itself omniscient. It may not have been directly responsible for the economic mess that Pakistan is in, but it has definitely contributed to the policies that led Pakistan to this sorry pass. Any other country would have thought this through and confronted the issue that was the cause of all its woes. Turkey has shown the way in this regard by bringing its army firmly under civilian control. A similar effort in Pakistan would benefit not just the country itself but the regional peace as well. In fact, some analysts also advocate the abolition of the ISI and its replacement with a new external intelligence agency under civilian control.

But that is unlikely to be. On the contrary, over the last decade, the Pakistani army has further strengthened its grip over national affairs. Moreover, over the last few years, Pakistan's weapons procurements have led to building up its conventional capability. Walter C. Ladwig in his 2015 study *Indian Military Modernization and Conventional Deterrence in South Asia* has pointed out:

> India's defense procurement continues to underperform, producing far less in terms of military power than its spending would suggest. Conversely, Pakistan—assisted by China and others—has prevented the emergence of sharp asymmetries in the conventional military balance and even narrowed previously existing gaps.[7]

And after Balakot, Pakistan's Army feels reasonably confident in limiting India's success in a short, sharp conventional conflict.

If on the military front Pakistan has reason to feel all powerful, its social, ethnic and economic health does not inspire confidence. That fragility, and the ethnic tensions within the country that it will lead to, poses a challenge that its leadership is likely to wish away rather than confront and correct.

The prognosis by foreign experts is also grim regarding Pakistan's macroeconomic situation. The IMF estimates that Pakistan's GDP growth had declined from 5.8 per cent in 2017–8 to 3.4 per cent in 2018–9. It is expected to decline further, to 2.7 per cent in 2019–20. The total debt-to-GDP ratio is likely to increase sharply from 77 per cent in 2018–9 to 85.6 per cent by 2023–4. The World Bank is equally despondent about the prospects for Pakistan in the years ahead. By its reckoning, Pakistan's fiscal deficit will increase to 8.7 per cent in 2019–20.

Whether these figures have taken fully into account the impact of various heavy borrowings by Pakistan in recent years remains to be seen. More importantly, they are not likely to have fully taken into account the financial burden that CPEC will add to Pakistan's resources. In 2015, when the CPEC was announced, Pakistan's then Prime Minister Nawaz Sharif had called it a game changer for the country and the South Asian region. Since then, the expectations from the project have been considerably scaled down. Instead of leading the way to an economic miracle, the CPEC is proving to be a financial drag for Pakistan. It is already, at least partly, responsible for Pakistan's mounting debt.

To take the example of a major investment, the Gwadar Port was inaugurated in November 2016 but has not earned much revenue due to competition from other ports in the region and lack of a hinterland industrial ecosystem. If and when it turns profitable, at that stage, according to the agreement, 91 per cent of the revenues generated from it are to go to China for the next 40 years. Besides, China and its companies have built clauses in the commercial contracts for CPEC that assure them returns as high as 30 per cent for the investment made by them.

Pakistan's economic problems are likely to increase as the combination of high debt and low revenues kicks in. But regardless of its difficulties, it is unlikely to turn against China as it frequently does against its other major benefactor, the US. Despite billions spent by the US in Pakistan, it remains one of the most anti-American countries in the world. Yet, it exercises demonic hold over the US. In fact, every time Islamabad's ties with China became stronger, the US was quick to further strengthen its alliance with Pakistan. India has borne the brunt of this recurring dynamic. To avoid ruffling India's feathers, the enduring aspects of US-

Pakistan ties have remained obscure, but still very real.

So, what is it that gives Pakistan that power over the most powerful? In the beginning, it was its strategic location—though whether that geographical assumption ever benefitted the US in a major way is open to doubt. Later, since the 1980s, it has been its role as the largest sponsor of terrorism that has really given it a vice-like hold over others.

On all other counts, especially political and economic, it verges on being a failed state. Consequently, and over the years, Pakistan has been slowly calcifying under different types of authoritarian regimes, elected or otherwise. But Pakistan has not learnt its lesson from history. It collapsed in 1971 to splinter into two states because of its mistakes. The question that is often asked in the background of the current unrest in Balochistan and the Frontier areas is this: How long will it remain safe from outright collapse?

Bringing Pakistan to heel has been the most fervent desire of most American presidents, but they have always stepped back, afraid of the consequences of confronting a nuclear-armed Pakistan. This American fear of the unknown is unlikely to change, and Pakistan is counting the gains that it feels will surely accrue from US's withdrawal from Afghanistan. As Bill Roggio maintains, 'It says much about America's ineptitude and confusion that not a single Pakistani official was ever sanctioned or designated as a terror supporter throughout 17+ years of war...'[8]

In March 2009, President Obama announced a new strategy for Afghanistan and Pakistan. He termed the situation in Afghanistan perilous and said, '...if Afghan government falls to the Taliban...that country will again be a base for terrorists who want to kill as many of our people as they possibly can. The future of Afghanistan is inextricably linked to the future of its neighbour, Pakistan.'[9]

As a follow-up, Obama asked for a fresh assessment of the situation. In November 2010, a Task Force chaired by Richard L. Armitage and former NSA Samuel R. Berger submitted a report on 'U.S. Strategy for Pakistan and Afghanistan.' It affirmed, '...militants in Pakistan and Afghanistan pose a direct threat to the United States and its allies. They jeopardize the stability of Pakistan, a nuclear power that lives in an uneasy peace with its rival, India.' The report was also clear about what needed to be done by Pakistan: '...a long-term partnership with Pakistan...is only sustainable if Pakistan takes action against all terrorist organizations based on its soil.'[10]

Alas, that is where all the diagnosis of the problem ended. Having successfully identified the cause and the symptoms of the disease, America hit a roadblock called the ISI. Nothing that Americans could do would move the Pakistani establishment to rein in the ISI or tinker with its priorities. But the Pakistani establishment alone was not at fault. The CIA had, among its own, some ardent sympathizers of the ISI: 'A major problem in confronting Pakistan was the mental make-up of the CIA officers posted in Islamabad, who felt that the ISI was a trusted associate.'[11]

Still, the US has the ability to put the squeeze on Pakistan, but it has continually put away that difficult decision in the hope that the problem would somehow disappear, that by some miracle, the Pakistani army and the ISI would have a change of heart and mend its ways, that somehow it would give up the bad company of the Taliban.

The basic reason for not going beyond hope and doing something concrete was the fear that Pakistan had grown far too strong even for the strongest army in the world to dare taking it on. This same complex was beginning to affect Indian policymakers. They had made the dilemma worse by turning the Indian army into a reactive force, one fed on the Maginot Line mentality—of being a stationary line of defence against the infiltrators across the LOC. Pakistan uses this to its military advantage; the infiltrators that it sends across the LOC act also as its testing probes to judge the vulnerabilities of the Indian security forces. Therefore the mantra that the fence is the best defence is an unsustainable option for an army.

Meanwhile, luck keeps favouring Pakistan. It was down and out by the beginning of 2019, counting its last dollar. Its usual benefactors were showing signs of aid fatigue. The IMF and World Bank were reluctant to give its economy pass marks and lend any more money, and the American squeeze on Pakistan's economic neck was beginning to hurt. Under pressure, Pakistan was beginning to show the first signs of compliance. Had the US maintained its pressure, Pakistan may finally have been compelled to show verifiable proof of disarming and disbanding its terror groups.

Alas, Trump did a volte face. His re-election campaign took priority over the long-term national interests, and Pakistan began being wooed again. The US wanted to withdraw its troops from Afghanistan before the US elections in 2020. So the economic squeeze on Pakistan started being loosened. The financial assistance started flowing in all over again. The overarching context of the situation in Afghanistan became one of America's need and Pakistan's opportunity. Ironically, the two are blending a third time in Afghanistan. They did so first in the 1980s to drive out the Soviet forces, and a second time post 9/11, when Pakistan pretended to be helping the American forces there. This third time, the US wants the Pakistani crutch to help get its forces to leave Afghanistan safely.

On its part, Pakistan is doing all it can to ensure that Afghanistan crumbles into helplessness and thus becomes Pakistan's virtual vassal. This Pakistani game is being played with transparency, but the US finds it politically convenient to play along, its great interest being that somehow it should be able to withdraw safely from Afghanistan. As a part of that bargain, the Taliban would step in to rule over Afghanistan, just as they were doing before 9/11. Once more, there would be reason for America to start feeling unsafe, as Michael Rubin warns:

> Zalmay Khalilzad was in Washington...to brief Capitol Hill on his ongoing talks with the Taliban. The senators were unimpressed, and with reason. There are many flaws in Khalilzad's plan: It revives the pre-9/11 formula of legitimizing Taliban rule in exchange for a Taliban pledge to close terror camps; it undercuts the legitimacy of the elected Afghan government; and it discounts the Taliban's long history of insincere diplomacy and fleeting commitments. The biggest problem with Khalilzad's approach, however, is it ignores a simple fact: There can be no peace in Afghanistan so long as Pakistan chooses to undercut Afghan stability and support extremism. The missing piece to the Khalilzad strategy, therefore, is how to bring Pakistan to heel.[12]

But bringing 'Pakistan to heel' is easier said than done. The senators may have desired it for all the right reasons; after all, abandoning Afghanistan at this stage would mean wasted US effort over the last 19 years. The blame then should go to the US, and Trump's re-election-related hurry to somehow call it quits. With that, America has taken a wrong policy turn and decided to sup with the devil. The Taliban, more than any other terrorist outfit, now carries out the world's deadliest terrorist attacks. Yet, it has compelled the US president to negotiate the terms of American surrender in Afghanistan and seek Pakistan's support to finalize the exit. As an Afghan insurgent once told an American reporter, 'You have the watches, we have the time.'[13] The Taliban's time seems to have come.

That return of the Taliban is what the ISI is waiting for, and it is this eventuality that worries the Indian strategic mind. India has reason to be greatly concerned, because whichever way you look, Afghanistan is heading towards a greater disaster than it is already in. Whichever way the toss of the Afghan coin falls, its effect on India will be immediate and perhaps fierce. In all likelihood, we might see history repeating itself. After the Russian retreat from Afghanistan in the late 1980s and the steady Taliban ascendancy, the ISI felt confident to divert its terror resources in a significant way to India. Terror in Punjab was followed by stepped-up violence in Kashmir. The signs that we are witnessing today are not reassuring at all. Even the Pakistani enthusiasm for the Kartarpur Sahib Corridor must be seen in that context.

In this background, the situation in the region is unlikely to improve in India's favour any time soon. A future Indian leader would have to contend with this and tread carefully around a geostrategic scenario that promises to be a virtual minefield. China is likely to remain antagonistic to India; Pakistan might continue to be in a wounding mode; and a Taliban-led anarchical Afghanistan will be a constant source of worry. A future Indian prime minister may well be receiving daily reports of increasing Chinese activity at the border and Pakistan-sponsored acts of terror within India.

The larger international context for India will not be ideal either. The US may have withdrawn all its forces from Afghanistan, leaving the region to fend for itself. If Pakistan helps America extricate itself safely out of Afghanistan, and with some dignity, then the shimmer of the earlier hope that India and the US are set for a new beginning will burn out. Unfortunately, in the anxiety to put all its eggs in the American basket, India had neglected its traditional relationship with Russia. But even as India tries to sew those pieces back into some favourable shape, there is time enough for the strategic thinkers to ask: Why is it that we tend to lose every time we are at the point of winning?

TRANSFORMATIVE REGIONAL ARRANGEMENT: A PIPE DREAM

Alas, the odds seem to be stacking up against India. For one reason or another, smaller neighbours around it, with the exception of Bhutan and to some extent Bangladesh, are in an uncomfortable zone with India. They maintain, with Chinese allurement and Pakistani prodding, that the fault lies with the big brotherly attitude of India. There may be a grain of truth in that complaint, but India's efforts to make it up to them reminds one of Diogenes's comment when he was asked why he was begging alms from a statue. The Greek philosopher replied, 'I am practising disappointment.'

The lack of regional cooperation is an oft-heard complaint. It is also added wistfully—'If only SAARC could be a catalyst for regional growth like some regional bodies elsewhere.' Ideally speaking, that is how it should have been, and that indeed was the hope, or a part of the ambition, when SAARC was first set up in 1985. It is true that a number of technical-level projects in fields like agriculture, education, etc. have shown that cooperation is possible and profitable for all concerned. But these examples, howsoever numerous they might be, are small in size and significance. The big ticket items of trade and communication have simply not taken off. The single biggest obstacle to meaningful action is the gulf between India and Pakistan, and their differences are unlikely to be resolved any time soon. As a result, India is shifting to cooperative arrangements on a bilateral basis with other SAARC countries, to the exclusion of Pakistan. Besides, it is trying to integrate itself with regional arrangements to the east, specifically the organizations in Southeast Asia.

Insofar as South Asia is concerned, the hopes for a truly transformative regional arrangement would remain on the drawing board for the foreseeable future. Besides the Indo-Pak friction, experience the world over has shown that regional organizations succeed when the member states are nearly equal in size and capacity, as is the case with the EU and the ASEAN. A second model is the one where a dominant state is a benevolent regional power that can regulate regional behaviour, as in the case of the US in the western hemisphere. Both these elements are missing in the South Asian case.

Even at the bilateral level, the signs are not encouraging. With the exception of Bhutan, any progress with the others in the region will be minimal, patchy and selective. With Nepal, for instance, our relations have always been balanced on a razor's edge; they are hypersensitive, yet we take their obedience for granted. A classic example that Nepalese diplomats have quoted for long is the case of a small hydel dam built on Indo-Nepal border in the early 1950s. When completed, the Nepalese found to their disbelief that their lands were flooded with the reservoir waters of the dam, whereas all the electricity produced by it was being transmitted to India. The sense that the big brother had cheated persisted, with the result that the bigger hydel projects that could have benefitted Nepal immensely were never allowed to be taken up, because the Indian word was not trusted.

A second round of India's intrusive activism in Nepal started around 2003 when the feeling began to gain ground in Kathmandu that India wanted monarchy to be abolished. This was followed by the move to mainstream the Maoists, and the support that the common Nepalese felt India was giving to the Madhesis. Ever since, there have been a series of missteps. Even an otherwise honourable and commendable effort like earthquake relief in 2015 was marred midway through by the pushy behaviour of some media personnel. It was followed a few months later in September 2015 by the economic and humanitarian goods blockade of Nepal by India, which included the stoppage of the supply of cooking gas cylinders. This measure directly affected people, and their resentment did not lessen for long after the blockade was lifted.

This sense of resentment against India is increasing at a time when South Asia is at an inflection point. Currently, both the nature and dynamics of its geopolitics is undergoing a change, slowly but surely. Consequently, the regional picture for a future Indian leader may be more troubled than reassuring. In the great power competition that is developing in the region, the US is now caught between its reluctance to part with its fading glory and an unwillingness to do what it takes to maintain its influence. It recoils instinctively when challenged by China and Russia in the region. But its pushback often leads to confused policies and mistaken decisions.

The Trump administration's desire to leave a lighter footprint in the world raises the very real possibility of scaled-down US engagement in this part of Asia. This could be both good and bad, depending on the perspective that the issue is viewed from. A downscaling of America here would strengthen China in a big way and constrain the regional security cooperation that New Delhi might have wished for.

Further, China's recent interest in expanding its naval presence in the Indian Ocean has added one more factor of strategic uncertainty to the area. Its string of pearls around India is not meant to strangle Japan or the US. It is largely aimed at containing India. A warning by Winston Churchill in the British House of Commons in March 1914 in the context of German naval expansion should apply equally to the situation that India is in now: 'They build navies so as to play a part in the world's affairs. It is sport to them. It is life and death to us.' China's hectic build-up of bases around the Indian Ocean could be, as Churchill said in a different context, a matter of life and death for India. If that is so, and assuming that neither the US nor Russia are going to be India's treaty friends in the manner that the Soviet Union was in 1971, then India will pretty much be on its own if, as in 1962, it finds itself in the deep end.

Sitting in the middle of this landmass, India is surrounded by unstable democracies and countries with which it has acrimonious relations. On its part, India has so far nurtured a strong democracy, a fact that helps maintain domestic stability. It is in India's interest to sustain it and encourage others in the region to follow its example.

That, of course, is the tricky part, because example alone is not sufficient to promote democracy in other countries. Nor is the hard power of military intervention a wise idea always. In considering such an option in future, India will do well to be wary after its disastrous military intervention Sri Lanka in the 1980s.

Among the threats that the Indian leader would have to guard against will be Pakistan and China's policies that aim to derogate India's domestic stability and its territorial integrity. Ironically, it could also get affected by the turbulence within these two countries. Their domestic turmoil, the

Baloch and Pashtun angst in Pakistan and the tensions in Tibet, Hong Kong and Xinjiang in China, will keep them suspicious and on edge and India wary.

Add to this mix, the trust deficit, or rather the scope for additional misunderstanding, which exists in varying degrees between China, India and Pakistan, besides the US, Russia and Iran. In this jostling, South Asia is at the cusp of a power transition that might prove to be destabilizing. India may also have to live with the emerging geopolitical reality that it will no longer dominate its neighbourhood. Its 'sphere of influence' in South Asia will now have to contend with the shadow of China's influence. At any rate, playing favourites in the domestic politics of neighbours is a blunt instrument, prone to failure. Therefore, it should only be employed as a last resort; and if employed, it cannot be seen to fail.

In this generally uncertain period, a future Indian leader would often need to reflect on India's past to carve the path ahead; sometimes just to ensure that history does not repeat itself. It is true that India's past is encrusted with history and legend. But it is equally true that if some countries are uncertain about their future, India is unsure about its past and future as well.

As an Indian leader, at a future date, wrestles with these issues, he would need to keep reminding himself of the core concerns, because the principal aim of 'foreign policy' is to protect and promote a nation's vital interests. To that extent, foreign policy cannot be rigid—it should evolve and adapt to the circumstances as they change.

It is particularly so in this age, because the international environment is dynamic and the instabilities are becoming acute. Yet the potential disruption, marked by the structural changes in great power relations and the global economic order, presents strategic opportunities as well.

TREADING CAREFULLY WITH IRAN AND RUSSIA

There may not actually be a law ordained by nature that world orders should collapse periodically. Yet it happens regularly, and when they crumble, it is often unexpected and violent. The late eighteenth century was the high point of the Enlightenment in Europe, before the continent suddenly fell into the abyss of the Napoleonic Wars. Later, World War II violently shook up the world and the empire that Hitler had nearly amassed. In quite a different manner, the collapse of the Soviet Union, while not violent, was cataclysmic in scope.

Russia is no longer the wreck it was in the 1990s, but it is still a pale shadow of the former Soviet Union. Its economy was not expected to transform magically in a generation. But the snail pace of change is far below even modest expectations. Between 1992 and 2016, the real compound annual growth rate of Russian per capita GDP has been 1.5 per cent. In contrast, India (5.1 per cent) and China (8.9 per cent) have performed far better during this period.

Over the past 10 years, Russia has increased its defence cooperation in Asia. But old stereotypes of Asia as inferior still dominate Russia's views and influence its traditional policy of regarding Asia as an adjunct or counterbalance to the West. The Russian political elite's West–centric worldview was to blame for this imbalance.

For the moment, however, Russia is keen on countering the US and cutting into its sphere of influence in Asia. In this scheme of things, India should have received special attention in Putin's plans, and he did try initially. Up to about 2005, he was attentive to India's concerns regarding both China and Pakistan. He made it a point to stay at least three days when it was his turn to visit India for the annual summit between the two leaders. Gradually, the relationship began to show signs of wear; its visible indicator was the cutting down of Putin's interest in the annual Indo-Russian summits and the length of his stay in India. The summit meetings started to give the appearance of an unavoidable formality. In part, this could have been a Russian reaction to India's wholehearted embrace of the US. A piqued Russia felt that the historic relationship that it had invested so much in no longer held great charm for the new India.

It did not take long for Russia to make its feelings public. Zamir Kabulov, Putin's special envoy for Afghanistan, said, 'Pakistan is a key regional player.'[14] There is nothing alarming as such about this statement, because others too, including the US, have repeated this mantra over and over again to propitiate Pakistan. But for a Russian diplomat, he went ahead surprisingly by adding, 'a key regional player that other countries should negotiate with.'[15]

This was unusual. At the Heart of Asia conference in December 2016, in Amritsar, Kabulov was even more direct and said Russia understands 'India's concerns but we cannot win the war on terror without Pakistan's support.'

The wheel had turned a full circle. Prior to 9/11, Russia was an active partner of the Northern Alliance with Iran and India, because it wanted to defeat the terror threat that the Taliban, with ISI's support, was posing to the Central Asian states. Yet the same Russia was now consorting with Pakistan and urging others to do so. This, despite the fact that once it consolidates its hold over Kabul, the Taliban could again pose a threat to the Central Asian states.

Add to this the fact that the US wants to lock India in as its exclusive arms client, regardless of India's compulsion in keeping its Russian line open. So, if it was possible earlier to seamlessly buy advanced military aircraft from America and air-defence missiles from Russia, that's not the case any longer. Now the purchase of S-400 missiles from Moscow invites the threat of sanctions from Washington. While that may suit the US, can India afford to cut off or even reduce its links with Russia? As it is, India's neglect has soured this important relationship that had provided considerable strategic comfort in the past. Moreover, if an aggressive China turns unfriendly, India's neighbourhood and near neighbourhood could turn into a nightmare. In that event, a simple nudge from Russia for restraint on China might work more effectively than American bluster.

India's other partner in the now-defunct Northern Alliance, Iran, is in the odd position of being stable in an unstable region. But its stability is balanced on a razor's edge. There are potent forces constantly testing its ability to stay coherent. A prime example is the ideological struggle it has been engaged in with its Arab neighbours, especially Saudi Arabia.

Saudi Arabia is following a perilous course under its whimsical crown prince. It has lit far too many fires within and outside. There is long suppressed discontent within the country and there are the setbacks it has received to its prestige abroad. A widely criticized war it waged against Yemen was a military disaster that can only be recalled for its bombing of the civilian population. Nor could it browbeat the tiny Qatar. And the crown prince's reputation, muddy as it already was for imprisoning in quick succession the business leaders of Saudi Arabia and then the visiting Prime Minister of Lebanon, nosedived to universal revulsion after the assassination of the journalist Jamal Khashoggi.

Yet, Saudi Arabia may continue flexing its regional muscle and pursuing a confrontational course with Iran out of the fear that the Shia state might consolidate the strategic gains it has made in Lebanon, Syria and Iraq. And that Iran's next step could be to incite further the Shia populations of the Gulf States. This possibility contains the potential for conflict because both Saudi Arabia and Iran are rigidly religious states and firm in their conviction that the other is not in an accommodative frame.

The American friction with Iran and the bitterness between Saudi Arabia and Iran could lead to violence in the region, as also in the West. When it happens at some future date, the Indian prime minister of the time would have to tread carefully, because our interests demand friendship with all three.

TANGLED LINES WITH THE US

India's strong bonds with Russia, its relationship with Iran, and its reluctance to endorse the intervention by foreign powers in Syria are examples where India's strategic interests and those of the US do not coincide. Though they do not always use the same prism, as the two largest democracies, they share a similar worldview on many issues. However, India is not a formal American ally, and that is how the relationship is likely to remain. If the experience of the former American allies around the world is any guide, it is a fickle, temperamental and petulant partner; forever demanding and expecting others to accept its foreign policy choices. But its policy choices, often driven by its domestic compulsions, are not the ones that its allies and friends would normally opt for.

Moreover, America is increasingly cramped by its systemic issues. Nearly three decades of largely puerile military interventions have increasingly weaponized its economic policies, variously sanctioning individuals, entities, governments and countries. Its partners are expected to fall in line with the US's decisions. It expects this compliance either on account of the support these countries may have received or may need, or in light of cost-benefit analysis, factoring in the deeper linkages with the US economy and society—or simply because these countries are unable to resist the US. This invariably results in strategic, political and economic costs to others.

It knows all this, yet India will find it difficult to resist a fresh American demand. Apart from the so-called strategic reasons, there are sound economic needs too. In global terms, India has for long posted a trade deficit, but its trade with the US represents an exceptional bright spot in India's favour. India has a nearly $25 billion surplus with it. At $140 billion exchange in 2018, it was India's largest trading partner in goods and services. The bulk of our global IT services exports go to it. Another important aspect is the population of nearly 4 million Indian- origin people settled there, making them the single largest Indian group anywhere outside the country. At any given time, almost 200,000 Indian students are attending its universities. Then there is the increasing investment interest both ways: American companies have invested around $28 billion in India, while Indian companies have invested around $18 billion in the US, especially over the past decade.

The defence orders by India are now a major new factor in the relationship. Indian orders for American defence equipment have risen from close to zero in 2008 to $18 billion now. This is significant because India is the single largest weapons importer in the world. The US realizes this, and it is also conscious that India can offer a continuing and long-term large market for its military products.

Though America is no longer the sole superpower it once was, its swagger has not reduced, nor has the list of its unreasonable demands. What is worse still is the fact that it does so at a time when it has lost its technological edge. Two separate recent events exemplify this. The first was the crash of a Boeing 737 Max plane in Ethiopia. The second was the downing, by Iran, of a US air force drone that had been considered invincible.

Besides these practical issues, there is growing concern internationally about the policy direction that America is taking. The war that Trump wants to end in Afghanistan, and the one that he wants to begin with Iran, both have major implications for India. Therefore, the Indian euphoria surrounding Trump's episodic tweets against Pakistan needs to be tempered down. Or to take another example, even as the US was campaigning to have Masood Azhar designated as a global terrorist, it was also seeking Pakistan's help to persuade the Taliban for a deal in Afghanistan. In a final show of his unpredictability, Trump felt it necessary to woo the visiting Imran Khan on Afghanistan by offering to mediate on the Kashmir issue.

This is illustrative of the tangled lines in today's world. As further proof of the crossed wires, consider this: Both China and the US have strategic partnership agreements with India. Can these agreements really be taken seriously?

It is not just with these two that India has signed agreements that in a classical sense, imply a defence and security relationship—just a little short of an alliance. Actually, India has promiscuously signed strategic partnership agreements with close to 40 countries, leaving people to wonder if the mystique of that bond has been blown away. They also question whether a country that had, till recently, professed non-alignment should be aligning itself strategically with so many countries.

Further, India is also apprehensive about the US moves in Afghanistan. If the US could so easily cast aside a policy it had fought for over the last 19 years, then a relationship with prickly and self-respecting India may not bind it for long.

INDIA'S MARCH TO GREATNESS

If the broader regional situation will demand his attention, the global developments will not give tomorrow's Indian leader any comfort either. The assurance that the world is in safe hands economically has lasted long enough. But a series of missteps have contributed to the present stage of doubt. One of them was the faith that globalization is here to stay. Like the ancient sages of India, Western economic wizards truly believed that 'the world is a family'. But this was the case as long as it suited their MNCs. Ever since that monopoly has been challenged by China, the Western advocacy in favour of globalization has become muted.

The shift away from globalization will not be limited to a change in economic philosophy. Had that been so, it could have been managed by new explanations and a different terminology. Alas, the effect would be wider, affecting the post-war fundamentals that had sustained the global economy so far. There are already signs that the turbulence is affecting the economic landscape. Argentina is in crisis; Pakistan finds itself without willing lenders. Markets are nervous in Indonesia, Myanmar, Italy and

Spain as financial conditions tighten. The trade war between the US and China continues to escalate and the fallout from Brexit is uncertain.

This combination of ill tidings is grim. Despite this early warning, the global financial safety net is not prepared for the next crisis, nor does it have sufficient financial resources to provide short-term liquidity. If the 2008 economic crisis was the result of overconfidence in free markets, the next might be triggered by the behaviour of an authoritarian leader; for example a leader like Erdogan of Turkey, whose presidency has knocked down an economy that was otherwise on an upward path. Or it could be a temperamental leader like Trump.

An Indian prime minister may, therefore, face the formidable task of weathering uncertain economic tides besides having to deal with some other emerging trends. The first is the declining will of the democratic world, led by the US, to maintain the dominant position it has held in the international system since 1945. In contrast, there is the activism of the two revisionist powers, Russia and China. Both of these feel threatened by the domination of democratic powers in the international system and consider the US as the principal obstacle to their ambitions. Increasingly, China views India as an adjunct to America's strategic calculus against it. Therefore, as it seeks to weaken the America-led international security order, it will consider checking India as well. This could happen on the heights of the mountains that they share, or in the waters around India. Going by the evidence of the build-up of its navy in the Indian Ocean and the rapid establishment of military bases around it, China is giving strategic priority to these waters as never before. And for good reasons too.

Annually, nearly $500 billion worth of trade passes through the Straits of Hormuz. The value of commerce flowing through the Malacca Straits every year is more than $3 trillion. So far, the safe passage of ships through these waters has been taken for granted. Even now there is no perceptible and immediate threat to shipping, but there is the apprehension that if the strategic situation in either of the two regions worsens and things get rough, then maritime traffic would be an easy target. In that event, even if India is not involved in a conflict, its shipping interests could get impacted by a misdirected hit from one of the combatants.

Since the US has become self-sufficient in its energy requirements, it is no longer energy-dependent on the oil supplies from Gulf. It is therefore pressing other countries that source their oil and gas from the gulf region, that they should do more to secure their supplies. This is not a new responsibility for India; it has successfully performed that role with other countries in the anti-piracy operations. But what would be new is the type of challenges this US demand throws up. India's stakes in the region are not just energy-dependent. The safety of its large NRI population based in the Gulf States is also a major responsibility in case of a war.

Clearly then, there are important reasons for India to undertake a protective role for its interests in the region and for the security of its energy supplies. But this carries major risks. In case hostilities break out and Indian shipping comes under attack, would India get involved in the fighting? By already committing two warships on patrol duty, India may have taken the first step in that uncertain direction.

Is India prepared for the consequences that could follow? Will a future prime minister order his navy to battle in the Gulf or, for that matter, in the South China Sea? Both of these are beyond the region that India has so far chosen to confine itself to. So what has changed? Is India already a major power?

Much as we would like to assert that yes, we are indeed a major power already, India is still many essentials short of it. It has just enough power to stand up to the influence of others in the region. But to say that it is a match for China at the global stage, or even in the near neighbourhood, would be stretching imagination. It still has many miles to go economically, and many gaps to fill strategically, before it can claim that it has enough ballast to effectively check and influence others.

As of now, India has the capabilities of a limited hegemon at the subcontinental level. Even there, the nature of its limited hegemony changed after the 1990s, from a relatively aggressive to a relatively benign role in the region. It has far more limited autonomous capabilities at the global level. But it has received encouragement and support as a player with potential from the US. It has been nudged to play a larger role in international affairs, particularly in the anti-piracy operations in the Indian Ocean and in the freedom of navigation in the South-China Sea. It has also been asked to put boots on ground in Afghanistan. But given its systemic shortfalls, it is neither expected, nor likely, to play the role of a major stabilizer should cataclysmic tensions appear in world affairs.

A country that aspires to become a stabilizer on a global scale should have the means to do so. Otherwise, those that try to punch above their weight end up as an economic mess. Alas, India is, as yet, far short of that essential muscle. Let us consider the economic and defence sides of it briefly.

If the struggle with China were only to be about the relative power of the Indian and the Chinese economies, India has long since lost that race. In 1980, India's GDP ($184 billion) was almost equal to China's ($191 billion). Since then, China has steadily outpaced India, reaching $14 trillion to India's $2.9 trillion in 2018.

Let's view this from a practical side too. In the two-year period between 2011 and 2013, China had produced and consumed more cement than America did in the entire twentieth century. By 2015, there were more billionaires in China than in the USA. Now it is adding a new billionaire to that list every week. A 2015 RAND Corporation study titled *The US-China Military Scorecard* says that over the next five to 15 years, 'Asia will witness a progressively receding frontier of US dominance.' Wherever the US recedes, China would want to fill the vacuum. India's capacity to respond to this explosive growth and revolutionary change is limited. It is the same story in defence; China is now competing with the US while India struggles to keep pace with Pakistan.

But the threat for India may be much greater than the economic race or a better gun. India sits next door as the first impediment to be overcome in China's march to greatness. Therefore, Indian and Chinese military readiness would deeply influence their strategic moves, or the lack of them.

In 2018, China spent nearly $177.5 billion for its defence forces, and this figure is set to increase further. In contrast, India had kept aside a much smaller $43.4 billion. While China does not face a clear and present danger, India cannot afford to relax its vigil, because of China and Pakistan. Even if India remains content with the lines as they are drawn presently on the ground, neither China nor Pakistan will be satisfied with the permanence of this condition. India may not want to start a conflict or a war; the same cannot be said of its rivals. A continuing challenge in the coming years would be the fact that India has two nuclear weapon states as hostile neighbours—China and Pakistan—and one would-be nuclear weapon state, Iran, in its near neighbourhood. Pakistan, in particular, has been hurling, rather cavalierly, nuclear challenges at India.

It is not just the direct nuclear threat that worries India; it also remains alert to the possibility of proliferation of nuclear weapons and technologies. China has been providing technology to Pakistan and helping it develop the nuclear arsenal in all its variety, besides a powerful delivery system. Pakistan itself has disseminated technology and materials to countries like Iran, North Korea and Libya. Moreover, there is the constant fear that a terrorist group might somehow get hold of one of Pakistan's nuclear weapons. These imponderables are daunting.

Yet two-thirds of India's defence budget is spent on salaries and routine maintenance. That leaves very little in the kitty for essentials like the upgradation of equipment. Consequently, the Army's spending on modernization is just about 14 per cent of its budget. India cannot keep its defence on a minimum budget and hope to ward off security threats through individual valour and collective prayers.

A criticism often levied against India is that despite its large-scale imports, it is arming without aiming. It may be an unduly harsh charge, but there is some basis to it, because when you are largely import-dependent for vital defence needs, then your options get restricted by what is on offer and the sales pressure by the other side.

Yet another criticism concerns the emphasis on equipping the forces largely for a conventional war. There is no denying the fact that wars will be fought as they have always been, but the new element that might increasingly come into play is the unconventional side of it. Tomorrow's India needs to pay greater attention to developing these capabilities, because without actually going to war, its adversaries could dent India's security through cyberattacks on power plants, energy pipelines and water supplies. It is only after optimally equipping the country for both a conventional and an unconventional war that a future Indian leader should think of the ways to exercise the power he or she has accumulated.

Responsibly and effectively exercised, power is one's ability to influence the behaviour of others to get what one wants. India has itself witnessed both sides of this; it had successfully engineered the outcome in the Bangladesh war and it retreated in disappointment from Sri Lanka, unable to influence the course of events there. But the larger question remains—is India prepared to battle by itself? Will a future Indian leader have the reassurance of the type Field Marshal Manekshaw gave to Indira Gandhi that the Indian armed forces will prevail in a conflict? The response of the army chief this next time could be iffy. Considering the state of its armaments, India seems to have forgotten the Roman injunction, 'If you want peace, prepare for war.'

In contrast, if China needs to fight, Xi is determined to win it. In that event, Chinese promises are irrelevant—what should worry the Indian leader are its capabilities.

The dilemma then, for an Indian prime minister in the coming years, will not be a Hamlet-like quandary but the possibility that the choice may already have been made for him by others. After all, increasingly diplomacy is under the gun. Defence ministries may still not be setting the foreign policy agenda, but they are, through their actions, often moulding the shape and direction of it.

Despite knowing that conflict will be inevitable at some stage, India's preparation for it so far has been piecemeal and lethargic. The root of the problem is India's reluctance to fully come to grips with the reality that its principal competitor is one of two great powers with extremely advanced military forces.

There is also the cardinal principle of war—that you don't start one unless you are sure you can end it by being better off. This is often cited as a major reason for India's restraint. The knowledge that any military action would not achieve the political objective of stopping cross-border terrorism has been cramping India's decision to punish Pakistan. Its dilemma was also influenced by the possibility that even if it were to inflict punishment, it may not be able to extract total compliance through a limited war. In that case, the gains it makes may not have a decisive edge. That's why India had, by and large, avoided using the option of hot pursuit or punitive air strikes, opting instead to follow a policy of strategic patience with Pakistan. This meant using no force but also offering no concessions. Simultaneously, it involved working with other countries to restrain Pakistan.

The hope that Pakistan would behave like a more responsible nation didn't work. To that extent, 'strategic patience' as a policy has been a failure. The Indian air strike in February 2019 on the terror training camp in Balakot signalled the end of that patience. It also meant that at long last, India had set itself free from the fear of consequences.

While that is a welcome change, it does not necessarily follow that the strike fully achieved its objective or that Pakistan has changed its behaviour. Resisting the Indian threat has been a cornerstone of Pakistan's military strategy ever since 1971. And China has enthusiastically built up Pakistan's capacities to be able do so. Within hours of serious hostilities breaking out, Pakistan could kill millions if, for example, it chooses to use the sarin gas.

If there is another war in the region, the costs would be radically higher than in the ones India had fought in the past, because this time the enemy will reach beyond the infantry lines to hit at the country's infrastructure. It is also possible that the next war might last longer. According to a 2016 study conducted by the RAND Corporation, just one year of an intense war without use of nuclear weapons could set back the American GDP by 10 per cent and the Chinese GDP by nearly 35 per cent. No such study is available for a war between India and China, or for that matter with Pakistan. It is, however, safe to say that going by the previous experience, neither war is likely to carry on for a full year. Still, even a short-duration war will significantly bleed India economically and in terms of combatants.

Regardless of the costs, a future leader must factor in the possibility of a war into India's strategic calculus because that is the necessary price a country must be prepared to pay for its integrity. As Adam Smith argues in *The Wealth of Nations*, 'Defence is of much more importance than opulence.'

But there is one area where China and Pakistan struggle to compete with India, and that is the battle of ideas. An autocracy like China and a military-ruled state like Pakistan are apprehensive of the Indian model of personal and political freedom, human rights and the rule-of-law. They spend a lot of time and energy repressing people and organizations that are attracted to democratic ideas. Alas, India is on the verge of losing this advantage too.

Therefore, the challenges that India is likely to face in future are going to be more complicated and complex than the ones it has faced so far. It is true that India has passed through difficult times in the past as well; from the trauma of Partition to a sputtering economy, from food shortages to terrorism and wars, to name just a few. But the future holds grimmer tests of a fatal kind in the form of a risen and restless China and a vengeful Pakistan. This will be compounded internally by acute water scarcity, a rising population, a stagnant economy and a crisis-prone security situation both inside the country and at its borders.

As in the past, the worries for India's future leader will mainly be from its west. And they will be Pakistan-centric, because it has too many ethnic, political and economic challenges of a fundamental, structural nature, which are bound to have an impact on its relations with India. If the Indian leadership of tomorrow chooses to follow the same path as before, it would keep repeating futilely the same old exercise of advancing one step to quickly take two steps back. This frustration would not just be limited to Kashmir or the issue of terrorism, but on the increasingly vital issue of water as well.

Close to 22 per cent of the world's population resides in South Asia, but it must make do with just about 8.3 per cent of the global water resources. Within South Asia, India faces the grimmest prospects, and its water woes are deepening steadily. The world's second most rapid rate of groundwater depletion, after the Arabian Peninsula, is in the Punjab-Haryana-Rajasthan belt.

A future Indian leader would be confronted by this water misery every time he peeps over Delhi to look at its neighbouring cities. Each time he does so, he will also be tempted to compare it with the water availability in Pakistan.

Pakistan has the luxury of water riches. A World Bank report, *Pakistan: Getting More from Water*, points out that Pakistan's per person water availability is 1,100 cubic meters. But it does not make the best use of its available water. It has poor water resource management and poor water service delivery. India watches ruefully as Pakistan wastes water. It could have done a lot to protect and promote its interests, as it has a unique riparian status as the upper, middle and lower riparian. It may not be very much off the mark to say that India has suffered in all three roles; it is the world's most generous upper riparian, it has been more than accommodative as a middle riparian and its interests have not been kept paramount as a lower riparian.

Considering the very grave water crisis facing India, it must reconsider its adherence to the Indus Waters Treaty. But till it picks up the courage to do so, it should at the very least make arrangements to draw to the full its share of waters.

Both the Kashmir issue and the Indus Treaty have been exploited to the fullest extent by Pakistan. These perennials will continue to baffle the Indian policymakers in the coming years too. Yet, even in their frustration, the Indian leaders of the future are likely to keep reminding themselves of the formula followed by generations of Indian leaders, that their actions should not rock any further the precariously balanced Indo-Pak boat. This caution has not been to India's advantage in the last seven decades, and it is unlikely to benefit India in future. If anything, the situation around India is likely to worsen.

If Pakistan were to have a charismatic leader, genuinely interested in course correction, it might still have a chance of stumbling along. But that rare leader is unlikely to be found there. Instead, it may gradually start eroding. This may take time and it might happen only in bits, but unless there is a major course correction by Pakistan's army and it decides to withdraw into its barracks, the break-up is likely.

Should India be concerned if Pakistan begins to dissipate?

It will, and should, naturally be concerned, both because of the accident of history and its contiguity. At a practical level, there could be large-scale migration into India if there is a major turbulence in Pakistan. But India will not be able to change the course of events, because if people are set on a path, they will have their way. A restless and discriminated Pakistani province will carry on along the road of protest if it feels alienated, as Balochistan and Khyber Pakhtunkhwa (KPK) already do. It is around a crumbling Pakistan that Robert Kaplan sees the contest in future between India and China:

...the political map may evolve over time: Pakistan can partially crumble into a rump-Greater Punjab with Baluchistan and Sind gaining de facto independence, with vast implications for India. And it is the Indian subcontinent that I am talking about: Since parts of

Afghanistan were incorporated into various Indian imperial dynasties, governments in New Delhi always have considered Afghanistan in conceptual terms as part of a Greater India, stretching from the Iranian Plateau in the west to the Burmese jungles in the east. Whereas China seeks to expand vertically south to the Indian Ocean, India seeks to expand horizontally along or close to the Indian Ocean, with a growing influence in the Persian Gulf. Therein lies the contest between these two faded empires.[16]

In a future contest between India and China, the 'two faded empires' as Kaplan terms them, Pakistan undoubtedly would side with China. Even in case of a conflict between Pakistan and India, the third party supporting Pakistan openly or behind the scenes would be China. In such a case, the weaker side would be subject to the stronger, and innovation will be the key to a favourable outcome. India still has the time to make up on both these accounts, but that time is finite and it is running out fast. Meanwhile, China is innovating and arming itself at a furious pace with a bewildering range of the latest in technology. Even if there are innumerable voices in the world wishing India speed in this looming contest, India's inability frustrates them. As Lee Kuan Yew wrote:

> Together with other democratic socialists of 1950s, I had wondered whether India or China would become the model for development. I wanted democratic India, not communist China, to win. But despite achievements such as the green revolution, population growth has kept down India's standard of living and quality of life.[17]

Lee Kuan Yew had wanted this in the 1950s. It was a part of his and almost everyone else's wishful thinking that in a contest between democracy and communism, democracy should prevail. Since then, the ideological lines have blurred. China is no longer the rigid communist state that it once was. It may still not be in the most likeable category of countries, but it is no longer the untouchable it was.

There have been material changes as well. Between 1820 and 1950, the per capita income of India and China was largely flat. From 1950 to 1973, it increased by 68 per cent. Then between 1973 and 2002, it grew by 245 per cent. As they prospered, their ambitions needed a wider footprint. Gradually, it became evident that the existing model of global business and trade was flawed. China took full advantage of that opening.

It is not just China and India that have changed; the world too has undergone many transformations. In this phase, and in the one that is coming, the US will watch exhaustedly as the world goes by. It will take a major effort on the part of the US to stand by India's side in any confrontation that it may be forced into with either of its big neighbours.

There are other developments, however, which could be opportunities if handled with care. The China-US contention, in particular, creates space for middle powers like India to pursue their interests in the region. As they seek partners in their confrontation, this should make both China and the US more attentive to these middle powers. The point of concern is whether India can convert this improved attention into substantive gains for itself.

India is not a stranger to a geo-political situation of this nature. In the 1960s, as India began to deal with the complexities of its strategic environment, the temptations of alignment kept intruding into its policy calculus. At first, it was a desperate appeal for help to the US in the middle of the Chinese invasion of 1962. Then, anticipating conflict with Pakistan in 1971, India signed a treaty with the Soviet Union. Euphemistically called the Treaty of Peace, Friendship and Co-operation, the terminology didn't fool people into believing that India continued to be equidistant from both blocs. So if the circumstances necessitate, India can manoeuver its way through its principles to a pragmatic path.

DILEMMAS OF A FUTURE PRIME MINISTER

If the neighbourhood and the international scene do not promise great tidings for a future Indian leader, is there enough chutzpah in our DNA to claw our way out of a difficult situation? Or does our DNA lack the killer instinct? Though convenient, it will be a fallacy to shrug off the blame for wrong policy choices by passing it onto flawed DNA. After all, Pakistan supposedly shares our DNA, and our administrative abilities were inherited in equal measure from the British example.

Among the many legacies that the British left behind were its bureaucratic practices. Both India and Pakistan followed them virtually to a tee, so much so that long after the British departed, it was difficult to distinguish between the laws and administrative forms of the two countries. The same practices were more or less followed in their respective armies and foreign offices. Yet, this is where the similarity ends.

The British were aggressive in pursuing their military and foreign policy. They did not hesitate in employing force, deception and diplomacy to achieve their ends. Pakistan has learnt that lesson well, and more or less followed that tradition. Its annexation of Gilgit-Baltistan was as audacious as it was illegal. Yet, 70 years later, if you were to ask a hundred Indians where exactly these two lie, not even one among them would be able to come up with the right geographical response.

The fact is that though some claim mistakenly that India and Pakistan were born of the same womb, it is a gross fallacy. Our DNA could not be more different. We are diffident, and we are shy of scenes. Pakistan is aggressive and shouts to drown out the rival voices.

Modi has done some course correction in this respect. But much more needs to be done, and not just in relation to Pakistan and China. The world itself will become a much more unpredictable place in the years to come. A prime minister at some future date will be confronted with a bewildering milieu where dangers lurk all around—on land, at sea, in air and in cyberspace as well. Modi and his successors may not have the ideal set of options available with them, but this is all that they will have.

A second qualification must be added to this, and that relates to the ability, or lack of it, of the leader. It is worthwhile to remember that no leader is perfect. Some maintain vehemently that a president or prime minister need not be too smart. As creatures of flesh and blood, they too are prone to error, anger and misjudgement like any other person. In their case, the chance of making a wrong decision or a less than appropriate choice increases, because of the sheer number of decisions that they are required to make. It is also a fact that a leader is in a constant struggle between the rules of political accountability and the law of unintended consequences. Henry Kissinger was referring to such agonies of high office when he wrote:

High office often involves harassment, frustrations, petty calculations. Rather than the dramatic peaks of the public imagination it usually means an accumulation of seemingly endless pressures and tensions in which every apparent solution appears to be only a ticket to a new set of problems. The character of leaders is tested by their willingness to persevere in the face of uncertainty and to build for a future they can neither demonstrate nor fully discern.[18]

This applies even more to the leader of 1.3 billion people who are still not out of the woods. Another daily reminder a future leader should whisper to himself is this: 'One great message of history is that a leader must avoid the illusion of his infallibility'. Alas, this sense of infallibility is precisely what happens when a leader accumulates enormous power. So, among other things, a future Indian leader must know when his time at the top is up and he should bow out.

It is with all this as background that a future Indian prime minister may have to put his thinking cap on as he arrives every morning in office. Let us assume this morning to be in 2030. India may have become the world's most populated country by then, and climbed up to the third spot in terms of GDP. At last, India may also have become a major power, adding that much to the leader's everyday worries. He will need to constantly tell himself that a great power always has a lot to fret about. He might begin the day by reminding himself of Clinton's words to the Indian parliament: 'Time and again in my time as President, America has found that it is the weakness of great nations, not their strength, that threatens their vision for tomorrow.'

He will also have to keep in view the fact that the modern world is shaped by the wild oscillation between the hunger for modernization and the determinism of nationalism. Both foreclose any real debate and both are inimical to genuine democracy. One licences domineering technocracy; the other, cruder forms of authoritarianism. The dilemma for the leader would be—should he let India go with the drift and follow one or the other? Or should he steer India towards the middle path, as it has usually done?

Among the many major issues that will confront him on a daily basis will be some that are reminders of his responsibility, and a few others that pose fresh challenges. Pakistan will continue to preoccupy an Indian prime minister, but India's principal challenge will be China, and the risks of getting it wrong are enormous. There were occasions in the past when a boundary settlement could have been reached with China. But it kept getting postponed. The issue will continue to linger, keeping the relations lukewarm.

Among other changes from now, there could be a dilution in the China-Pakistan equation. Where its interests are concerned, China has shown that if it comes to deal-making and tackling international pressure, the Pakistan card is negotiable. For Pakistan, too, China is not a costless option. Sooner rather than later, China will demand its pound of flesh. Some of it is already in evidence due to the Shylockian commercial terms of the CPEC. Consequently, their relations are already showing signs of strain. It will remain the Indian leader's challenge to see whether these strains can be deepened.

On the broader scale, both the US and China see India as 'a swing power'. Both are wary that India's shift to the other would decisively shift the global power balance that way. In this background, and at long last, the US administration may realize that its strategic interests lie with India, which has actually become the state that US dollars had tried to create in Pakistan.

But India is too proud to be tied to American coattails, and prudence demands that India should not become an ally. Moreover, in this increasingly sensitive age, India is geographically too close to China to ally with its greatest competitor. Since China has a phobia that America will sooner or later try to contain it, it will not be in India's interest to be seen openly siding with the US. However, India's demographic, economic and military strength, and its location dominating the Indian Ocean, is by itself a counterpoise to China. Therein lies the quandary for the future Indian prime minister.

Troubles might come in unexpected ways too. The cultural purity that India seeks in the face of the influx of immigrants from Bangladesh is simply impossible in a world of increasing human interaction. So the dilemma, both moral and practical, for a future Indian prime minister would be: Should the migrants be pushed back into an unwilling Bangladesh or must they remain in detention camps? Both are unpleasant options and both spell long-lasting political problems for India.

A similar dilemma may face him in case the civic disturbances in a Pakistani province lead to mass migration into India. Should he then put up a board on the border saying 'No Entry', or allow them in and risk another confrontation with Pakistan? To make the picture more complex, add to all this the possibility that within India, its secular fabric might show strains.

As the reach of cyber information becomes all-pervasive, and governments become regular participants in influencing the behaviour of other people, India will need to match the well-directed and well-crafted psy-war and fake news capabilities of other countries. If it does not match up to them and their latest, it will have to suffer the consequences of a campaign that could psychologically degrade India and exploit its fault-lines, vulnerabilities and insecurities.

Hybrid warfare is another challenge that a future Indian leader would struggle to understand as a matter of daily routine. These multi-layered conflicts combine conventional military force with non-state actors, making them difficult to tackle. It might become doubly so in future, posing a continuing challenge for India.

As this future leader settles down with a sigh into the prime ministerial chair, he allows himself a fleeting thought: Will this timeless country ever change?

He lets the cup of tea go cold as his attention is caught by the flash on one of the many computer screens on his table. As over the last seven decades and more, the news that has just flashed on the screen is about a major infiltration attempt. He leans back into his chair, smiles sardonically, and whispers to himself, '*Plus ça change, plus c'est la même chose* (the more it changes the more it remains the same).'

If a wise advisor happens to be in the room at this moment, he might be heard repeating softly Mahatma Gandhi's words, 'Be the change that you wish to see in the world.'

NOTES

PROLOGUE: AN INDEPENDENT PATH IN THE WORLD

1 *Public Papers of the Presidents of the United States: William J. Clinton*, United States Government Printing, 1 February 1999

2 'China to mark emergence as leader of Third World', *The New York Times*, 9 April 2005

3 *World Order*, Henry Kissinger, Penguin, 2015

4 Madhumita Das; 'Continuity and Change in India's Early Tibet Policy: 1905-1960'; *South Asia Chronicle*, 2019; https://edoc.hu-berlin.de/bitstream/handle/18452/20495/07%20-%20Forum%20-%20Das%2c%20Madhumita%20-%20Continuity%20and%20Change%20in%20India%e2%80%99s%20Early%20Tibet%20Policy.%201947%20to%201960.pdf?sequence=1&isAllowed=y

5 US Department of State, Diplomacy in action, Archived content, Former Secretary Clinton's remarks

6 'How Sharp Power Threatens Soft Power: The Right and Wrong Ways to Respond to Authoritarian Influence', Joseph S. Nye Jr., *Foreign Affairs*, 24 January 2018

7 '*Memento homo, quia pulvis es, et in pulverem reverteris* (Remember, man, that you are dust. And unto dust you shall return).'

8 This excludes Gulzari Lal Nanda, who was twice the interim prime minister for a few days each.

9 Becky Little; 'JFK was completely unprepared for his summit with Khrushchev'; History Stories; 13 July 2018; https://www.history.com/news/kennedy-krushchev-vienna-summit-meeting-1961 Accessed on 12 February 2020

CHAPTER 1: JAWAHARLAL NEHRU: GANDHI'S CHOICE

1 Makkhan Lal; 'In Patel vs Nehru saga, remember that India's first PM wasn't elected unanimously'; *The Print*; 9 February 2018; https://theprint.in/opinion/jawaharlal-nehrus-election-as-indias-first-prime-minister-wasnt-unanimous/34519/ Accessed on 31 January 2020

2 *India Wins Freedom*, Maulana Abul Kalam Azad, Orient Black Swan 1988

3 Jawaharlal Nehru, *Selected Speeches: Volume-2 : 1949-1953*, Publications Division, India

4   Pervez Hoodbhoy; 'What India owes to Nehru'; *Dawn*; April 21, 2018; https://www.dawn.com/news/1402940 Accessed on 1 February 2020

5   Alex Von Tunzelmann; *Indian Summer: The Secret History of the End of an Empire*, Simon & Schuster, London, 2008

6   S.Y. Quraishi; *The Great March of Democracy: Seven Decades of India's Elections*; Penguin Viking; 2019

7   Pervez Hoodbhoy; 'What India owes to Nehru'; *Dawn*; April 21, 2018; https://www.dawn.com/news/1402940 Accessed on 1 February 2020

8   Jawaharlal Nehru; Sarvepalli Gopal, Uma Iyengar (eds.); *The Essential Writings of Jawaharlal Nehru, vol. 2*; Oxford University Press; 2003

9   Srinath Raghavan; *The Most Dangerous Place*, Penguin Allen Lane, New Delhi, 2018

10 Jawaharlal Nehru; *India's Foreign Policy: Selected Speeches, September 1946–April 1961*; Publications Division, Ministry of Information and Broadcasting, Govt. of India (1961)

11 Ibid

12 Ibid

13 Praveen K. Chaudhry & Marta Vanduzer-Snow(eds.);*The United States and India: A History Through Archives*; Sage Publications Pvt. Ltd (2011)

14 Bruce Riedel; *JFK's Forgotten Crisis*; Brookings Institution Press (2017)

15 Robert J. McMahon, Stanley Shaloff (Eds); *Foreign Relations of the United States: 1955–1957, South Asia, Volume VIII*; United States Government Printing Office, Washington, 1987

16 Memorandum of a Conversation Between President Eisenhower and Prime Minister Nehru, The White House

17 Atal Bihari Vajpayee (edited by N.M. Ghatate); *Four Decades in Parliament*; Shipra Publications, 1996

18 Jawaharlal Nehru; *India's Foreign Policy: Selected Speeches, September 1946-April 1961*; Publications Division, Ministry of Information and Broadcasting, Govt. of India (1961)

19 Atal Bihari Vajpayee (edited by N.M. Ghatate); *Four Decades in Parliament*; Shipra Publications, 1996

20 'Ambedkar's 124th Birth Anniversary Today', *The Hindu*, 14 April 2015

21 Faizan Mustafa; 'Explained: What are Articles 370 and 35A?'; *The* Indian Express, 6 August 2019; https://indianexpress.com/article/explained/understanding-articles-370-35a-jammu-kashmir-indian-constitution-5610996/ Accessed on 1 February 2020

22 Atal Bihari Vajpayee (edited by N.M. Ghatate); *Four Decades in Parliament*; Shipra Publications, 1996

23 *Not at the Cost of China: India and the United Nations Security Council, 1950*, Anton Harder, Wilson Centre, March 2015

24 John Foster Dulles occupied many senior positions in the US State Department, culminating finally in his post as secretary of state from 1953 to 1959. Philip Jessup was an expert in international law and in that capacity, he was associated

closely in the initial setting up of the UN. Between 1949 and 1953, he was an ambassador-at-large for the US.

25 G.S. Bajpai, an ICS officer, was the first Secretary General of India's Ministry of External Affairs.

26 Ashali Varma; 'A seat for India on UN Security Council: What Modi is asking for is what Nehru lost'; *The Times of India*; 26 September 2015; https://timesofindia. indiatimes.com/blogs/no-free-lunch/a-seat-for-india-on-un-security-council-what-modi-is-asking-for-is-what-nehru-lost/Accessed on 1 February 2020

27 Ibid

28 Minhaz Merchant; 'Did Nehru refuse Kennedy's nuclear weapons technology offer?' *DailyO*; 15 July 2016; https://www.dailyo.in/politics/did-nehru-refuse-kennedys-nuclear-technology-offer-nsg-china/story/1/11779.html Accessed on 1 February 2020

29 Anton Harder; *Not at the Cost of China: India and the United Nations Security Council, 1950*; Wilson Centre; 11 March 2015; https://www.wilsoncenter. org/publication/not-the-cost-china-india-and-the-united-nations-security-council-1950 Accessed on 1 February 2020

30 From Sardar Patel to Nehru; http://www.claudearpi.net/wp-content/uploads/2016/12/P-18b-Patel-to-Nehru.pdf Accessed on 1 February 2020

31 Jawaharlal Nehru, Edited by H.Y. Sharada Prasad; *Selected Works of Jawaharlal Nehru: Second Series, Volume 29: 1 June - 31 August 1955*; OUP India

32 Ibid

33 From Sardar Patel to Nehru; http://www.claudearpi.net/wp-content/uploads/2016/12/P-18b-Patel-to-Nehru.pdf Accessed on 1 February 2020

34 Bruce Riedel; *JFK's Forgotten Crisis*; Brookings Institution Press (2017)

35 The Panchsheel treaty, also known as the Five Principles of Peaceful Coexistence, is a 1954 declaration that defined the relationship between the Republic of India and the People's Republic of China

36 Srinath Raghavan; 'Intelligence failures and reforms'; The Centre for Policy Research; 1 July 2009; https://www.cprindia.org/articles/intelligence-failures-and-reforms Accessed on 1 February 2020

37 Ibid

38 'What China means when it says, "India needs to remember the lessons from history"', Prem Shankar Jha, *The Wire*, 6 July 2017

39 Ibid

40 Lee Kuan Yew; *From Third World to First*; HarperCollins 2000

41 Nehru Memorial Museum & Library, Nehru to Pandit, 8 June 1948, Panditpps, subject file 1, no 54

42 Rudra Chaudhuri; *Forged in Crisis: India and the United States Since 1947*; Oxford University Press (2014)

43 Bruce Riedel; *JFK's Forgotten Crisis*; Brookings Institution Press (2017)

44 Pervez Hoodbhoy; 'What India owes to Nehru'; *Dawn*; 21 April 2018; https://www.dawn.com/news/1402940 Accessed on 1 February 2020

45 Andrew Glass; 'Prime Minister Nehru visits Capitol Hill', 13 October 1949; *Politico*; 13 October, 2015; https://www.politico.com/story/2015/10/prime-minister-nehru-visits-capitol-hill-october-13-1949-214690 Accessed on 2 February 2020

46 *India and the United States: Estranged Democracies, 1941-1991,* Dennis Kux, Diane Publishing Co, 1994

47 Jawaharlal Nehru; *An Autobiography*; Penguin Random House India (2017)

48 Shashi Tharoor; *Nehru: The Invention Of India*; Arcade Publishing (2003)

49 'The death of Mr Nehru, hero and architect of modern India'; *The Guardian*; 28 May 1964; https://www.theguardian.com/world/2014/may/28/nehru-india-death-1964-archive Accessed on 2 February, 2020

50 Lee Kuan Yew; *From Third World to First*; HarperCollins 2000

CHAPTER 2: LAL BAHADUR SHASTRI: NO SMALL MAN

1 'After Nehru—What?' *The New York Times*, 3 June 1964; https://www.nytimes.com/1964/06/03/archives/after-nehruwhat.html; Accessed on 29 January 2020

2 *Succession in India: A Study in Decision-Making*; Michael Brecher, Oxford University Press, 1966

3 'The Original Accidental Prime Minister', Manu S. Pillai, *Live Mint*, 12 October 2018

4 'India's Nuclear Program', Atomic Heritage Foundation, 23 August 2018

5 *Indira Gandhi, the 'Emergency' and Indian Democracy*, P.N. Dhar, Oxford University Press, 2001

6 Areas that rise above the salt level in the Rann of Kutch are known as Bets. These can be inhabited.

7 *Defeat is an Orphan: How Pakistan Lost the Great South Asian War*, Myra MacDonald, C Hurst & Co Publishers Ltd, 2016

8 *Ayub Khan: Pakistan's First Military Ruler*, Altaf Gauhar, Sang-e-Meel Publications, Pakistan, 1998

9 Kuldip Nayar; 'Shastri did not want the war'; *The Week*; 23 August 2015; https://www.theweek.in/theweek/cover/INDO-PAK-WAR-1965-Lal-Bahadur-Shastri-did-not-want-the-war.html; Accessed on 4 February 2020

10 *India after Gandhi: The History of the World's Largest Democracy*, Ramachandra Guha, Pan Macmillan, 2008

11 'Shastri, Ayub and a War', Syed Badrul Ahsan, *The Daily Star*, 28 May 2018

12 By the Tashkent Declaration, the two countries bound themselves to pull back their forces to pre-war positions. They also agreed not to interfere in each other's internal affairs, to restore economic and diplomatic relations and work towards improving bilateral relations

13 'The Falling out at Tashkent' (1966), *The Friday Times*, 4 November 2016; https://www.thefridaytimes.com/the-falling-out-at-tashkent-1966/Accessed on 29 January 2020

14   Atal Bihari Vajpayee; *Four Decades in Parliament*, volume 3; ed. N.M. Ghatate; Shipra Publications, Delhi, 1996

CHAPTER 3: INDIRA GANDHI: A GODDESS EMERGES

1   'CIA thought Kamraj would succeed Shastri', Amit Baruah, *The Hindu*, 13 February 2017
2   By October 1963, the regional leadership of Congress party had started thinking of 'what after Nehru.' They were K. Kamaraj, S. Nijalingappa, S.K. Patil, Atulya Ghosh and N. Sanjeeva Reddy. Over time, they became known as the Syndicate, which began to wield overwhelming influence over the party and in the policies of the Government. But their right- of-centre policies were in conflict with Indira Gandhi's socialist agenda. Finally, on 12 November 1969, Prime Minister Indira Gandhi was expelled from the Congress party for violating the party discipline. In the party split that followed, 445 of 705 members of All India Congress Committee (AICC) opted to side with Indira. The Syndicate faction of Congress limped along, but just about.
3   *Two Alone, Two Together: Letters Between Indira Gandhi And Jawaharlal Nehru 1922-1964*, Edited By Sonia Gandhi, Viking/Penguin (2005)
4   *Indira Gandhi: Letters to an American Friend*, 1950-1984, Dorothy Norman, 1985, Harcourt
5   *Indira Gandhi: A Personal and Political Biography*, Inder Malhotra, Hay House, 2014
6   *Mother India: A Political Biography of Indira Gandhi*, Pranay Gupte, Penguin, 2009
7   *Indira: The Life of Indira Nehru Gandhi*, Katherine Frank, Harper Perrenial, 2007
8   https://mea.gov.in/bilateral-documents.htm?dtl/5139/Treaty+of
9   'Kissinger sorry for deriding Mrs Gandhi', Randeep Ramesh, *The Guardian*, 2 July 2005; https://www.theguardian.com/world/2005/jul/02/india.randeepramesh2; Accessed on 29 January 2020
10   'Kissinger memoirs: An American dilemma', *India Today*, 20 February 2014; https://www.indiatoday.in/magazine/nation/story/19791031-henry-kissinger-richard-nixon-white-house-indira-gandhi-jawaharlal-nehru-822457-2014-02-20; Accessed on 29 January 2020
11   *Indira: India's Most Powerful Prime Minister*, Sagarika Ghosh, Juggernaut Books, 2017
12   *The Blood Telegram: India's Secret War in East Pakistan*, Gary J. Bass, Knopf, New York, 2013
13   *India-Pakistan Relations, 1947-2007*, Volume I to X, A.S. Bhasin, Public Diplomacy Division, MEA
14   Ibid
15   Ibid
16   Ibid
17   Ibid
18   Ibid

19 The Mukti Bahini (Freedom Force) was formed after the declaration of Bangladesh's independence from Pakistan on 26 March 1971. It consisted of security forces, regulars and civilians of the then East Pakistan. They played a vital role as an effective guerrilla force against the Pakistani army

20 *Indira Gandhi: A Biography*, Pupul Jaykar, Penguin, 2000

21 'The True Story of India's Decision to Release 93,000 Pakistani POWs After 1971 War', S.K. Banerjee, *The Wire*, 2 March 2019; https://thewire.in/history/the-untold-story-behind-indira-gandhis-decision-to-release-93000-pakistani-pows-after-the-bangladesh-war; Accessed on 29 January 2020

22 Zorawar Daulet Singh; 'The Puzzle of the 1972 Shimla Summit, Or Why India Did Not Impose Its Will'; *The Wire;* 22 November 2017; https://thewire.in/external-affairs/puzzle-1972-shimla-summit-india-not-impose-will; Accessed on 29 January 2020

23 Ibid

24 *Indian Foreign Affairs Journal,* Vol. 2, No. 3, July-September, 2007, 105-119

25 'The collapse of the Shimla accord', Inder Malhotra, *The Indian Express*, 9 June 2014; https://indianexpress.com/article/opinion/columns/the-collapse-of-the-shimla-accord/Accessed on 29 January 2020

26 *Where Borders Bleed*, Rajiv Dogra, Rupa Publications, 2005

27 Zorawar Daulet Singh; 'The Puzzle of the 1972 Shimla Summit, Or Why India Did Not Impose Its Will'; *The Wire*; 22 November 2017; https://thewire.in/external-affairs/puzzle-1972-shimla-summit-india-not-impose-will; Accessed on 29 January 2020

28 *From Third World to First*, Lee Kuan Yew, HarperCollins 2000

29 P.N. Haksar, Instalment IIIrd, Subject File 290, NMML, New Delhi, 'LONG TELEGRAM'

30 Vivek Prahladan, 'The Recent Declassification of India's Secret 'Long Telegram' Shows Why It Went Nuclear', *The National Interest*, 9 December 2016https://nationalinterest.org/feature/the-recent-declassification-indias-secret-long-telegram-18673; Accessed on 29 January 2020

31 'When the Buddha Smiled', Rediff.com, 22 August 2007

32 *India's Nuclear Limbo and the Fatalism of the Nuclear Non-Proliferation Regime, 1974–1983,* Jayita Sarkar, 9 May 2013, Taylor & Francis

33 From Third World to First, Lee Kuan Yew, HarperCollins 2000

34 John Elliott; 'Indira Gandhi—a flawed legacy'; *Financial Times*; 2 November 2009; https://www.ft.com/content/ff57d648-c7a5-11de-8ba8-00144feab49a; Accessed on 29 January 2020

35 *Mother India: A Political Biography of Indira Gandhi*, Pranay Gupte, Penguin, 2009

36 *The Years of Endeavor: Selected Speeches of Indira Gandhi August 1969 to August 1972*, Publicatons Division

37 *Indira Gandhi: A Biography*, Pupul Jaykar, Penguin, 2000

38 *The Years of Endeavor: Selected Speeches of Indira Gandhi August 1969 to August 1972*, Publicatons Division

39 'Assassination in India: A Leader of Will and Force; Indira Gandhi, Born to Politics, Left Her Own Imprint on India', Linda Charlton, *The New York Times*, 1 November 1984; https://www.nytimes.com/1984/11/01/obituaries/assassination-in-india-a-leader-of-will-and-force-indira-gandhi.html; Accessed on 29 January 2020

40 Ibid

41 'Indira Gandhi', *National Herald*, 31 October 2018

CHAPTER 4: RAJIV GANDHI: INDIA'S RELUCTANT PRINCE

1 *The Turbulent Years:1980-96*; Pranab Mukherjee; Rupa

2 Ibid

3 'Rajiv Gandhi faces big foreign policy task', *New York Times*, 6 November 1984

4 Essentially, the Government of India acknowledged under this accord the political, social, cultural and economic concerns of the Assamese people and agreed to identify and deport the refugees and migrants into the state after 25 March 1971.

5 'Remarks at the Welcoming Ceremony for Prime Minister Rajiv Gandhi of India', Ronald Reagan Presidential library and Museum, 12 June 1985

6 The pasturage of Sumdorong Chu lies north-east of the confluence of the rivers Namka Chu and Nyamjang Chu. The Chinese claimed that the area was north of the LAC, whereas India contested that claim. There was also the additional element of retrieving some of the honour lost in 1962 as this part of Arunachal Pradesh was close to Thag La ridge, where the Indian army had lost a major battle. By the end of 1986, the Indian army had landed a brigade in the region, prompting China to scramble its forces. The resulting eyeball to eyeball confrontation lasted upto the summer of 1987. Along the way, the Chinese statements became almost as shrill in tone as they were before the 1962 war. Gradually, however, both sides started the diplomatic efforts to scale down tensions; one result of which was Rajiv's visit to China. Another, and lasting, effect of this stalemate was the 1993 agreement between India and China to ensure peace along the LAC.

7 'Modi should note how Rajiv Gandhi handled China', Mani Shankar Aiyar, NDTV, 16 August 2016; https://www.ndtv.com/opinion/big-progress-with-china-made-without-modis-usual-hi-jinks-1444643

8 'Defining Moments', N. Ram, *Frontline*, 12-25 September 1998; https://frontline.thehindu.com/static/html/fl1519/15190100.htm; Accessed on 29 January 2020

9 'Rajiv Gandhi missed opportunity to resolve border issue: former Chinese diplomat', Sutirtho Patranobis, *Hindustan Times*, 13 April 2015

10 'South Asia's Northern Frontier', A.G. Noorani, *Criterion Quarterly*, Vol 10 no 4, 29 January 2016

11 'The Truth About 1962', A.G. Noorani, *Frontline*, Vol. 29, Issue 23, 17–30 November 2012

12 Rajan Hoole; 'Handing Over Arms To The LTTE'; *Colombo Telegraph*; 23 May 2015; https://www.colombotelegraph.com/index.php/handing-over-arms-to-the-ltte/Accessed on 29 January 2020

13 'Rajiv Gandhi's Sri Lanka policy led to his death: Natwar Singh', *Hindustan Times*, 1 August 2014; https://www.hindustantimes.com/india/rajiv-gandhi-s-sri-lanka-policy-led-to-his-death-natwar-singh/story-0JLTRSHTUF92n32q904rnL.html; Accessed on 29 January 2020

14 Lalit K Jha; 'Rajiv Gandhi was genuinely interested in US military ties: CIA'; *Live Mint*; 4 August 2017; https://www.livemint.com/Politics/q6xoc52bqbTg9nDU4JIvbM/Rajiv-Gandhi-was-genuinely-interested-about-US-military-ties.html; Accessed on 29 January 2020

15 *The Illustrated Weekly of India*, 11 June 1989

16 *The Economist*, 15 April 1989

17 Shaikh Aziz; 'The 'dawn of a new era' that remained a dream'; *Dawn*; 21 August 2016; https://www.dawn.com/news/1278747; Accessed on 29 January 2020

18 'Accidental Politicians', *The Friday Times*, 15 June 2018; https://www.thefridaytimes.com/accidental-politicians-islamabad-1989; Accessed on 29 January 2020

19 https://www.cia.gov/library/readingroom/docs/CIA-RDP88T00096R000100150003-3.pdf

20 *Kaoboys of R&AW*, B. Raman, Lancer Publishers, Delhi, 2013

21 'Indira Gandhi: Death in the Garden', William E. Smith, *Time*, 12 November 1984

CHAPTER 5: NARASIMHA RAO: THE REAL CHANAKYA?

1 Charmy Harikrishnan; '25 years of reforms: How a PM with zero knowledge of economics scripted India's biggest turnaround story'; *The Economic Times*; 21 July 2016; https://economictimes.indiatimes.com/news/politics-and-nation/25-years-of-reforms-how-a-pm-with-zero-knowledge-of-economics-scripted-indias-biggest-turnaround-story/articleshow/53309051.cms?from=mdr; Accessed on 29 January 2020

2 K. Natwar Singh; 'How PV became PM', *The Hindu*, 2 July 2012; https://www.thehindu.com/opinion/op-ed/how-pv-became-pm/article3592050.ece; Accessed on 29 January 2020

3 Kapil Komireddi; 'Farewell to Manmohan Singh, India's Puppet Prime Minister'; *Daily Beast*; 12 July 2017;https://www.thedailybeast.com/farewell-to-manmohan-singh-indias-puppet-prime-minister; Accessed on 29 January 2020

4 Kapil Komireddi; 'PV Narasimha Rao reinvented India – so why is he the forgotten man?' *The National*; 19 May 2012; https://www.thenational.ae/lifestyle/pv-narasimha-rao-reinvented-india-so-why-is-he-the-forgotten-man-1.455990; Accessed on 29 January 2020

5 'P.V. Narasimha Rao reinvented India', Kapil Komireddi, *The National*, 19 May 2012

6   *Half-Lion: How P.V. Narasimha Rao Transformed India*, Vinay Sitapati, Penguin, 2016

7   Derek Brown; 'PV Narasimha Rao'; *The Guardian*, 24 December 2004; https://www.theguardian.com/news/2004/dec/24/guardianobituaries.india; Accessed on 29 January 2020

8   *Dragon on Our Doorstep*, Pravin Sawhney & Ghazala Wahab, Aleph, 2017

9   'Pragmatic | The 1994 Parliamentary Resolution on Jammu & Kashmir', Takshashila Institution, June 2011

10   'P.V. Narasimha Rao reinvented India', Kapil Komireddi, *The National*, 19 May 2012

11   A.P.J. Abdul Kalam; 'Make The Black Swan A White Swan'; *Outlook*; 25 January 2013; https://www.outlookindia.com/website/story/make-the-black-swan-a-white-swan/283731; Accessed on 29 January 2020

12   Rasheed Kidwai; 'Atal Bihari Vajpayee, a true democrat', *DailyO*, 16 August, 2018; https://www.dailyo.in/politics/atal-bihari-vajpayee-bjp-congress-relationship-kargil-bofors-emergency-shahbano-babri-masjid-ayodhya-dispute/story/1/26090.html; Accessed on 29 January 2020

13   Derek Brown; 'PV Narasimha Rao'; *The Guardian*, 24 December 2004; https://www.theguardian.com/news/2004/dec/24/guardianobituaries.india; Accessed on 29 January 2020

14   Sunanda K Datta-Ray; 'PV Narasimha Rao: The Saga of the Southerner'; *Open*, 13 October 2016; https://openthemagazine.com/essay/pv-narasimha-rao-the-saga-of-the-southerner/; Accessed on 29 January 2020

CHAPTER 6: ATAL BIHARI VAJPAYEE: POET, POLITICIAN, PATRIOT

1   *Engaging India: Diplomacy, Democracy and the Bomb*, Strobe Talbott, Penguin, 2007

2   'Crisis in South Asia: India's Nuclear Tests; Pakistan's Nuclear Tests; India and Pakistan: What Next?' Hearings of the Committee on Foreign Relations, U S Senate, second session, 13 May, 3 June & 13 July 1998

3   'India's Deterrence and Disarmament: The Impact of Pokhran-II', Jayant Prasad, *Strategic Analysis*, Vol 42, Issue 3, 2018, Pages 260-280

4   S. Jaishankar; 'India-Japan relations after Pokhran II'; https://www.india-seminar.com/2000/487/487%20jaishankar.htm; Accessed on 30 January 2020

5   Kate Sullivan; 'How the world warmed to a nuclear India'; *Inside Story*; 3 May 2012; https://insidestory.org.au/how-the-world-warmed-to-a-nuclear-india/ Accessed on 30 January 2020

6   A.G. Noorani; 'The truth about Agra'; *Frontline*, 16–29 July 2005; https://frontline.thehindu.com/static/html/fl2215/stories/20050729002104400.htm; Accessed on 30 January 2020

7   Atal Bihari Vajpayee; *Four Decades in Parliament*, vol-3, ed. N.M. Ghatate, Shipra Publications, Delhi, 1996

8   Sushant Sareen; 'Modi Season 2, Episode Pakistan: Give pressure a chance'; Observer Research Foundation; 25 May 2019; https://www.orfonline.org/

expert-speak/modi-season-2-episode-pakistan-give-pressure-a-chance-51223/ Accessed on 30 January 2020

9   'Weeks before Kargil conflict, Pervez Musharraf crossed LoC, spent night in India: Aide'; PTI; 1 February 2013; https://economictimes.indiatimes.com/news/politics-and-nation/weeks-before-kargil-conflict-pervez-musharraf-crossed-loc-spent-night-in-india-aide/articleshow/18291792.cms; Accessed on 30 January 2020

10 Srinath Raghavan; 'Intelligence failures and reforms'; Centre for Policy Research; https://www.cprindia.org/articles/intelligence-failures-and-reforms; Accessed on 30 January 2020

11 'Releasing Masood Azhar was a political decision'; Vivekananda International Foundation; 19 February 2010; https://www.vifindia.org/node/231; Accessed on 30 January 2020

12 'Armed forces tribunal indicts Lt Gen for fake Kargil battle accounts'; ET Bureau; *Economic Times*; 28 May 2010; https://economictimes.indiatimes.com/news/politics-and-nation/armed-forces-tribunal-indicts-lt-gen-for-fake-kargil-battle-accounts/articleshow/5983320.cms?from=mdr; Accessed on 30 January 2020

13 Ejaz Haider; 'The Heights of Folly: A Pakistani Account of the Kargil War'; *The Wire*, 24 September 2018; https://thewire.in/security/the-heights-of-folly-a-critical-look-at-the-kargil-operation; Accessed on 30 January 2020

14 'Pakistan was to deploy nukes against India during Kargil war'; *PTI*; 12 July 2018; https://economictimes.indiatimes.com/news/defence/pakistan-was-to-deploy-nukes-against-india-during-kargil-war/articleshow/50019153.cms?from=mdr; Accessed on 30 January 2020

15 Anwar Iqbal; 'Clinton adviser: confusion gripped Islamabad during Kargil crisis'; *Dawn*; 23 October 2006; https://www.dawn.com/news/216034/clinton-adviser-confusion-gripped-islamabad-during-kargil-crisis; Accessed on 30 January 2020

16 Ibid

17 *The Clinton Tapes, A President's Secret Diary*, Taylor Branch, Simon & Schuster, 2009

18 Ibid

19 'When Nawaz Sharif gave Bill Clinton a hard time over Kargil', Rediff, 21 October 2013

20 Ibid

21 Arifa Akbar; 'Trail of Terror: Boarding Card Blunder Allowed Hijackers On Jet Plane, Muslim Hijackers Boarded Plane On One Card'; *Independent*, 27 December 1999; https://www.independent.co.uk/news/world/trail-of-terror-boarding-card-blunder-allowed-hijackers-on-jet-plane-muslim-hijackers-boarded-plane-1134764.html; Accessed on 30 January 2020

22 'Handling of Kandahar Hijack Was "Goofed Up", Says Former RAW Chief A S Dulat'; *PTI*, 3 July 2015; https://www.ndtv.com/india-news/handling-of-kandahar-hijack-was-goofed-up-says-former-raw-chief-a-s-dulat-777744;

Accessed on 30 January 2020

23 'The Truth about Agra', A.G. Noorani, *Frontline*, 29 July 2005

24 Anuja Jaiswal; 'How Vajpayee stayed optimistic about Indo-Pak ties despite Agra summit failure', *TNN*, 17 August 2018; https://timesofindia.indiatimes.com/city/agra/how-vajpayee-stayed-optimistic-about-indo-pak-ties-despite-agra-summit-failure/articleshow/65444302.cms; Accessed on 30 January 2020

25 Praveen Swami; 'Beating the retreat'; *Frontline*, 26 October–8 November 2002; https://frontline.thehindu.com/static/html/fl1922/stories/20021108007101200.htm; Accessed on 30 January 2020

26 Alex Perry; 'Asleep at The Wheel?'; *Time*; 10 June 2002; http://content.time.com/time/magazine/article/0,9171,260747,00.html; Accessed on 30 January 2020

27 Sudheendra Kulkarni; 'The one who reached out to China: On Atal Bihari Vajpayee'; *The Hindu*, 11 September 2018; https://www.thehindu.com/opinion/op-ed/the-one-who-reached-out-to-china/article24918999.ece; Accessed on 30 January 2020

28 Brahma Chellaney; 'India's Betrayal of Tibet'; *The Wall Street Journal*; 28 July 2003; https://www.wsj.com/articles/SB105934174617047500; Accessed on 30 January 2020; 29 Brahma Chellaney; 'An insecurity trap of India's own making'; *Mint*; 15 August, 2013; https://chellaney.net/2013/08/14/an-insecurity-trap-of-indias-making/Accessed on 30 January 2020

30 Randeep Ramesh; 'Atal Bihari Vajpayee—Obituary'; *The Guardian*, 17 August 2018; https://www.theguardian.com/world/2018/aug/17/atal-bihari-vajpayee-obituary; Accessed on 30 January 2020

31 Alex Perry; 'Atal Bihari Vajpayee'; *Time*; 26 April 2004;http://content.time.com/time/specials/packages/article/   0,28804,1970858_1970888_1971081,00.html; Accessed on 30 January 2020

32 *An Anthropologist Among the Marxists and Other Essays*, Ramachandra Guha, Orient Blackswan, 2001

33 'This young man will be PM one day', Sanjay Basak, *Asian Age*, 16 August 2018

CHAPTER 7: MANMOHAN SINGH: WILL HISTORY BE KINDER?

1 'After 10 years as PM, Manmohan Singh's legacy to go down like Narasimha Rao', Ajmer Singh, *Economic Times*, 11 March 2014

2 *India Booms: The Breathtaking Development and Influence of Modern India*, John Farndon, Virgin Digital, 2009

3 'One more push', *The Economist*, 21 July 2011

4 'The legacy of Manmohan Singh', *Financial Times*, Gideon Rachman, 3 January 2014

5 *Zero-Sum Future: American Power in an Age of Anxiety*, Gideon Rachman, Simon and Schuster, 2012

6 'Manmohan Singh—India's saviour or just "the underachiever"', Andrew Buncombe, *Independent*, 16 July 2012

7   Paranjoy Guha Thakurta; 'Illusion of consensus'; *India Seminar*; https://www.india-seminar.com/2004/541/541%20paranjoy%20guha%20thakurta.htm; Accessed on 31 January 2020

8   Ibid

9   *Mandate: Will of the People*, Vir Sanghvi, Westland, 2015

10 *The Accidental Prime Minister: The Making and Unmaking of Manmohan Singh*; Sanjaya Baru; Penguin, 2014

11 Jonathan Power; Talking to the new prime minister of India; *The Transnational Foundation for Peace and Future Research*, 24 May 2004; http://www.oldsite.transnational.org/SAJT/forum/power/2004/05.04_IndiaPrimeMinster.htm; Accessed on 31 January 2020

12 *The Most Dangerous Place*; Srinath Raghavan, Penguin Allen Lane, New Delhi, 2018

13 Steve Coll; 'The Back Channel'; *The New Yorker*; 2 March 2009

14 Nitin Gokhale; '26/11: Sheer Paralysis had gripped the government'; *Rediff*
26 November 2014; https://www.rediff.com/news/column/nitin-gokhale-2611-sheer-paralysis-gripped-the-government/20141126.htm; Accessed on 31 January 2020

15 Emma Garman; 'When India Failed in the Mumbai Terrorist Attacks'; *Daily Beast*, 2 November 2013; https://www.thedailybeast.com/when-india-failed-in-the-mumbai-terrorist-attacks; Accessed on 31 January 2020

16 Ibid

17 Bharat Bhushan; 'Manmohan Singh's Balochistan blunder'; *India Today*, 20 July 2009;   https://www.indiatoday.in/latest-headlines/story/mammohan-singhs-balochistan-blunder-52425-2009-07-20 Accessed on 31 January 2020

18 Brahma Chellaney; 'An insecurity trap of India's own making'; *Mint*; 15 August 2013;   https://chellaney.net/2013/08/14/an-insecurity-trap-of-indias-making/ Accessed on 31 January 2020

19 *The Indo-US Nuclear Agreement: Advantage US*, Garima Singh, 20 January 2006, IPC

20 Simon Denyer; 'India's "silent" prime minister becomes a tragic figure', *The Washington Post*; 4 September 2012; https://www.washingtonpost.com/world/indias-silent-prime-minister-becomes-a-tragic-figure/2012/09/04/a88662c4-f396-11e1-adc6-87dfa8eff430_story.html; Accessed on 31 January 2020

21 'History will be kinder to me than the media, says Manmohan', *The Hindu*, 4 January 2014

CHAPTER 8: NARENDRA MODI: THE RULE MAKER

1   *The NaMo Story: A Political Life*, Kingshuk Nag, Lotus, 2013; *Narendra Modi: The Man, the Times*; Nilanjan Mukhopadhyay; Tranquebar, 2013

2   Ram Madhav; 'This election result is a positive mandate in favour of Narendra Modi'; *Indian Express*, 24 May 2019; https://indianexpress.com/article/

opinion/columns/lok-sabha-elections-result-narendra-modi-bjp-government-congress-5745313/; Accessed on 31 January 2020

3   PM to Heads of Indian Missions, Press Information Bureau, Government of India, Prime Minister's Office 7 February 2015

4   John Elliott; 'Long Read: Modi's foreign policy performance'; *LSE blogs*; https://blogs.lse.ac.uk/southasia/2019/04/25/long-read-modis-foreign-policy-and-performance/; Accessed on 31 January 2020

5   Rahul Shrivastava; '92 nations in 55 months: PM Modi's travel costs hit Rs 2,021 crore'; *India Today*; 29 December 2018; https://www.indiatoday.in/india/story/92-nations-in-55-months-pm-modi-travel-costs-hit-rs-2021-crore-1419337-2018-12-29; Accessed on 31 January 2020

6   Happymon Jacob; 'Losing the Neighbourhood', *The Hindu*, 18 May 2016; https://www.thehindu.com/opinion/lead/modis-neighbourhood-first-policy-losing-the-neighbourhood/article14324718.ece; Accessed on 31 January 2020

7   Jyoti Malhotra; What happened during Narendra Modi's 2015 visit to Pakistan and why it still matters; *The Print*, 3 October, 2018; https://theprint.in/opinion/global-print/what-happened-during-narendra-modis-2015-visit-to-pakistan-and-why-it-still-matters/128746/; Accessed on 31 January 2020

8   'A fatal friendship?' Opinion, *Wall Street Journal*, 17 December 2010

9   Philip Rucker & Carol Leonnig; *A Very Stable Genius*; Penguin Random House

10 'Asia will have a better future if India, China work together: PM Modi at Shangri La', *The Statesman*, 1 June 2018

11 Michael Kugelman; 'Modi's Bold New World'; *The Cairo Review of Global Affairs*; Spring 2017; https://www.thecairoreview.com/essays/modis-bold-new-world/; Accessed on 31 January 2020

12 'The Guardian view on Modi's mistakes: the high costs of India's demonetization'; *The* Guardian; 31August 2018; https://www.theguardian.com/commentisfree/2018/aug/31/the-guardian-view-on-modis-mistakes-the-high-costs-of-indias-demonetization; Accessed on 31 January 2020

13 Ibid

14 Gideon Rachman; 'How India's Narendra Modi will shape the world'; *Financial Times*, 14 May 2018; https://www.ft.com/content/42912706-574f-11e8-bdb7-f6677d2e1ce8; Accessed on 31 January 2020

EPILOGUE: THE MORE IT CHANGES, THE MORE IT REMAINS THE SAME

1   Lee Kuan Yew; *From Third World to First*; HarperCollins, 2000

2   Strobe Talbott; *Engaging India: Diplomacy, Democracy and the Bomb*; Penguin India 2007

3   Yang Xiaoping; 'When India's Strategic Backyard Meets China's Strategic Periphery: The View From Beijing'; *War on the Rocks*, 20 April 2018; https://warontherocks.com/2018/04/when-indias-strategic-backyard-meets-chinas-strategic-periphery-the-view-from-beijing/; Accessed on 3 February 2020

4   'The Biggest Vote', William Safire, *The New York Times*, 18 May 2000

5   The Kargil Committee Report; https://nuclearweaponarchive.org/India/ KargilRCA.html; Accessed on 3 February 2020

6   Pakistan's future: "the most dangerous country in the world"; *Axios*, 4 August 2018; https://www.axios.com/pakistans-future-most-dangerous-country-in-the-world-09691d14-52a5-4485-9738-e8d6abebd872.html; Accessed on 3 February 2020

7   Walter C. Ladwig III; *Indian Military Modernization and Conventional Deterrence in South Asia*; Taylor & Francis 2015; http://www.walterladwig.com/Articles/ Conventional%20Deterrence%20in%20South%20Asia.pdf   Accessed   on   3 February 2020

8   Thomas Joscelyn & Bill Roggio; 'Analysis: The costs of withdrawal from Afghanistan'; *FDD's Long War Journal*; 21 December 2018; https://www. longwarjournal.org/archives/2018/12/analysis-the-costs-of-withdrawal-from-afghanistan.php; Accessed on 3 February 2020

9   'President Obama's Remarks on New Strategy for Afghanistan and Pakistan', *The New York Times,* 27 March 2009

10 ASG Chair Samuel R. Berger on U.S. Strategy for Pakistan and Afghanistan, Council on Foreign Relations: U.S. Strategy for Pakistan and Afghanistan Council on Foreign Relations Task Force Report, Albright Stonebridge Group ASG, 10 November 2010

11 Steve Coll; *Directorate S: The C.I.A. and America's Secret Wars in Afghanistan and Pakistan, 2001–2016*; Allen Lane 2018

12 'Winning in Afghanistan Requires Taking the Fight to Pakistan', Michael Rubin,*National Interest*, 3 June 2019

13 '10 Years of Afghan War: How the Taliban Go On', Sami Yousafzai, *Newsweek*, 2 October 2011

14 'Pakistan's pivot to Russia', Kamran Yousaf, *The Express Tribune*, Pakistan, 7 May 2018

15 'Exploring new drivers in India-Russia cooperation', Aleksei Zakharov, ORF, 12 October 2017

16 Robert D. Kaplan; 'The Return of Marco Polo's World and the U.S. Military Response'; Center for a New American Security; May 2017; http://stories. cnas.org/wp-content/uploads/2017/05/CNASSTORY-MarcoPolo-Final.pdf Accessed on 3 February 2020

17 Lee Kuan Yew; *From Third World to First*; HarperCollins 2000

18 Henry Kissinger; *White House Years*; Simon & Schuster; 2011

BIBLIOGRAPHY

Every effort has been made to include all references/material sourced for the book, into this list. However, any omission here and/or in the text is inadvertent. It will be corrected as and when noticed.

- Madhumita Das, 'Continuity and Change in India's Early Tibet Policy: 1905-1960', *South Asia Chronicle*, 2019
- Alex von Tunzelmann, *Indian Summer: The Secret History of the End of an Empire*, Simon & Schuster, London, 2007
- S. Gopal, *The Essential Writings of Jawaharlal Nehru*, vol. 2, OUP, 2003
- Srinath Raghavan, *The Most Dangerous Place*, Penguin Random House, New Delhi, 2018
- Jawaharlal Nehru, *India's Foreign Policy: Selected Speeches*, September 1946-April 1961, Ministry of I & B, India
- Bruce Riedel, *JFK's Forgotten Crisis: Tibet, the CIA, and Sino-Indian War*, Brookings Institution Press, 2015
- N.M. Ghatate, *Atal Bihari Vajpayee: Four Decades in Parliament*, Vol 1, Shipra Publications, Delhi, 1996
- Anton Harder, *Not at the Cost of China: India and the United Nations Security Council, 1950*, 11 March 2015, Wilson Centre
- H.Y. Sharada Prasad and A.K. Damodaran (ed), *Selected Works of Jawaharlal Nehru*, Second Series, Volume XXXI, A Project of Jawaharlal Nehru Fund, distributed by OUP, p.578
- Lee Kuan Yew, *From Third World to First*, Times Media Private Ltd, Singapore, 2000
- Nehru Memorial Museum & Library, Nehru to Pandit, 8 June 1948, Pandit papers, subject file 1, no 54
- Shashi Tharoor, *Nehru: The Invention of India*, Arcade Publishing, 2003
- Joseph Stiglitz, *Globalization and its Discontents*, Penguin, New York, 2002
- Vikram Sood, *The Unending Game*, Penguin, New Delhi, 2018
- Jairam Ramesh, *Intertwined Lives*, Penguin, New Delhi, 2018
- Tim Marshall, *Prisoners of Geography*, Elliott & Thompson ltd, London, 2015
- Stephen Kinzer, *The Brothers*, Times Books, New York, 2013
- Robert D. Kaplan, *The Revenge of Geography*, Random House, New York, 2012
- Robert D. Kaplan, *Warrior Politics*, Vintage Books, 2002, New York

- Shivshankar Menon, *Choices*, The Brookings Institution, Washington, 2016
- Kishore Mahbubani, *The Great Convergence*, Public Affairs, New York, 2013
- Pranab Mukherjee, *The Turbulent Years: 1980-96*, Rupa Publications India
- Juan Mascaro, *The Bhagavad Gita*, Translation from Sanskrit, Penguin, 1962
- Farid Zakaria, *The Post American World*, WW Norton & Co, New York, 2008
- George Perkovich, *India's Nuclear Bomb*, OUP, New Delhi, 2000
- L.N. Rangarajan, *The Arthashastra*, Penguin Books, New Delhi, 1992
- Kingshuk Nag, *Atal Bihari Vajpayee: A Man for All Seasons*, Rupa, 2015
- Pranay Gupte, *Mother India*, Penguin, 2009
- P.V. Narasimha Rao, *The Insider*, Penguin, 2000
- Sanjaya Baru, *The Accidental Prime Minister: The Making and Unmaking of Manmohan Singh*, Penguin, 2015
- Vir Sanghvi, *Mandate: Will of the People*, Westland, 2015
- Kingshuk Nag, *The NaMo story: A Political Life*, Lotus, 2013
- Nilanjan Mukhopadhyay, *Narendra Modi: The Man, the Times*, Tranquebar, 2013

INDEX

www.ingramcontent.com/pod-product-compliance
Lightning Source LLC
Chambersburg PA
CBHW070438100426
42812CB00031B/3330/J